The Fourth World

George Manuel is a man of unspoken
determination. As he came of age,
colonization had just started in the
Shuswap, far into the interior of British
Columbia. He was Chief of his Neskonlith
band of Chase, British Columbia. He was
elected Chairman of the National Indian
Advisory Council, and President of the
North American Indian Brotherhood. He
is presently the President of the National
Indian Brotherhood.

Michael Posluns is a free-lance
broadcaster and writer. He is presently
associated with Akwesasne *Notes*, an
international newspaper reporting on
Indian and aboriginal concerns throughout
Europe and North America.

The Fourth World

An Indian Reality

GEORGE MANUEL
MICHAEL POSLUNS

Foreword by Vine Deloria, Jr.

THE FREE PRESS
A Division of Macmillan Publishing Co., Inc.
New York

Design: Robert Burgess Garbutt
Cover illustration: Gordon McLean
Illustrations: John Fadden
Cartography: Research by Maralyn Horsdal
              Artwork by Frank Zsigo
Library of Congress Catalogue Card Number: 73-8040

The Free Press
A Division of Macmillan Publishing Co., Inc.
866 Third Avenue, New York, N.Y. 10022

Printed and Bound in Canada
5 4 3 2 1   78 77 76 75 74

These words are written for my grandchildren, Roland,
Geraldine, Genevieve, and for their children's children.

G.M.

And to the memory of three grandfathers who do not otherwise appear in the story, Abraham Posluns, Samuel Brenzel,
and John McIlvride. Stories about Zeide Posluns and my recollections of Zeide Brenzel and Granda McIlvride nurtured in
me the feelings that we have both tried to convey in this book.

M.P.

Contents

Foreword

~~~~~~

IT IS MY good fortune to be asked to write a foreword to George Manuel's book, *The Fourth World*. Not only are we good friends of some years standing, but with this book I become a student of his thinking and I am happy to acknowledge that status. Just as I was considering writing a book to illustrate the relationship between the various aboriginal peoples of the globe, he called me and asked me to write a foreword to *his* book. So I am doubly happy: first, that a book of this nature is being written, and second, that George had already considered many of the theories that were beginning to come to me in a vague and undefined manner. But let me relate the sequence of what happened.

Some years ago, as the social movement of the United States began to spin its wheels in frustration over Viet Nam, a pernicious doctrine known as the "Third World" began to spread in North America. The "Third World" was to be a great coalition of oppressed peoples of the world rising up against the technology and tyranny of the western European peoples. During a speech on fishing rights at an eastern college, I was asked why the Nisquallies didn't take up guns and shoot it out. I replied that there were so few Nisquallies and so many Washington state Game Wardens that it wouldn't be a contest at all, just another massacre. Then I was told that the "Third World" was waiting to support any effort that we undertook. Such was the fanatic ideology of the American New Left.

The doctrine of the Third World was, of course, based upon a partial examination of a world in which the emergence of African and Asian nations from their century of colonialism seemed to indicate a radical shift in the realities of world politics. I remembered, while hearing this inflammatory rhetoric, the great disappointment of Stokely Carmichael when he learned that the new African nations were, after all, not going to introduce the problem of the American black in the forum of the United Nations. Thus it was that I mistrusted this ideology since it attributed to people of foreign lands a sophisticated knowledge of North American domestic affairs that they did not have or feel.

My next confrontation with the Third World ideology was during the recent occupation at Wounded Knee when the Lakota protestors were surrounded by federal officers and the Third World was either nowhere in sight or busy making speeches on behalf of the Palestine Liberation Front, (Indians having passed out of favour at that point). I was uncertain about the future of both Canadian and American Indians, certain that both the Canadian and American governments would remain cloaked in lethargy, and still uncertain about how Indians really related to either the modern world or the past.

The only person that I could find who understood what was happening was George Manuel. He had travelled to various countries in an effort to learn who the other aboriginal peoples were, what their problems were, and what their history and present conditions really meant. When the Same (Lapp) peoples were having their problems with the Swedish government, George Manuel went to Sweden and met with their leaders. While they did not win their lawsuit against the Swedish government, George's demonstration of concern for them was probably more valuable than a legal victory which could be restricted in significance to a small European nation and hidden from sight.

With this book, therefore, I believe that George Manuel has

opened a whole new chapter in the experiences of mankind. He has told the story of the Canadian Indian in brilliant fashion, without the harsh clamour of militant rhetoric but with the wisdom and compassion that typifies the North American Indian at his best. Yet while telling us what has happened to the Canadian Indians, he somehow weaves into his story the experiences and conditions of all aboriginal peoples around the globe. He rebels at the thought of the national state which is so rigid and shortsighted as to attempt to substitute "citizenship" of whatever grade and quality for the living cultural traditions of peoples.

The idea of the supernational state which incorporates diverse groups of peoples within its borders is a relatively recent idea in man's experience. There is presently no place on earth that a people can live without either asserting their own political independence against the European nations or attaching themselves to a European nation, (or nation deriving its government from that tradition), in some weird political relationship—be it Puerto Rico's "Commonwealth" arrangement with the United States, or a "protectorate" status with Great Britain, France, Portugal, or Holland. On the North American continent, because of the continuous and seemingly endless stretches of land, Indian nations have become a strange form of "domestic Nation" in relation to Canada and the United States. Only when we visualize this condition occurring everywhere and ask why it should be that way, why it *has to be that way*, are we prepared to learn from George Manuel what the Fourth World really is.

The Fourth World is a reality because it describes most eloquently the nature of the world as we now confront it. But having grasped Manuel's vision of the Fourth World, we come to realize that it calls forth in us the morality of law and human existence in a more profound manner than any other vision of the world has ever done. The aboriginal peoples can only argue the morality of their case. Overwhelmed by the European peoples, they cannot look forward to the day when they regain control of their lands. Their cause is not less important and the legality of their demands should invoke no less a response.

The world has come to a détente with history. The rapid depletion of resources, coupled with their inequitable allocation, calls forth in humanity the necessity of re-evaluating its beliefs and values. When George Manuel calls for the Canadian Parliament to fulfil its responsibilities and for the churches of the Christian tradition to assume their burdens, he is not merely calling for new programs, more money, or additional sympathy. Rather, he calls the institutions of the world to re-examine their own origins, the beliefs which brought them into being, and the basis of integrity that lies beneath their formal structures. One can fulfil the letter of the law in such a manner as to violate dreadfully its spirit, and this tendency to pervert the reason for existence is all too familiar in today's world.

What makes a "nation"? How do peoples come into existence? How do peoples relate to each other? These are some of the questions that plague us today. If we continue to view the world as the combination of political and economic forces of recent vintage which seem to control our lives and properties, we do violence to the very core of our existence. Thus it is that the Fourth World of George Manuel offers a vision of human existence beyond that of expediency and the balancing of powers and speaks to the identity crisis that has gripped every land and its peoples. No contemporary political and economic structure *has to be*. Whatever structures do exist must eventually find a reason for their existence above and beyond the political and economic values of today. George Manuel has provided us with the vision by which that reason can be found.

I cannot help but think that the two nations of North America, Canada and the United States, which today are both struggling to find a new understanding of themselves, must understand and adopt George Manuel's vision of the world of tomorrow. The non-Indian citizens of these countries must cease their relentless cultural warfare against the Indian people and become as we are, the children of the land. George Manuel may be Canada's greatest prophet and to refuse to consider his words of advice may be the ultimate folly of our times.

VINE DELORIA, JR.

Authors' Note

IT MAY SEEM somewhat peculiar that a story told entirely in the voice of one man is the work of two authors. There is no convenient division of labour to which we can point that would allow us to say "researched by" or "as told to." The greater part of the research was developed through half a century of living and working on the part of one of us, although the technical research, especially in the sections dealing with political and legal events, was done mainly by the other. One of us had to sit down and draw the material together into its present form. However, that form was largely suggested by the course of our many recorded conversations, in which the major events of that half-century and their significance were explored. Looking back at the experience of working together we can only say that *The Fourth World* emerged—as a story and as a book—through a dialogue between two men.

Far from being strange that a single voice should be the work of two authors, we should like to think that the dialogue from which that voice arose is in itself a sign of the Fourth World.

Acknowledgements

I AM VERY fortunate that the personal nature of some of the latter portions of this story has allowed me to acknowledge my debts to some of the people who most contributed to my own growth and particularly to my consciousness of the philosophy of the Fourth World. There are others whose lives have become intertwined with mine more recently, to whom I am no less indebted.

My special gratitude goes to my cousin, Ida Rogas, who first encouraged me to write.

Paul Orth, an ethnologist in Lillooet, British Columbia, was the first friend who encouraged me to draw my ideas together into a broad overview that could be presented as a book.

Marie Smallface Marule, who has been secretary-treasurer of the National Indian Brotherhood during much of my term as president, cultivated in me the idea of pulling my thoughts together into the form of a book. Marie was also the first person to be able to show me, from direct and personal experience, the close relationship and common bonds between our own condition as Indian people, and the struggles of other aboriginal peoples and the nations of the Third World.

Mbutu Milando, who was for some time First Secretary of the Tanzanian High Commission in Ottawa, was the first diplomat to welcome a closer relationship with the Indian people through the National Indian Brotherhood. It was Mbutu who first suggested to me the concept and nature of the Fourth World—an idea that grew into a framework for much of my own thought.

Douglas Sanders' friendship and legal studies have combined to give me what I hope is a far deeper understanding of both the binds in which Indian people have been caught and the opportunities that might be open to us.

Harold Cardinal has successfully combined a traditional Indian knowledge with higher academic learning, and the strength and vigour of youth. Although others, including some of my own children, have followed this example, Harold has been the first leader in recent years to demonstrate the success that this combination can offer.

The other presidents of the provincial Indian organizations who have formed the executive of the NIB have given me constant feedback and a sounding board throughout my two terms as president. Though they did not know I might draw on their ideas in this particular way, many of the historical and personal examples told here were brought back to mind by the contemporary problems and policy questions we debated as a body. This group has included Dave Courchene, Manitoba Indian Brotherhood; Dave Ahenakew, Federation of Saskatchewan Indians; Andrew Delisle, Indians of Quebec Association; Tony Francis, Union of New Brunswick Indians; Noel Doucette and later John Knockwood, Union of Nova Scotia Indians; Jack Sark, Lennox Island Development Corporation; Elijah Smith, Yukon Native Brotherhood; James Wah-Shee, Indian Brotherhood of the North West Territories; Fred Plain and later Bill Sault, Union of Ontario Indians; Philip Paul, Victor Adolph, Heber Maitland, and Bill Mussell of the Union of British Columbia Indian Chiefs. I am indebted and grateful to them all.

Although all these people have contributed substantially to my reflection on the Indian reality and to my own personal experience, it is we, and not they, who must accept final responsibility for what is said here.

The Fourth World

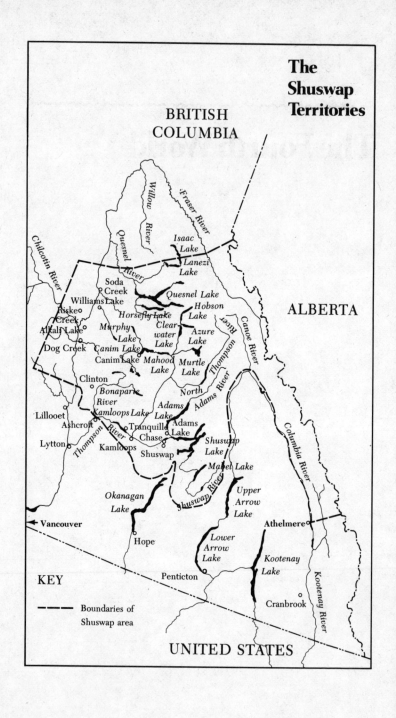

The Shuswap Territories

BRITISH COLUMBIA

ALBERTA

Willow River

Fraser River

Chilcotin River

Quesnel River

Isaac Lake

Lanezi Lake

Soda Creek

Williams Lake

Quesnel Lake

Hobson Lake

Riske Creek

Horsefly Lake

Alkali Lake

Murphy Lake

Clearwater Lake

Azure Lake

Canoe River

Dog Creek

Canim Lake

Canim Lake

Mahood Lake

Murtle Lake

Thompson River

Clinton

Bonaparte River

North

Lillooet

Kamloops Lake

Adams Lake

Adams River

Ashcroft

Tranquille

Adams Lake

Thompson River

Chase

Lytton

Kamloops

Shuswap

Shuswap Lake

Columbia River

Mabel Lake

Okanagan Lake

Shuswap River

Upper Arrow Lake

Vancouver

Athelmere

Hope

Lower Arrow Lake

Kootenay Lake

Penticton

Cranbrook

Kootenay River

UNITED STATES

KEY

— — — Boundaries of Shuswap area

Introduction

"Does Indians Have Feelings?"

THE TERRITORIES OF the Shuswap Nation in the interior of British Columbia encompass an area from Williams' Lake to Athelmere on the Kootenay River and south from that line to the Okanagan. It touches on, or includes within its boundaries the Fraser and North Thompson rivers, providing access to the sea, and the Okanagan Boundary. The land is a mixture of river valleys, lakeshore plateaus, forested hills, and snow-capped mountain peaks. It is diverse enough in its offerings to support the largest Indian nation in the area now occupied by British Columbia.

My recollections of the Shuswap Nation belong to the time when it was just beginning to come under the domination of the Indian agent. Although the process had been set in motion long before, the forces of conquest and colonial rule did not become fully effective in the Shuswap until after World War 1. However precarious our existence may have been in the 1920's, we still maintained our traditional means of livelihood, our language—the key to any culture—and our own internal decision-making processes, the essence of government. We had dignity and self-respect.

Within my own lifetime I have seen my people, the Shuswap nation, fall from a proud state of independence — when we looked to no man's generosity outside our own bounds but only to our own strength and skill and the raw materials with which we had been blessed for our survival — to a condition of degeneration, servitude, and dependence as shameful as any people have ever known. I have also seen my people make the beginning of the long, hard struggle back to the plateau that is our proper place in the world.

What has happened to the Shuswap within my lifetime is a repetition-in-miniature of the last two centuries of North American history. My people, the Shuswap, are a microcosm of the whole Aboriginal World. Only to the extent that for us it has happened in a single lifetime are we more of a microcosm than other Indian nations. Nor were we the last to be colonized. The Waswanapi (James Bay) Cree have only been seriously threatened within the last two years. The peoples of the Northwest Territories and the Yukon only experienced active colonization beginning with the Second Great European War.

The broad overview I offer is a summary of the understanding I have received from listening to both Indian thinkers and other people throughout my life. It reflects, I think, something close to a consensus of how we understand our history. I think that if scholars trouble themselves to prepare the appropriate footnotes and citations, they will find that the story I tell resembles their standard of truth as well as ours. I hope that when that is done, it is presented in a way that is useful, both for Indian people and also for those Europeans for whom the future of North America is as compelling as it is for us.

The gap between the myth of the Indian world as it has been generally represented to European North Americans and the reality I have known has not really closed very much in my lifetime, and what little change there has been has occurred in the decade of the 1960's.

A cornerstone of the mythical structure that has stood in the way of the Indian reality has been a belief that an Indian way of life meant something barbaric and savage, frozen in time and incapable of meeting the test of changing social conditions brought about by new technology. This myth was created by confusing the

2

particular forms in use at one time with the values and beliefs they helped to realize. A man who is wedded to the soil is not necessarily married to a wooden plough. A man of letters is not committed to a fountain pen or a microphone.

It is true that there have been any number of surface changes that have increased understanding. Our children now often go to provincial schools rather than church schools, and we are now allowed into most hotels and protected against the more blatant forms of discrimination.

While these changes may be important for their own sake, few if any of them reach below the surface and touch on the fundamental ways in which two cultures, so different in their roots, meet and touch each other.

Only with that meeting and touching can the gap be closed. Only the closing of the gap—not a domination of one over the other but a real meeting—can result in a real change.

Let me give you an example from my early work experience. I have never forgotten a certain conversation during a coffee break on the first job where I worked side by side with white people on an equal footing. I was a boom man on the Thompson River for a lumber mill that employed about forty men. Maybe two or three of us were Indians.

Another worker with whom I often sat at coffee breaks said to me as he sat down, "Can I ask you a question that's been on my mind for some time?"

"Sure," I said.

"Does Indians have feelings"? he asked.

"Yes, Indians have feelings," I told him.

"You know, my wife and I often talked about this, and since you're my friend I felt you wouldn't be offended if I asked you. We actually feel Indians is no different from dogs, no feelings at all for kinship."

A second incident occurred one Monday, as we were sitting in the mill yard having coffee. From the mill yard you could look across the river and see the Catholic church on our reserve. The priest would come around to that church once a month on a Sunday and stay until Tuesday. During those three days almost everybody went to church every day, as though to make up for the time lost between his visits. This sight amused the white men, who on that day started to laugh so that I thought they would split their ribs. They were laughing at all the Indians going to church on a Monday, a working day.

I was still a long way from learning to project an aggressive and forceful personality. I must have been provoked past the point of caring when I said, "You're laughing at my people. It's you who brainwashed my people to go to church."

"What do you mean, 'we'? We had nothing to do with it."

"Your people did. The white people did. We had our own religion. It was your ancestors, whether you were there or not, who compelled the Indian people to go to church and give up our own religion. Now, after you did this to my people, you laugh at them."

Perhaps neither of these conversations would be so likely to take place today. But how often has a dialogue, however crude, been replaced by silence? If this is change it is certainly not progress.

For a people who have fallen from a proud state of independence and self-sufficiency, progress—substantial change—can come about only when we again achieve that degree of security and control over our own destinies. We do not need to re-create the exact forms by which our grandfathers lived their lives—the clothes, the houses, the political systems, or the means of travel. We do need to create new forms that will allow the future generations to inherit the values, the strengths, and the basic spiritual beliefs—the way of understanding the world—that is the fruit of a thousand generations' cultivation of North American soil by Indian people.

At this point in our struggle for survival, the Indian peoples of North America are entitled to declare a victory. We have survived. If others have also prospered on our land, let it stand as a sign between us that the Mother Earth can be good to all her children without confusing one with another. It is a myth of European warfare that one man's victory requires another's defeat.

Perhaps the one true change of substance I have seen is the growing number of non-Indian people who are coming to value the land, the air, the water, and the light as we do. It is no coincidence that at a time when Indian people are looking to our old ways for strength and guidance, others are also learning that if we too long abuse the medicines of nature, they will no longer work for us.

An awareness of another common bond has also been growing among the colonized peoples of the world. Whenever a tribal people have come under the domination of a European power, there has been the common experience of colonialism. Were this a political experience that did not reach to the very roots of our being, striking at the very heart of our view of the world, it would not have forged such a compelling bond between such distant peoples.

Were there not already a common understanding of the universe shared by many, if not all, of these people before the coming of the Europeans, the mere fact that we had all had a period of foreign domination would not be an enduring link. The bond of colonialism we share with the Third World peoples is the shared values that distinguish the Aboriginal world from the nation-states of the Third World.

Each time that I have visited another aboriginal people in their homeland—the Maoris and Australian aborigines, the Polynesians, the Lapps, the Africans—I have been touched by two kinds of common bond I held with the people I was greeting. (It was the Maoris who taught me the use of the name "European," rather than white. In New Zealand even the more progressive whites use the Maori word *Pakeha*, meaning "European," to describe themselves. If Europeans can come to terms with their own origins, they may no longer need to insist upon their purity, i.e., whiteness.)

First, the distinction between the Third World and the Aboriginal World is at present political, but will eventually be seen as religious and economic. The Third World is emerging at this time primarily because it is rapidly learning to adapt its life-style to Western technology; it reacts to Western political concepts; and it uses racial issues to pivot its expanding influence between the super-powers, gathering concessions from both sides while struggling to imitate them.

It was a Tanzanian diplomat who said to me, "When the Indian peoples come into their own, that will be the Fourth World." I do not think he meant that we would create nation-states like his own, but that, like Tanzania, the nation-state would learn to contain within itself many different cultures and life-ways, some highly tribal and traditional, some highly urban and individual. At that point the Third World will no longer need to imitate and compete with the European empires from which they have so recently escaped.

The Aboriginal World has so far lacked the political muscle to emerge: it is without economic power; it rejects Western political techniques; it is unable to comprehend Western technology unless it can be used to extend and enhance traditional life forms; and it finds its strength above and beyond Western ideas of historical process. While the Third World can eventually emerge as a force capable of maintaining its freedom in the struggle between East and West, the Aboriginal World is almost wholly dependent upon the good faith and morality of the nations of East and West within which it finds itself.

Second, when I met with the Maori people, on my first trip beyond the shores of North America, if I had said, "Our culture is every inch of our land," the meaning would have been obvious to them. Wherever I have travelled in the Aboriginal World, there has been a common attachment to the land.

This is not the land that can be speculated, bought, sold, mortgaged, claimed by one state, surrendered or counter-claimed by another. Those are things that men do only on the land claimed by a king who rules by the grace of God, and through whose grace and favour men must make their fortunes on this earth.

The land from which our culture springs is like the water and the air, one and indivisible. The land is our Mother Earth. The animals who grow on that land are our spiritual brothers. We are a part of that Creation that the Mother Earth brought forth. More complicated, more sophisticated than the other creatures, but no nearer to the Creator who infused us with life.

The struggle of the past four centuries has been between these two ideas of land. Lurking behind this struggle for land was a conflict over the nature of man himself. Aboriginal people were not born with the debit balance of original sin to work off in this world to assure their place in the next. We did not think of the individual existing prior to his being a part of the tribe or clan. If a task was incomplete at the time of his departure, it was an inheritance of the nation to carry on, not a judgement against man.

Political processes reflect the same difference in world views. In a society where all are related, where everybody is someone else's mother, father, brother, sister, aunt, or cousin, and where you cannot leave without eventually coming home, simple decisions require the approval of nearly everyone in that society. It is the society as a whole, not merely a part of it, that must survive.

A society like European North America, which avoids stability at all costs and keeps all its social factors in a perpetual state of change, demands only that a majority of people consent to proposed actions. At any one time there are those who are "in" and those who are "out." If the outs cannot gain the majority to make more changes, they always have the option of getting out of the society altogether.

Although there are as wide variations between different Indian cultures as between different European cultures, it seems to me that all of our structures and values have developed out of a spiritual relationship with the land on which we have lived. Our customs and practices vary as the different landscapes of the continent, but underlying this forest of legitimate differences is a common soil of social and spiritual experience.

The Fourth World emerges as each people develops customs and practices that wed it to the land as the forest is to the soil, and as people stop expecting that there is some unnamed thing that grows equally well from sea to sea. As each of our underdeveloped nations begins to mature, we may learn to share this common bed without persisting in a relationship of violence and abduction. Such mutuality can come only as each respects the wholeness of the other, and also acknowledges his own roots.

The first years of contact between Europeans and various Indian nations often provided a new flowering for both the local and the visiting cultures. Both the native people and the visitors developed a mutual dependence that assured that even when relations were not friendly they would at least be respectful and, for the most part, peaceable. This pattern seems to apply both on the east coast and, almost two centuries later, on the west coast, including to some degree those Indian nations who maintained regular trade routes by river from interior homelands to either coast.

Both cultures had many things to give each other. As long as the trading continued on the basis of mutual interdependence, it cannot be said that either one got the better of the other. By what standard do you measure?

One of the earliest treaties between Europeans and North American Indians was recorded by the Iroquois as the Two Row Wampum Belt. The two rows that are woven into the pattern symbolize the path of two vessels travelling on parallel paths but neither interfering with the other. It is only through the mutual acknowledgement of the other's reality that it is possible to travel on parallel courses and avoid collision. It is the emergence of this kind of mutual acknowledgement that I would understand to be the only standard of positive change and integration.

There is another, secondary but important, interpretation of the Two Row Wampum. What is the fate of the man who stands with one foot on the bow plate of each of the two vessels when those boats hit rough water?

I have spent much of my adult life straddling the two vessels in the hope that some honest coming-together was possible. If there has not been substantial change in my lifetime in relations between the two main cultures of Canada—Indian and European—the problem has its roots in the failure to look at North American history as we are taught to look at European history, as the trunk and the roots, not as the borrowed branch. When we do this we see that the culture of North America is that of the Indian nations.

It is not, of course, the school-book histories that have kept us apart. They are but a shortened statement of European consciousness in North America. The reason we have not come together is far simpler than the racial myth of the schoolbooks.

We have not come together in three hundred years of living on the same land because neither side would accept the other's terms of union.

Canadian authorities, since Confederation, have offered an open hand to an Indian who, as one major-general recruiting Indians for the Canadian army in the far north recently put it, "becomes one of us"—that is, an enfranchised, tax-paying Christian who brings nothing from his past, unless it is saleable.

As Indian nations were "discovered," one after another, we responded to the European offers with the Two Row Wampum

Our celebration honours the emergence of the Fourth World: the utilization of technology and its life-enhancing potential within the framework of the values of the peoples of the Aboriginal World...(Note the Two Row Wampum Belt at the bottom.)

Belt or some variation on that basic idea. Our terms were found unacceptable. Another solution was found.

I do not know whether Europe is such a poor place that its peoples have always had to travel and plunder to sustain themselves, or whether its peoples have been placed at a strategic crossroads that has furnished them with a unique opportunity. That is too great a question to have an answer. Certainly, the role of town crier within the global village is both vital and valid. But it is common knowledge that the messenger is not the scribe. And the scribe is not the thinker who originates the message. The town crier need not be a chief in anyone's culture.

No one can make an exclusive claim to the making of the global village, or to the wisdom to guide it. Similarly, the political leaders and scholars who have been saying, "The Indians' old world is disappearing. He must make the change to the white man's civilization whether he likes it or not," are pretending to speak with the voice of the Creator.

Throughout the nineteenth and early twentieth centuries, enquiry after enquiry assured the Canadian government that we Indians were dying off of our own accord. With the epidemics of disease and famine that these commissions catalogued, the rate of conversion to Christianity was so great that the vanishing souls of our ancestors would all arrive safely at their proper place.

Indian spiritual leaders have been telling our people for a very long time that every man answers directly to his Creator through his own conscience, that he is judged by that Creator according to his service to his community, and that every man has the potential to make that service. My grandfather, who raised me from my infancy until his death when I was twelve years old, was an Indian doctor. It was on such a view of the world that he based all his teachings, both spiritual and medical, for the two were never very far apart.

It has been difficult to communicate his knowledge to a culture that published pictures of him burning in hell, and made his spiritual practices an indictable offence. So much gets lost in the translation when two cultures cannot find a common language. Today, when more and more young people in North America, of all races, are trying to understand his wisdom, some translation of what he was saying, and its political implications, may be possible.

The National Indian Brotherhood will celebrate the victory of the Indian peoples by bringing together aboriginal peoples from every corner of the globe.

Our celebration will embrace the aboriginal peoples of the world: the Indians of the Americas, the Lapps of Northern Scandinavia, the Polynesian and Pacific Basin peoples, the Basques of Spain, the Welsh and Celts of Great Britain, the Maori and Australian aborigines. These are the people whom we know, but there are more. Within the Soviet Union, China, Japan, and Ceylon are numerous peoples unknown in the Western world who share the status and perhaps the fate of Western aborigines. If no other way is open to them, we will be with them in spirit.

Our victory celebration will honour the fact of our survival, that we have not forgotten the words and deeds of our grandfathers, and that today Indian people throughout North America are undergoing a rebirth, as self-conscious societies aware of our own unique role in the history of this continent.

Our cultures have survived because they possess a strength and vitality with which the visitors to our continent have not yet been prepared to credit us. The ancients, both in Europe and in America, would have said, "Your gods are as strong as our gods."

Does it matter how many battles others say you have lost if on the day of reckoning you have survived? In a Christian framework, victory means to make it to the day of reckoning. In an Indian framework, every day is the day of reckoning.

Our celebration honours our grandfathers who kept it alive.

The present concern with ecological disasters visited upon Western man by his failure to recognize land, water, and air as social, not individual, commodities, testifies to aboriginal man's sophistication in his conception of universal values.

As we view the North American Indian world today, we must keep in mind two things: Indians have not yet left the aboriginal universe in which they have always dwelt emotionally and intellectually, and the Western world is gradually working its way out of its former value system and into the value system of the Aboriginal World.

Our celebration honours the emergence of the Fourth World: the utilization of technology and its life-enhancing potential within the framework of the values of the peoples of the Aboriginal

World—not a single messianic moment after which there will never be another raging storm, but the free use of power by natural human groupings, immediate communities, people who are in direct contact with one another, to harness the strength of the torrent for the growth of their own community. Neither apartheid nor assimilation can be allowed to discolour the community of man in the Fourth World. An integration of free communities and the free exchange of people between those communities according to their talents and temperaments is the only kind of confederation that is not an imperial domination.

The Fourth World is a vision of the future history of North America and of the Indian peoples. The two histories are inseparable. It has been the insistence on the separation of the people from the land that has characterized much of recent history. It is this same insistence that has prevented European North Americans from developing their own identity in terms of the land so that they can be happy and secure in the knowledge of that identity.

1

~~~~~~

Mutual Dependence

TECHNOLOGIES ARE ONLY the tools through which we carry on our relationships with nature. The great accomplishments of Indian technology are almost all related to food, clothing, housing, and medicine. In the early days of colonization in North America, there was a meeting of technologies — Indian and European.

Measured by the needs of the common man, the commodities Indian nations had to offer in the greatest abundance were the ones European man most lacked. What the Europeans had to offer in consideration for having their basic needs met was the techniques with which to do the same job better.

Europeans, for instance, were already highly skilled at making knives, axes, and other steel products that easily out-performed the equivalent Indian tools. But how much food, medicine, and clothing did they produce with these tools? How well did the average European peasant eat in the course of a long winter? How well did he meet the ravages of disease brought home by the aristocratic explorers he helped to support?

It has been estimated that the average European at the time of Columbus was five feet tall. One out of ten Europeans in those days was deformed in some way due to insufficient diet—hunchbacked, crippled, lame, deaf, blind, or retarded. That does not include those who simply died in their infancy from the same root causes. This was Europe after its Renaissance.

At that time North American Indians were cultivating six hundred different types of corn; all the different kinds of beans known today (except horse and soy beans, which came from China); potatoes; peanuts; and a host of other foodstuffs on which our present civilization is far more dependent than it is on whatever Europeans were eating before they got here. Nothing in this list was then on their diets.

The preparation of "Boston-baked beans" was taught by the Wampanoag Indians to the Pilgrims. Other east coast Indians taught Europeans to enjoy such dishes as clam chowder, oyster stew, baked pumpkin, cranberry sauce, and popcorn, and introduced them to squash, celery, buckwheat, maple sugar, pepper, chocolate, and tapioca. The list is virtually endless.

How much meat was available to the average European? The movies treat us to the sight of men feasting on venison and wild boar. But the books tell us that a prosperous peasant might have owned a cow and a few sheep, and only his lord was permitted to hunt in the forest. The distribution of food is part of the story of social relations to which I'll return when I talk about my own people. What is important here is that whether the Indians cultivated meat through animal husbandry or harvested it from the natural state, it was in abundant supply, because it was carefully conserved both in the harvesting and in the storing. No people have been entirely free of the scourge of famine, but few Indian societies were familiar with protein deficiency in the normal cycle of a generation.

Our technology was not limited to good eating. The first time Europeans saw rubber was when they observed Indians playing a game similar to basketball. These same Indians had such practical uses for rubber as waterproof clothing and rubber boots.

We had developed a highly sophisticated use of medicinal herbs. In the four hundred years since Europeans came to this continent, there has not been a single medicinal plant discovered that was not known to the Indian people of the region in which that plant grows.

Among our contributions to the world pool of technology are manufactured items as well—toboggans, canoes, and snowshoes on which we still rely when more sophisticated transportation breaks down.

Europeans today are actually living closer to the way that *our* grandfathers lived at the time of Columbus—not only in their food, clothing, medicine, and recreation, but also in their style of government and ease of travel—than in the ways of their own ancestors at the same time.

The Indian nations have given more to the world's technology than they have received from it. But the calculation cannot be made in terms of levels of technology as a measure of civilization. If every race prepared a list as long as this one, no one list would detract from the strength and value of any other. Similarly, it was not to Europeans that the gifts were given, but to whoever had need of them. Technology is the stew-pot of the global village. Every technical development from every culture, nation, or race is contributed to the feeding of the whole community of man.

What is important about such a list in general is the evidence it offers of creativity, imagination, and humanity. The Indian list, in contrast to the European one, also gives some important clues about differences in values and goals. Europe's most important contributions that are still of value today seem either to be means of transport or instruments of war: ships, wagons, steelware, certain breeds of horses, guns. Most of the other things that were brought to North America by Europeans came from other parts of the world: paper, print, gunpowder, glass, mathematics, and Christianity.

I do not think it does anyone discredit to say that our efforts at technological development have focused most sharply on meeting the needs of the common man, and raising the mere act of physical survival to a high art in which all could participate. If Europeans learned to travel because of poverty, perhaps we cultivated our relationship with the land out of the need to survive. What matters is that two different paths were taken and two different bodies of knowledge and life-ways developed.

What happened when two so different life-ways met?

15

No general statement can fully describe the full range of responses that occurred between such a variety of European and North American nations on first sight, or during the first year.

The Spanish replayed their homeland inquisition against both the island-dwelling Arawaks and Caribs and, when they arrived on the mainland, in the nations of the Aztecs and the Incas. The only thing in this land in which they could find value was gold. So they proceeded to make slaves of the islanders and kill off those who were not immediately useful to them.

Not every group of early visitors was seeking riches. French aristocrats, for example, who landed on the Pacific islands spent many years sharing knowledge with their native counterparts, whom they clearly regarded as their equals in every respect. They learned each other's language in order to share different ideas of the Creation and the universe. They exchanged vast amounts of technical information. And these civilized Frenchmen warned their Polynesian friends against the barbarian element who held power in their native France.[1]

North of the area invaded by Spain, the Dutch, French, and English were developing trading posts and small plantations whose relationships with the host nations were more moderate and more practical than either of these extremes. In almost all these contacts, after the initial shock of learning of one another's existence, very little happened during the first generation — and often for several generations — that could be considered a major conflict.

The European settlements on the east coast could not have existed without the good will and tacit support of the east coast Indian nations. In fact, it is most unlikely that the colonists and traders could have survived their first winter without the hospitality of the people to whose land they had come. And there were as many "first winters" as there were separate European settlements isolated from other Europeans. Ships leaving Europe in the spring at that time were fortunate if they arrived on our east coast by the fall. But by then it would be too late to prepare for the winters to which we are accustomed. And who would have had the knowledge of the terrain, the animals, or the other forms of food supply with which to prepare for a winter?

Much has been made of the "first winter's hospitality," even by

European writers. European settlement began on the east coast in the early 1600's. Eastern Indian civilizations did not begin to collapse until the revolt of the English Colonies against their mother country, 150 years later. It was not for just a single winter, but a period of five human generations, that people avoided a major outbreak of hostilities.

Even the deeply spiritual commitment to hospitality shared by all Indian cultures could not have justified this extended period of cooperation. This was the period of mutual dependence for that part of the world, when both Europeans and North Americans believed themselves to be benefiting from an exchange which allowed both cultures to better meet their own needs.

Of course, there were periodic conflicts of the sort that arise spontaneously between any neighbouring societies whose ways differ sharply. But, like brush fires, these were easily extinguishable unless the powers of the time chose to allow or even to encourage them to spread. Most of these conflicts arose either out of the presence of alcohol, or out of a failure of the newcomers to understand and respect local custom. So long as the period of mutual dependence continued, the governors of the European settlements, whenever such a misunderstanding arose, considered it to be in their interest to ensure a conciliation rather than to fan the flames of hate.

The disasters that befell our brothers of the eastern nations at the end of the eighteenth and beginning of the nineteenth centuries came about because of their unavoidable participation in European wars fought on our soil, and the simultaneous spreading of disease. Small pox, tuberculosis, syphilis and trachoma—all were new diseases against which neither Indian nor European medicine of that time could prevail. As they spread, once powerful peoples were reduced to momentary impotence. The combined plagues of war and disease cut their numbers in half.

By the end of the War of 1812—more than 200 years after the founding of the Hudson's Bay Company, the Virginia Company, and the Dutch East India Company—the eastern nations were no longer a power to be reckoned with. Up to that time their influence had been decisive in each European war fought on this continent. Nor was the option of neutrality ever open in these wars. There were many who explored that avenue in the variety of

17

wars between the Spanish, French, English, Dutch, and colonials. When they attempted to remain neutral, they found themselves under attack from both sides for "trading with the enemy."

Reduced to impotence, the eastern nations were no longer seen as useful allies either by the English, whose authority continued in British North America, or by the newly established Republic of the United States. The economic relationships cultivated over the preceding centuries were no longer needed by Europeans, who were already developing their own trade routes into the interior of the continent. Both William Johnson, on behalf of George III, and George Washington, on behalf of the new republic, had made treaties and alliances recognizing the sovereignty and valuing the friendship of the Indian nations who allied with them. When the body politic of these nations was weakened by the ravages of disease and war, these alliances became like spent money. Gone.

Concepts of honour, tradition, law, and order could not prevail against the more purely economic motives of an acquisitive society religiously committed to possessive individualism.

Imagine Europe immediately after the bubonic plagues of the fourteenth century had swept across every natural boundary including the English Channel. Many towns have lost two-thirds of their people within less time than it takes for a new-born baby to grow to manhood. Half the people who were living in western Europe a decade ago have been carried away by the plague. Now, imagine an invasion from some other territory into England, France, Germany, and Spain similar in size and force to the invasions of the Roman Empire a thousand years earlier. When you imagine that single addition to the actual events of European history, you are picturing the fate of the Seminoles, Cherokees, Penobscots, Wampanoags, Micmacs, Malecites, Algonquins, Hurons, and Iroquois between 1760 and 1830.

If our instruments of war had been as highly developed as our social structures, our agriculture, and our medicine, the result might have been still different again.

The possible directions in which history might move at any one moment are endless. The reason for looking at the possibilities is not to change the reality but to better understand it. What happened to those Indian nations at that point is not really different from what has happened to many other peoples at some time in their history, a momentary weakness due to events beyond any living person's understanding. *Only when the internal disorganization was coupled with a threat from outside did the situation become unmanageable.* What has so often been put forward as the superiority of the English race seems clearly to have been an historical accident, the combination of two forces, both the result of the total history of two different cultures.

The Plains nations had a much different history of relations with European settlements than did peoples of either coast. For them there was no period of mutual dependence and beneficial contact when they were in direct contact with European settlements. The influence of European settlement to the south and on the coast was felt through trade long before the period of westward expansion.

The horses that were to revolutionize their hunting economy came to them from herds of wild horses that had escaped during uprisings against the Spanish in the late seventeenth century.[2] The steel utensils, canvas, and guns came through established trade routes with their southern and eastern neighbours.

By the time the Europeans were ready to move west of the Mississippi and renounce the sacred promises made both by George Washington and George III, the basic European attitude had already been consolidated. The Indian nations were an inconvenience that stood in the way of the Manifest Destiny with which the eastern god had blessed his new empire. Their main historic asset had been land. It was the surrender of that land that the new American empire demanded of them.

By this time, extermination through massacre and the deliberate spreading of disease had become institutionalized as the standard way in which European powers sought to relate to Indian peoples. General Sheridan's discovery that destroying the buffalo cut off the principal source of food, clothing, and housing materials for many peoples raised these instruments of westward expansion from an affair of occasional convenience to an officially sanctified marriage that would bear the death of nation after nation.

The Buffalo Hunters have done more in the last two years to settle the vexed Indian Question than the entire regular army in the last thirty years. They are destroying the Indians' commissary. Send them powder and lead, if you will, and let them kill,

19

skin and sell until they have exterminated the buffalo. Then your prairies will be covered with speckled cattle and the festive cowboy, who follows the hunter as a second forerunner of civilization.[3]

The record of European relations, and the clear intent to exterminate people as well as the supplies, is nowhere more obvious, or more widely published, than on the Plains.

The record in Canada, though less widely published, is no less clear than it is in the United States. *Canada resorted to major acts of violence less often than the United States because she was a prime beneficiary of the American aggression against the peoples of the Plains.* John A. Macdonald was Canada's first Minister of Indian Affairs as well as her first Prime Minister. Neither he nor his Liberal successor, William Mackenzie, were restrained in their use of violence where it appeared expedient.

It was Macdonald who waged war on the new Métis Nation, formed in a land then claimed by no other state. It was he who promised pardons—which ought not to have been needed—and then refused to provide them. It was he who refused to receive Sitting Bull's Sioux as loyal subjects of the Queen and forced them to return to certain death.

Macdonald may not have spoken in terms of Manifest Destiny, but he advised Queen Victoria, when she would not make Canada a kingdom in its own right, to call it a dominion, a term taken from the biblical statement,

> ... and let them have dominion over the fish of the sea, and over the fowl of the air, and over the cattle, and over all the earth, and over every creeping thing that creepeth upon the earth.

It was his administration that negotiated most of the treaties in Canada—treaties the Indian leaders signed because, they confessed, during many of the official discussions recorded by the Governor's secretary, their people had not enough food to see their way through the next winter.

American treaties, in contrast to Canada's, required confirmation by the Senate, as well as the signature of the president. Once confirmed, they had the force of law. But very often the next administration broke its predecessor's treaties. Sometimes the

Senate refused to ratify a treaty made by the president, who then broke his earlier word. And Indian leaders often pointed out that they were not allowed time to consult with their councils as the president could with the Senate.

Macdonald and Mackenzie perfected the American game with a formula that meant that treaties were not enforceable in law in the first place. Typically, the government was represented by a lieutenant-governor, the Queen's personal representative as head of state at the provincial level, a man who could lend sufficient prestige to the proceedings that he could claim to speak directly on behalf of Her Majesty. Once signed, all the clauses of surrender were taken as valid, but no court to which there was ready access had the power to oblige the government to fulfil its obligations. The lieutenant-governor could not bind Parliament to spend money, nor could he exempt people from paying taxes that Parliament had levied.

The Indian Act, on the other hand, was passed into law by Parliament without any reference to the realities of Indian life as Indian spokesmen might have explained them.

It was Macdonald's first administration that passed an "Act providing for the organization of the Department of the Secretary of State and for the management of Indian and Ordinance Lands." The title is deceiving—this was Canada's first Indian Act. Perhaps the first Indian law was officially described as land legislation because even the constitution recognizes that the land and the people are inseparable. "Indians and lands reserved for the Indians" is the twenty-fourth in a series of exclusively federal powers listed in Section 91 of the British North America Act.

This Act was not as repressive as later legislation, but it did continue in force a provincial statute inherited by the federal government at Confederation called, "An Act respecting the civilization and enfranchisement of certain Indians." The rule that an Indian could only become civilized and enfranchised by ceasing to be an Indian was applied to the rest of Canada, beyond Ontario and Quebec, by "An Act for the gradual enfranchisement of Indians," a week short of Canada's second birthday. Before the western provinces were acquired and before the treaties were negotiated, the basic terms under which the people would live were already clearly spelled out, by John A. Macdonald.

It was Mackenzie's government that created the first Indian Act called by that name, and in doing so changed the legislation from being protective to restrictive. The definition of who was an Indian was narrowed for the first time. It was no longer a question of a person being "reputed to be an Indian," a phrase that could be taken to mean accepted by the band as a member rather than a strict tracing of male blood line, an English way of tracing lineage not accepted by very many Indian societies.

It was Mackenzie who prohibited Indians in the newly acquired territories from acquiring a homestead, without withdrawing from his treaty in the way Macdonald had already provided. He also compelled every judge receiving evidence from an Indian, to

> caution every such Indian, or non-treaty Indian, as aforesaid, that he will be liable to incur punishment if he did not . . . tell the truth. (*Statutes of Canada, 1868*)

With Macdonald's return to power, the Indian Act achieved its clearest statement of intent when it defined a person as "any individual other than an Indian."

This was the mind of Canada's Parliament, elected to represent the people of the northeastern half of the continent, as they began their period of western expansion.

The early Macdonald government purchased the Northwest Territories from the Hudson's Bay Company. The Territories at that time included what is now the prairie provinces, northern Ontario, and northern Quebec. In the proclamations confirming the transactions, the Government promised always to respect the rights of the native people then occupying the land, and to extinguish their title with compensation before granting rights to anyone else. Like the unenforceable treaties, the writing of this proclamation still remains, but the spirit of its promises was written on the wind.

Canada shed less blood and fought fewer wars because she was the beneficiary of American policy. Troops were sent west twice—on the two occasions when there was resistance to policies that consistently ignored peaceful petitions for aid from starving and diseased peoples. It was not even armed resistance, so much as an effort to set up a government to meet the needs that Ottawa so consistently ignored.

If such resistance appears to have happened only twice, it is because the boundary that had been agreed upon between Britain and the United States bore no relation to the realities of the great North American plains. Neither the Indian people nor the buffalo had ever seen the invisible boundary that now cut through the hearts of many nations. Even the few white settlers who had come to the northern prairies traded through towns on the American side of the line that had river access to the coast.

But the strength of the prairie people had been eroded in the same way as the eastern nations had been undermined. There was less fighting because there was less resistance. There was less resistance because by the time Canada was making her presence felt in the prairies the people were exhausted. They had been starved into submission.

Macdonald and Mackenzie had only to take care not to offend the United States by giving aid and comfort to her sick and starving enemies to reap the harvest of death from the seeds of destruction sown to the south.

There is a story that when the first governor of Vancouver Island was sent out from London he found only one permanently settled colonist to govern. The governor took the next boat home, and the British government appointed the chief factor of the Hudson's Bay Company Governor of Vancouver Island.

Until the gold rush of 1858, European settlement had not become a serious threat to the mainland of British Columbia. Settlement up to that time had occurred only slowly and almost entirely on Vancouver Island, where it was carried on under a governor who sought to prevent grievances, on the part of either the colonists or the native peoples, before they could emerge.

Before the gold rush, for some eighty years the coastal Indian nations had had a growing trade with both the Hudson's Bay Company and the Yankee traders from New England. England had claimed the northern interior under the name of New Caledonia but had made no move to actually exercise sovereignty. Although the area may have been coloured pink on some maps to resemble the rest of the British Empire, London felt no need to actively pursue her claim to such a vast territory as British Columbia.[4]

This was a period of mutual dependence between the west coast native nations and the European traders. It was the sea otter that brought scores of ships to visit the coast while the North West Company was sending men overland to establish posts in the interior to trade for other kinds of fur. It is said that the Yankee Clipper ships took the design of their hull from the great whaling canoes of the west coast, to which they added a superstructure. Even this was a fair exchange, for the coastal people soon had sails on their whalers.

Through the first half of the nineteenth century the Yankee Clippers out of New England traded iron, copper, brass, muskets, cloth, rum, and beads for sea otter furs, which they carried to China for tea, spices, silk, ginger, and porcelain for the European and New England markets. Far from being mere pawns in a game, the Haida, Kwakiutl, Tsimshian, Nishga, and Salish peoples could have seen themselves as part of the first truly round-the-world trading partnership.

These people were by no means passive recipients of whatever trinkets the traders chose to offer. They held out for goods they wanted, and drove hard bargains. In the earliest years, iron, in the form of chisels, was the most popular item. Later, they began to demand that it be forged, or would reject it altogether in favour of other goods in short supply. Copper was also in high demand at first, and its value was set by the small amount of native copper already available. By 1800 the coast was saturated with copper and the demand fell off. Clothing, blankets, muskets, and ammunition remained in steady demand. Blankets and cloth became the standard unit of trade after a while, like the dollar today. The trinkets most commonly described to school children as goods sold to Indians were always secondary items: beads, buttons, brass wire, thread, knives, scissors, stockings, and apples.

The new wealth furnished by the fur trade strengthened rather than weakened the existing social and economic systems. As one scholar put it, "The Northwest Coast society rush out to meet the sea otter trade, to use it, and to shape it to the society's own ends."[5]

The first chiefs to contact the traders were able to turn the Europeans' desire for furs to their own advantage. To the furs they obtained by hunting they could add large numbers obtained by an easier method: trade with other tribes not yet visited by Euro-

These people were by no means passive recipients of whatever trinkets the traders chose to offer. They held out for goods they wanted, and drove hard bargains.

peans. This required only an expansion of native trade routes that existed before the advent of European trade.

Some of the Nootka and Haida chiefs very early tried to claim monopolies and act as middlemen between the traders and other tribes. Later, in the 1830's, Kwakiutl traders travelled along the coast, buying furs at higher prices than the Hudson's Bay Company was paying and selling them to the Yankee ships. Tsimshian and Tlingit chiefs took control over all the trade along the Skeena and Strikine Rivers. So profitable was their business that they fought the white traders to keep them away. One Tlingit chief even led an inland raid that wiped out a small Hudson's Bay post that threatened his trade monopoly. He must have caught the fever of free trade and not realized that only selected European diseases were open to dark-skinned people.

In the interior, the European presence was felt through the pre-established trade routes before any real contact was established. Horses, guns, and other trade items passed into the interior from the south and east in advance of the first explorers. The coastal peoples trading into the interior soon came to dominate neighbouring tribes socially and culturally. The Carrier and Tahltan began to adopt the social systems and ceremonies of their more powerful coastal neighbours. The Athapaskan people around Atlin and Teslin Lakes took on so much coastal custom and language that they are now regarded as "Inland Tlingit."

It should be understood that this kind of cultural adaptation did not so much grow out of the increased volume of trade as from the increased social contacts, exchange of ideas, and actual intermarriages made possible by the trading activity. The increase in economic activity increased the opportunity for social contacts of which people on both sides could take advantage.

Hearing the stories of this period, both from our old people and from scholars, it seems that both the material and cultural exchanges were on a level of meeting mutual needs quite unrelated to the era that followed.

The key that links the period of trade with the time of conquest of the northwest coast was, as in the East and throughout the plains, disease.

The west coast generally was the most densely populated part of the continent. It is estimated that before contact with Europeans, a million native people lived north of Mexico. Thirty per cent of this number lived on the west coast on about 6 per cent of the land area of North America. Estimates of the numbers in British Columbia range from 80,000 to 125,000, or about 40 per cent of the population living north of the present Canadian border. Even taking the most conservative estimates, it is clear that the Indian population of British Columbia as a whole dropped by 60 per cent in the fifty years following 1835. Some tribes lost as much as 90 per cent of their population. None lost less than 40 per cent.

Smallpox, malaria, and typhoid made wars of conquest unnecessary. The introduction of liquor compounded the effects of the natural plagues. Firearms may have escalated traditional feuds to the level of warfare. It is certain they did nothing to stop the decline of the general strength of the people. Still, when the effects of liquor and firearms are compared to the impact of the greater scourges, they cannot be generally called major causes of the decline.

Much, for instance, has been made of the disunity of the small Indian nations. Toward the end of this fifty-year period, when a clear threat from the outside was seen, all the peoples of southern British Columbia were able to organize and unite effectively enough to force the federal government to intervene in a provincial land grab.[6]

If it was the gold rush that prompted London to establish a colonial administration, it was a trading governor who had already spent many years in the area who made a peaceful transition possible. James Douglas was already Chief Factor of the Hudson's Bay Company on Vancouver Island when it was declared a colony. When James Blanshard returned home because there was nobody needing to be governed, Douglas was given authority as governor of the colony. When the mainland was declared the colony of British Columbia, he became the governor of the two still separate colonies.

As colonization progressed, his main concerns, in addition to maintaining an administration, were to purchase the Indian ownership rights to the land and to set aside adequate reserves for our use. Douglas, too, had the usual British view at that time, that although the absolute title to the land was vested in the Crown, the Indians did own proprietary rights to the land that should be respected. Where land was wanted, those rights should be extinguished by making treaties and paying compensation. Between 1850 and 1854, acting as the agent of the Hudson's Bay Company, he made fourteen treaties with the peoples living around Victoria, Nanaimo, and Fort Rupert.

Douglas believed that all cause for discontent would be removed if he gave the Indians as much land as they requested. By the time of his retirement, he had set aside a large number of reserves on Vancouver Island and along the Fraser River. His policy was to give each band whatever plots they chose and as much acreage as they requested. Farming had hardly begun, so that these fishing people never asked for more than ten acres. The pattern of small, scattered reserves often adjoining white communities would, he hoped, provide the close contact needed to integrate the two cultures.

There are many Douglasses today on Leskete Island who call themselves descendants of British Columbia's first governor. Many reports have it that Douglas was related to Napoleon's wife, Josephine. Like her, he was a mixed black and white West Indian.[7] There is a story that indicates the esteem in which he was held. Spence's Bridge is one of the few areas of British Columbia where most of the Indian people joined a major Protestant Church. According to the story, when Douglas went to that area it was seen that the governor was at least partly African.

"If being a Protestant," people said, "can make an African governor, we'll all become Protestants."

If any man could have laid the foundation for a harmonious relationship within the context of British or Canadian sovereignty, Douglas would have done it. But Douglas failed to establish that foundation, because his policy misunderstood the popular will and general sentiment of the colonists at least as much as it misunderstood the thinking of the Indian peoples over whom his authority extended. It is beyond the power of any man, even in the name of the Queen, to create harmony, alone and unaided, against the general will of the people. It is also hard to fault the man who tries.

By 1860, when he was representing only the Crown and was no longer working for the Hudson's Bay Company, Douglas made determined efforts to continue the policy of buying out the Indian rights to the land that was wanted for settlement. The local assembly agreed that it was necessary but, rather than vote the money themselves, they petitioned the Imperial Government in London. The colonial secretary also agreed that the step was an absolute necessity, but maintained that the funds should be raised locally. Neither the Imperial nor the local legislatures were prepared to spend money to extend the rule of law to Indian people whose lands, bodies, and souls they pretended to govern.

When Governor Douglas retired in 1864, his successors did not feel that they had to recognize aboriginal title. When Douglas's hands had been tied during the last years of his administration, colonists still continued to move onto land to which they had no claim. And they do not appear to have suffered any great wrath for their actions.[8]

His successors cut back the size of many of the reserves he had established, and where farming was coming into use in the interior regions they tried to apply the same standard allotment per family that was given to fishing people.

British Columbia entered Confederation in 1871. Control over Indian matters now passed from the local governor to the Secretary of State in Ottawa. Generally, if a people must be subjected to colonial rule, the greater their distance from the conquering power, the less harsh the rule will be. It is a lesser of evils. The problem here was in the transition.

The federal government's responsibility would now extend to "the charge of the Indians and the trusteeship and management of the lands reserved for their use and benefit." But the province retained possession of public or Crown lands within the province, at a time when for many bands no lands had been reserved at all. Others had just had their allotments cut back.

The result of these conflicting powers was that, five years after British Columbia entered Confederation, the Indian nations of the southern interior, according to reports wired to Ottawa, were at the point of open warfare.

The Dominion had agreed, in the terms of Union, to continue a policy "as liberal as that hitherto pursued by the British Columbia Government."[9] If the statement referred to the post-Douglas administration, it was a cruel mockery. If it rested on the remains of Douglas's reputation for generosity, it was a measure of Ottawa's ignorance of almost everything west of the mountains,

Indian or otherwise, and her disinterest in becoming informed.

On the prairies, the federal government had made treaties allowing one square mile per family or 160 acres per person compared to 10 acres per family on the coast. Only the threat of war could create a spark of curiosity about British Columbian matters in Ottawa.

Basically, Douglas had guaranteed each small Indian band the land it was occupying at the time of the negotiations. This often ignored the Indian reality that the band would move to several specific and identifiable camps during their annual cycle of food gathering. Which camp they received might depend on the time of year in which the negotiations were carried on. Still, it had the virtue that Douglas, who had already consulted with the assembly elected by the colonists, did actually inquire of the different bands about their actual needs.

After Confederation there were no longer two parties involved, but three: the different Indian bands and nations; the province; and the Dominion. To keep matters simple, the party most directly affected was left out of the negotiations. A federal-provincial reserve commission was set up to establish reserves on the mainland coastal territory and the lands lying along the gold rush routes into the interior. One claimed they owned the land. The other claimed they owned the Indians. This commission had no authority to make treaties or to negotiate title, but only to establish reserves on the basis of an agreed formula.

Since the time of Union, the interior and mainland Indians from the Shuswap down to the American border had been organizing to make their demands known. When the reserve commission began to function in 1876, the commissioners observed that the interior of the province was on the verge of open war.

Chief Joseph, the Nez Perce leader, was still holding off the U.S. Cavalry's attacks just south of the border. By strength of numbers there is no doubt the Indian nations could have won. Unlike Manitoba, where Riel had stood a few years before, there was no way that troops could have been moved into the area in large numbers on an overland route within Canada.[10]

Ottawa instructed the commission that if war should result because of the failure of the province to be as generous as possible, Ottawa would take the necessary steps. With these new instructions the commission found a formula for allotting the size of lands to be reserved that avoided the threat of war and postponed the more fundamental questions.

The B.C. land question that took root at this time has come to dominate Indian legal and political action in each generation of Indian leadership down to the present. In June 1972, the Union of B.C. Indian Chiefs presented a brief to the federal cabinet on the nature of the Aboriginal Title to British Columbia. The Nishga Tribal Council had taken their case for the title to the Nass River Valley to the Supreme Court of Canada the previous November. This was sixty-one years after Sir Wilfrid Laurier promised B.C. Indians he would find a way to have their case heard in the Privy Council and forty-five years after a parliamentary committee decided the claim "had not been proven." Throughout the century since the Terms of Union were drawn up, the B.C. land question has been raised through every channel that appeared to open from time to time. The response, almost invariably, was to close that channel. But, that is another story.

British Columbia was the first British colony to deny that native people held an aboriginal title. In the territories ceded directly from the Hudson's Bay Company to Canada, this was the major treaty-making period. These treaties cover all the area from northwestern Ontario to the Rocky Mountains and north into the lower regions of the Yukon and Northwest Territories.

Canada's official stand was that it would follow whatever policy had been laid down by those who preceded it. If the Hudson's Bay Company had honoured title, Canada would honour title. If a colonial administration had not honoured title, Canada would deny title. Honour, to Ottawa, is attached to the land, like timber and minerals. If the honour does not come with the land, Ottawa has none to lend it.

Once the Dominion declared Indians to be non-persons, it could have a consistent policy from sea-to-sea simply by maintaining the light of whatever facet of the British Crown reflected on that particular territory.

The period of mutual dependence had ended by the time Douglas had retired. From a European point of view, the Indian in Canada was moving from a period of nuisance to a period of irrelevance. Now we were merely a small obstruction in the Plan of Providence for her Northern Empire. Like a bad debt we were to be written off in the most expeditious manner possible.[11]

From an Indian point of view, we were entering into a period which, in European terms, can only be compared to a time of exile. There is no single Trail of Tears that can be drawn on Canadian maps as it must be drawn for the Cherokee Nation. We were not banished from our land. It is as though the land was moved from under us.

The struggle that was to come was for the mind and soul of the Indian people. We had lost our land. Now they would try to convince us it was for our own good.

2

Strong Medicine

"*WHAT WAS THE* low point of Indian history in the interior of British Columbia? Economically?" The question was posed by a journalist to a friend of mine who is a scholar of native history.

My friend, looking at his calendar watch, hesitated before speaking. "It may be 1972," he said. "The grandfathers of the present generation were often in a better economic relationship with the surrounding culture than their grandchildren have now," he explained. "The surrounding culture was not so mechanized. The economic situation of the Indian people sixty, seventy years ago has to be called better than it is today. Maybe we haven't reached the low point yet."

The transition from a hunting-and-gathering economy within a strong, well-defined social order to an economy of farming, hunting, and gathering was fairly easy when you compare it to the move from reserve to city without any change of skills. The Plains people[12] objected to farming as women's work, and sometimes as irreligious. The people of the plateau saw farming differently; it

33

was an addition to the existing economy and not a second-rate substitute. It did not bring down our whole social order. It did not take children away from the family circle. It did not take men away from jobs at which they were skilled to do menial work for strange men far away. Farming, for us, was a change in land use that did not require a complete renunciation of the relationship between the land and the men who lived on it.

So long as that relationship could grow, our way of life was strong, however it might change. Economically, and therefore socially, we were really threatened only when the thrust of government policy was to separate the people from their land.

The traditional Shuswap economy did not collapse with the Act of Union that joined British Columbia to Canada. Nor did it die out with the work of the reserve commissions. In fact, it took the federal government quite a long time to build up an administrative structure to control Indian communities in the interior at all. At first there was only a single commissioner, Dr. Powell, for the whole of British Columbia. Later, they appointed a second commissioner, a Mr. Lenahan, to govern the interior. But it was only in the late 1880's that there were actually Indian agents for each district within that vast territory.

Chase, my home town, was eighty miles from the gold rush trail of the 1850's. Before the birth of Kamloops, the nearest Hudson's Bay Trail had been at Cache Creek. The first wave of European migration passed us by. Indeed, my grandfather was a married man with children before horses became common in our immediate area. When he was first married, sometime in the 1860's or 70's, he worked for a time with the Hudson's Bay Company packing in supplies on his back.

The human leftovers, who had failed to find a niche for themselves in the California gold rush of the 1840's, came northward, often crossing into present-day British Columbia. When the British Columbia gold rush was on in 1858, this riffraff was followed by a massive American migration. Along with the positive virtues these pioneers may have had, they also brought the habit of shooting Indians for sport. The first Bishop of New Westminster tells in his memoirs of travelling the freight route with the district court judge of the day, Judge Begbie, when he first began to hear cases against white men who shot Indians. What was noteworthy about these prosecutions was not the crime—which had been going on for many years—but the decision to extend the protection of the courts, and the authority of the colonial government, to Indian people. It would still be many years before a dispute between two Indians would be heard before a government court. The decision to assert British authority over the territory north of the forty-ninth parallel must have been seen as a very mixed blessing.

The first years that I remember are the 1920's, when I was a young boy living with my grandparents on the reserve at Shuswap. I did not grow up with my own parents; my father had died when I was a baby and I had gone to stay with my grandparents, where I remained even when my mother remarried. At that time it was just as common for children to grow up with their grandparents as with their parents, so my own situation did not seem very much out of the ordinary.

There was so much in our life then that was good. We were still free to follow our own way of life. If the years that followed had brought the skills and prosperity of urban middle-class life, as many thought and hoped it would, perhaps that time would be remembered as one of hardship. Looking back from where we stand today, when 56 per cent of our people are unemployed at the best of times—and most of those who have regular jobs have had to leave their homes and families—it was not a time of hardship but simply a time when there was hard work to be done by everybody.

My grandfather was an Indian doctor. Other people have called him a shaman, but I prefer to describe him as an Indian doctor, or a psychologist. That is what he was.

His medical rituals and formulas were not strictly passive, from the sick person's standpoint, as you see in the movies. He talked to his patients and he listened to them. The patient went away with definite instructions to follow. After living in European society I have come to think that he was doing what they call "psychotherapy." The songs and rituals were one way of drawing out the anxiety and pains that were troubling the patient. The power of those Indian doctors, like my grandfather, who relied mainly on songs and rituals was really aimed at producing the same effects as modern psychotherapy. And if you studied the matter further you might find that his methods were not very different from the ones being newly discovered in the universities today.

There were other Indian medical people who mastered the use of drugs and different forms of natural chemicals. That was another profession altogether. My grandmother was always experimenting with different forms of medicines, herbs and syrups, barks and roots. She was not so much a doctor as a pharmacist.

My grandfather had a strong influence as a spiritual leader, not only on the Shuswap Reserve itself but over the whole Shuswap Territory. Even people from other tribes would come to consult with him on medical problems, on spiritual problems, or on a political or social problem.

Grandfather was not only a doctor and spiritual leader. He was a long-distance runner, an athletic skill that had great practical value in those days. Many of his sayings and stories, in which he expressed his wisdom, came from his experience in travelling and treating people.

"If you don't train fully in the way you need to," he would tell visitors who felt they were not succeeding in their lives, "you are really cheating yourself. It's your own conscience that you have to deal with, not another man. Even though everyone watching the race knows from watching whether you have trained or not, it is you who really knows."

For him life was both the training and the race. Not too many years later, as the church took a stronger hold, this thinking would get him into great difficulties with the priests, who always seemed to present life as a training period for the Big Race in the Sky. He could never comprehend why you might need to go to another man to confess your sins in order to receive forgiveness. Purity was a state of being within yourself. "If you cannot be honest with yourself you will never be honest with anyone else. If it is a prayer you need, it does not matter whether you do it out in the forest or prairie field where nobody will see you or if you do it to another person. Unless you are such a weak person that you need somebody to lean on."

His whole basis of teaching was that the strength to fulfil one's self lay within each man. The preachers who came from outside sought to make people dependent upon them as a link with a Higher Authority.

Cleanliness, honesty, and strength were inseparable in his mind. "If you cannot be clean within yourself you will not be clean in your dealings with anyone else. But if you are not going to be clean, then you will not be helped by kneeling down before another man and telling him about it."

His way of teaching was by telling stories. Story-telling was often used among native peoples, not only for moral teaching, but for practical instruction, to help you remember the details of a craft or skill, and for theoretical instruction, whether about political organization or the location of the stars.

One advantage of telling a story to a person rather than preaching at him directly is that the listener is free to make his own interpretation. If it varies a little from yours, that is all right. Perhaps the distance between the two interpretations is the distance between two human lives bound by the same basic laws of nature illustrated by the outline of the story. However many generations have heard the story before the youth who hears it today, it is he who must now apply it to his own life.

There is a story about a fat little asthmatic type of boy who had a big belly from living off the scrapings from the bottom of the pot, the sort of boy you would not trust to walk to the corner store and back without having a major accident. You'd wonder how a boy like him could get out of bed in the morning without breaking a leg or cracking his skull. Not content merely to be clumsy, he would always be doing foolish things that would be an embarrassment to his family.

One day his two brothers invited him for a ride in the canoe. They arrived at quite a distant point of land where they landed for a time. Suddenly, he saw that his two brothers had hopped into the canoe and left him alone on this very isolated clearing.

Because he was so clumsy, nobody had ever tried to teach him to hunt. He was so alone and afraid that he sat down and cried. He cried until he fell asleep. When he woke up he saw a grizzly bear and two cubs in the clearing. The big mother bear came and talked to him until he calmed down. Then she took him back to the den with her two young cubs, who took him for a brother.

When he had begun to eat properly and find his way around the woods, the mother bear opened him up and cleaned out his stomach to get rid of all the scrapings from eating so much fat.

After that he began to sit up straighter and taller and to take on all the handsome features of his fathers.

One day the grizzly told him it was time to go back to his own people. She led him to the path of the village and told him, "Always remember where your new strength came from. Always remember what you had to endure to be able to learn what I have taught to you. Nobody will taunt you or be mean to you if you remember those two things."

Needless to say, every young girl in the village who had teased and taunted him and laughed in his face now approached him with far more friendly greetings. But the only one he would spend time with was a very old woman who was so hairy that she reminded him of the bear. Finally, when the day came that he asked her to marry him, she said, "So you know who I really am." Thereupon she turned into the most beautiful young girl, tall and slender with flowing black hair.

A story such as this can be shaped to illustrate many aspects of daily life and to include very clearly the situation on which you want to comment. Even the brief outline I have given touches on customs of our life that we would take for granted while strangers might fail to notice that those details were even present.

When a boy began to enter manhood he would go up into the mountains to find his true self. Manhood begins when the boy's voice began to change, about the age of twelve years. It would not be unusual for him to stay there by himself for several months. Some young men were known to stay for two years.

Try to imagine what was expected of a twelve-year-old boy. He had to learn to live on his own strength and on the resources that the Creator had put at his disposal. His years with his parents and grandparents were like the years spent in elementary school. Now he was beginning his secondary education. He would learn to apply the many stories he had been told from his earliest childhood.

If he had learned all his lessons well, he would have all the knowledge he might need to live comfortably. Perhaps he would take a few basic tools. Nothing more. With these he must learn to express appreciation for the many values of the land and the water. The swift water for swimming and cleaning, the calm waters for travel. The saplings for building shelter, the seedlings for thatch-work. The barks of the different trees—for weaving, for stringing roots to dry, for medicine, for building a canoe if he was good. The animals who would feed and clothe him. He would learn to meet all his basic material needs.

What boy ever learned his lessons so well that he did not experience an inner panic when put to the test? The value of the test was that he discovered for himself how much he had learned. The test of manhood was to learn to live.

That meant his learning had to take a young man beyond the basic material needs. He would learn to converse with the animals. An animal would present himself to the youth, but only if he had completely isolated himself from other people and had developed sufficient peace within himself to leave the panic of the first few days a good distance behind him. If the young man stayed and conversed with the animal, the animal became his spiritual power. The longer he stayed and learned the animal's language, the more power the young man gained.

If he stayed long enough the animal would teach a song to him. Each time that an animal comes to the youth and gives a song to him, the young man is said to have received a snam, a degree of harmony with nature. It is also a degree of power that the youth has acquired through his harmony with nature.

When he came back among the people the young man would sing that song, or the several songs, at festivals and ceremonies, especially the mid-winter feasts. That song was uniquely his. Nobody else could ever sing it unless he willed it to them to carry on the power of his spirit when his strength would wane in later years. While it is a great honour to inherit a spirit, it is no substitute for power personally gained. An inherited spirit is old and weak. Only the power gained through the youth's own effort gains the full recognition of the Shuswap Nation.

A sceptic might insist that the youth conversing with the animal was only meeting his own solitude. His song gave voice to no more than his own sorrow at being separated from his people. The sceptics I have met are always the ones who deny other peoples' experience because they have not had one of their own. But even if his own solitude is all that he met, and he learned to live with it well, he would then have prepared himself to give as well to other people as he had given to himself.

39

It is customary for the youth in many Indian societies to seek a manhood vision. The details of the exact conditions under which the vision is sought vary from place to place. Not everybody has mountains available into which they can go. What is common to all our cultures is the recognition by the community of the power the person has gained and the expectations of how he will use it.

In many ways our daily material life, in fact our whole economy, worked along lines that were parallel with the kind of spiritual life that my grandfather taught. Perhaps it is for that reason, and not because it is at all primitive, that our way of life should be seen as a natural economy.

Each family had its own berry-picking grounds. We also had our own campsites, where we would stay on our way to and from the harvest. These places were called Slheechumun camp, or Clear-Head's bushes. When you set out from home in the morning, you did not just walk until sundown or until your feet hurt or until you came to the first set of berry bushes. You had a fixed destination, a definite route that you would follow, and a designated campsite. The route was well known, and a good runner might overtake you if there was a sudden need for you to return to the village.

It was not just berries that we picked. Carrots, potatoes, and parsnips all grew wild—no different in shape from the cultivated kind, but a lot smaller. We used to thread the parsnips with a length of tough grass or the inner lining of a spruce sapling to hang them up to dry.

Everything was dried so that it would keep for the winter, even different kinds of mosses—some for scouring pots and pans, others because they are softer than Flush-a-byes.

At salmon-fishing time the smoke houses and drying racks were set up next to the river so that the fish could be cut and set to dry as they were brought in.

Organized agriculture was becoming stronger than hunting and gathering in those years, but the two activities did not conflict. They complemented each other. Just as each family had its own berry-picking area, its own fishing spot, or its own trap line, now each had its own land for farming.

Long before I can remember even hearing of an Indian agent, I recall our traditional chiefs leading the people into the fields to tend the crops. The men would work at the harvesting or planting or clearing the irrigation ditches according to the season. The women cooked for them on open fires. The children gathered wood or packed water. No one was idle. Everyone had a job to do, and the community needed the labour each person could contribute to the process.

I did not go away to school until almost my tenth birthday. In the years just before I went away, I travelled to many of the Indian communities of the Shuswap with my grandfather. In all those many trips I do not think I ever heard any language spoken besides Shuswap, or some other dialect of Salish, and Chinook, a trade jargon made up from many languages with the chief European ingredient being French. I am certain that I did not hear English spoken until the first day I arrived at boarding school.

Many years later I learned that there had indeed been an Indian agent in Kamloops in the years I am recalling. Legally, I suppose, he held the same power and authority over each person's daily life that would later make him the main reality of reserve life. If the agent's presence failed to make an impression on a curious and well-travelled boy who spent so many hours listening to the conversations of his elders, it can only be that his presence was not yet that strongly felt. The agent had not yet become all-powerful because our customs and traditions were still strong. Our legal and political structures had been undermined before the turn of the century, but those structures were still functioning. There was no vacuum the agent could occupy without the use of force. So long as our traditional economy remained strong, the social fabric could withstand the pressure that was being put upon it.

Our economy carried on because it was being held together by a substance much stronger than the simple list of raw materials with which we worked. The roots and berries, fish and meat, bark and moss are a list of ingredients that cannot by themselves make a whole cloth. There is only economic organization when those raw materials are brought together on the loom of social values toward which people choose to work.

The whole foundation of our society—not just for Shuswap or Salish, but for Indian societies generally—is summed up in one word: *giving*. If someone gives something to you, sooner or later you find a way to give something back to him. It is a vital part of your life's work to find or create the opportunity to repay the people who have given to you. Indian people who live this way believe that things come back when they are needed the most.

The strongest example among my own peoples' day-to-day life is in the deer hunt. When you kill a deer, it is not just food for your own family. There are other people to whom you will give each section of the animal. You know who these people are before you go on the hunt. Some may be immediately related to you, some only very distantly related. All are close to you by the bonds of human necessity. The only part of that animal which you will keep for yourself is the neck, the least-favoured part. Each of those people to whom you give will someday repay you. For every person to whom you assign some special portion, a fore-quarter, a heart, or a liver, there is someone who has assigned as good a meal to your table.

A family whose berry crop or fish catch is especially good do not stop picking or fishing when they have enough for themselves alone. They stop when there is enough for all the people with whom they are in contact, as if to say, "If there are so many fish in our pool there may not be so many upstream or down. And next year there is no assurance that the fish will favour us."

Whenever we would go to visit somebody my grandmother would say to me, "Take a loaf of bread. When we get there take a look around and see what needs to be done. Are there buckets that need to be filled? Is there wood that needs to be fetched?"

The real value of taking bread is not in the bread but in the taking. If you did not have bread you could still bring some dried meat, fish, berries or roots, some sugar or some flour. If you had nothing to give—and there were times when we did not—that did not make any difference. There was always something you could do to make yourself a part of the household where you were a guest. Even if you did bring something, you did not just leave it at that. There was wood to be gathered, water to be drawn and packed.

"Always keep your eyes open," was the way they used to express it.

It was a way of making your host feel good. A guest honoured his host by making himself part of the household. He was honoured in return by being allowed to be part of the family—not by being allowed to do nothing.

Nature is not always kind. And it is not any kinder to Indian people than to anybody else. What made you secure in living with nature, in a traditional economy, was the security of the community. A community that had its roots in that soil, however barren and rocky it might appear to the outsider, had developed a knowledge that allowed its people to gather in as much as they needed to see the winter through.

I tried to explain this to a reporter recently. "You were never to think only of yourself," I told him.

"The deprived . . . " he began to cut in.

"They weren't deprived. Just unlucky."

A community that had learned to survive through mutual support was not plagued with the worry that the other fellow might catch more fish or kill a bigger moose than you. The slimmer your pickings, the more you hoped for the other man's good fortune. At the same time, if you could prove yourself a great hunter, fisherman, or farmer, this was the chief source of status and prestige.

Our ideal of leadership is closely related to developing to a fine art the life-way of giving. Spiritual and material power have never been wholly separated in the Indian world as they seem to have been elsewhere. In many Indian societies, especially those with a less formal structure, a leader may better be described as a person who gives well and who gives often. Even within the most highly structured Indian societies, in which one could earn a title or office only through routes which combined family lines with outstanding ability, there were few nations that based status solely on family lines. There was something basically democratic in the recognition of status through giving. Anyone of sufficient ability and generosity could achieve a status that would almost rival that of an office holder. The opportunity to develop the absolute power of a duke or baron simply did not exist.

Perhaps this brief excerpt from the journal of a hypothetical and so far entirely fictitious Indian scholar inquiring into European folkways will better make my point than a more serious analysis:

> Among European peoples there are some who believe that spiritual power is to be saved up to assure a life in the world hereafter. This allows material wealth to be used for personal pleasure or converted from wealth into political power. On the other hand, these same people have developed a practice called

banking, which seems to provide the material equivalent of spiritual salvation. In either case, among these strange people an individual acquires his status according to the wealth he commands and not according to what he does with it. Although their belief in a separation of material and spiritual power or wealth seems either unclear or inconsistent, and certainly deserves further study, it has impressed North American Indian observers as uniformly barbaric and uncivilized.

This is why it would have been rare, even at the height of prosperity, to find an Indian chief who was wealthy in his own right, in European terms. Any man who has accumulated a great deal of wealth for himself has not been very good at giving, and would not be much of a leader. On the other hand, a leader who exhausted his material wealth giving to his people and caring for them would be invested with greater wealth by those people.

It would be tempting to compare a good leader to a good financier and say, "His assets are all out on loan." The trouble with such a neat and tidy translation is that it is not very accurate. It leaves the impression that the Indian leader and the financier have a common goal. We do not measure a leader's wealth as a banker measures his, by the loans he has outstanding. The gift is a gift. The leader's wealth is the status, prestige, and respect that he enjoys on account of how well he has given. And when Indian leaders are judged this way, they are not being measured by a different standard than dancers, doctors, carvers, housewives, or fishermen in the same community.

I can find no comparison to the forms of European culture I have seen. It is one of many practices and ideas for which there is no direct translation, because European cultures have not developed the concepts sufficiently to coin a word for it. Those who want to understand our ways can either wait for European cultures to catch up, or they can simply learn to understand our language.

Giving, in the way I have described, is the most commonly recurring theme of social and spiritual relationships among every Indian society I have visited, regardless of the corner of the continent in which the people find themselves.

The spiritual significance of giving and sharing is celebrated in many Indian religious ceremonies. George Clutesi, the great west coast Indian scholar, says that "the feast to which guests were invited from any number of tribes — Tloo-qwah-nah — later came to be known as Potlatch by the early Europeans because the Nootka verb *Pa-chitle*, to give, was often heard during these festivities so naturally the early settlers mistook that verb for the name of the feast."

In the more general sense, potlatch has come to refer to any ceremony of which the main element is the giving away of large amounts of valuable possessions. It was this concept of human relations that led the missionaries to petition Ottawa until the potlatch was outlawed. Such ceremonies are common all along the west coast, north into Alaska, and far into the interior plateau.

The potlatch ceremonies contain another ingredient that is no less essential to the way of life that they are celebrating. Even when it is a ceremony to which guests have been invited from any number of tribes, it is a system of kinship, of the interrelatedness of all the people present, that is being celebrated.

There is a Coast Salish story of the origin of the masks that are worn by the dancers at the celebrations. A young man who is always getting into trouble and can never do anything useful becomes so frustrated with himself that he sets out to find a high cliff from which he can jump so that he will no longer be a burden on his family. The route that he follows, in looking for an appropriately high cliff, or seeking for a voice that will set him on the right path, leads him through the entire Salish territory. After he jumps he meets the masks under the water and they deliver him back to his island home, a new man.

Even the dancing symbolizes the invisible bonds of mutual support between each individual and the community. Only one person dances at a time. When he dances he sings his song, the song that is uniquely his, given to him either by an animal when he went into the mountains, or by inheritance. Nobody else can ever sing it. Yet the chief value that song holds for him, although he may also sing it to himself at times of trouble, is when he sings it in his moment of ecstasy during his dance. Any number of people may drum, or support a dancer. When you are asked to give such support the request is not made with words. You are simply handed a coin, or some other object of value. You help. Nobody marks down what is owed, but everybody knows what they have received and from whom they have received it.

45

The kinship that is being celebrated goes deeper than the fact that everyone is related to everyone else in a certain village. The kinship ties, the giving, and the celebration of mutual support are all one. It is the recognition of this unity or brotherhood that makes meaningful a mid-winter ceremony that brings together all the villages of a wide-spread nation.

Many parts of the potlatch ceremony re-create, in the presence of the whole community, aspects of the solitary trip each singer made up into the mountains of his youth. That meeting with your own spirit can, under very special circumstances, be a proper thing to share with the whole community who gave you the strength to climb in the first place. It is a way of reminding ourselves who we are and where we came from. The daily economic life built on a foundation of giving would not stand without the framework which is rebuilt in each mid-winter ceremony.

Perhaps, as some non-Indian observers have said, the quest for a manhood vision was a test of strength. I think it was more a seeking for new strength than a test to prove the strength a person already had. It is not so much a needless hardship imposed to prove what already is as a way of acquiring the strength to face the hardships that must be met in the course of life.

When the potlatch, on the petition of Christian missionaries, was outlawed and made a criminal offence, it was this way of life that the Parliament of Canada declared intolerable to the Christian conscience.

The Potlatch Law was a declaration of war against a people who had still not surrendered when the law was repealed seventy years later. What followed for the people of the interior plateau was a very long period of phoney war, a time when there was a great deal of sniping and undermining that in many ways sapped away our strength. But the full-scale frontal assault was yet to come. Perhaps the frontal assault was only postponed for us because the government was occupied with attacking our most eastern brothers and our brothers of the west coast. We were also ignored while they took time off to fight in the First Great European War. What I can say with certainty is that our way of life continued for five decades into the phoney war and that it touched and shaped many of the people who are alive today.

Even when the frontal assault came, the ceremonies and the values that they contain endured. Among our people today these ways are still very much present in our relations among ourselves. They are strongest in the most remote areas of Canada that are only now being undermined as we were in the years between the European Wars.

When my grandfather died in 1941, I was in the hospital with tuberculosis of the hip. I did not see him in his last days. Some time later I was told that the day before he died he went to see my mother eight miles away. At the age of 101 years he had walked both ways. When he got home that evening he had supper, lay down, and went to sleep.

His lifetime on the plateau had spanned the years from the first European settlement until the final collapse of our traditional economy. He had seen the trading years when the settlers needed our manufactures at least as much as we needed theirs. The generations of Indian people who had tried to adapt European technology to traditional values and institutions had been his own and his children's generations. He saw those values and institutions that he was rebuilding undermined by the missionaries and the agents. He saw his people ravaged by disease like the children of Job. He challenged his Creator's will for permitting such plagues. But he did not surrender the way that the Creator had taught him to live.

So long as there is a single thread that links us to the ways of our grandfathers, our lives are strong. However thin and delicate that thread may be, it will support the weight of a stronger cord that will tie us securely to the land.

3

The Earth
and My Grandmother

BERRY-PICKING TIME. Late summer in my eighth year. The mountains were filled with life up to their snow-capped peaks. My grandmother had risen with the first sign of dawn that morning to get us ready for the long walk to our first berry-picking after the strawberries had ripened. Before she had stirred from her bed, I had already been awake long enough to walk the whole trail in my mind. Last year my grandfather had had to carry me the last part of the walk. This year I was determined to make it on my own and carry my filled basket home as well.

Now the sun was high and we had been on the trail for several hours. Soon we would reach the shady spot by the creek where we would have a bite of lunch. Then we would be a little less than two hours from the first bushes where we would pick.

I must have been thinking about that lunch and not looking straight ahead. Suddenly there was a gate blocking our way with a barbed-wire fence running away from it in both directions into the bushes. On the gate there was a lock and a white board with black

Suddenly there was a gate blocking our way with a barbed-wire fence running away from it in both directions into the bushes. On the gate there was a lock and a white board with black letters.

letters. I could not read them then, but they are still clear in my mind's eye today.

My grandparents talked awhile in quiet voices. Then my grandmother held her skirts with one hand and lifted herself over the gate with the other hand. My grandfather looked at her strangely when he handed her the walking stick and baskets. But he followed her, and so did I.

We were not a hundred steps beyond the gate when a white man came around a bend in the trail. As soon as he saw us he began to shout and wave his arms at my grandfather. Grandfather talked back to him in Chinook. I did not need to understand the words to know that they were both angered.

Grandfather had put down his baskets when the man had begun to speak to him. He was just bending over to gather them up when my grandmother picked up her stick and began to chase the white man. She spoke only our own Shuswap language but she had made herself well understood. He left. We stayed.

That woman was quite convinced that our people owned the land and that we had a special right to the bushes for which we were heading. No one had a right to fence it off.

Her victory was very short-lived. We completed our walk to the berry bushes. It was a good crop. Three weeks later we came back to the village with our baskets filled with berries already dried for the long winter. But my grandparents had a heavy sadness about them I had never seen before. They did not speak the rest of that trip. When they had sung their voices had been very low, as if each one were alone and had to work hard just to remember the tunes they had sung each day of their lives.

There were other signs that the strength of the old order was being sapped away, in that last year before I went away to school.

The word went around very quickly when someone had killed a deer. It meant fresh meat on the tables in many different homes. If the animal had been killed near the village the hunter would return for help to carry it home. If the kill was made at some distance from home, he cleaned and quartered it on the spot, unless it was a smaller animal that he could sling across his shoulders. It was a grand sight to see a man walk into the village like that. The drying racks were prepared. The smoke houses were fired up. Even in the best of seasons, when it was an everyday sight, your eyes did not tire of seeing good food brought home. When I remember those days I still feel a deep longing for food that was a true gift of nature.

An animal was more than good food. Skins for mitts and gloves and bed-covers. Sinews for sewing. Oils for working the skin.

That fall, I remember, was the first time when a man of our village refused to share a deer he had killed. Instead of giving away the heart, the hind quarters, and the forequarters, he gave only the neck and kept the real meat for himself.

The man was disgraced and totally ostracized. Ostracism was the only punishment we knew in those days. It had many different forms according to the nature and seriousness of the offence. A child might be ignored by his parents for an hour if he was insolent; a thief might be banished from the village by the elders for some months.

What that man had done was worse then thieving; it was as if he had beaten an old woman or molested an infant girl. Even that comparison is uncertain, for those offences were as unknown to our village as a refusal to share. But the power of the elders and the chief were declining. He could not be banished. I doubt that anyone talked to that man before that winter's snow was gone.

That same man was the first person to own a car on our reserve. He had been disgraced and ridiculed throughout the Shuswap. But he was a pioneer in introducing European progress.

So many of my memories of that year before I went to school are related to food. This is surely because it was the last winter for years to come in which I was not hungry.

Grandfather was always going on trips to one or another Shuswap village to make medicine and to counsel together with the other elders. Sometimes he even went beyond the Shuswap. When he went long distances on the open road he had a horse and wagon or sleigh in which he rode. That last winter he took me along several times. It was good to sit up there behind him on the high seat behind the horse, or to surround myself with the piles of blankets and skins and clothes which people had given him to take to friends or relatives who lived along the route of our journey. It was also good not to be tied to apron strings any longer, even my grandmother's. Travelling with grandfather was almost like being allowed to go out in the woods on your own, only you got to go more places and do more things than could ever happen in the woods.

It was our first trip after the snow had begun to melt. The ground was still hard, but you could see the water dripping off the long icicles hanging from the cliff walls as we rode down the valley.

Two white men in uniforms blocked our way. They spoke to my grandfather in the same harsh language the white farmer had used the summer before. He spoke back to them quietly in Chinook, shaking his head to say, "No."

The next thing I knew they were behind us in the wagon, throwing all our bundles onto the ground. Then the two men looked at each other, shrugged and muttered something, and told us we could go.

When we had repacked our wagon, we rode in silence for the longest time. Finally grandfather began to speak, not to me or anyone in particular. "You can't pick berries. You can't hunt deer except when townsfolk are in the bush, during what they decide is the right time to hunt. You can't bring down a bird to feed yourself when you're trapping. You can only fish four days a week, and they choose the days. They show us better ways to use nets and then say we can't use them.

"When the new sicknesses were killing us they gave us blankets of death to warm ourselves, but at least they let us eat. Now they only want us to eat what we buy in their stores or grow with their tools."

Let me pick up the story of what was happening to our people where my grandfather left off.

At the very time when every sign indicated that a new prosperity and a resurgence of strength should have been approaching the Shuswap—and I believe now Indian peoples across Canada—we were being caught in a stranglehold of new laws or laws applied with new vigour that would always succeed in keeping strength and prosperity just beyond our grasp.

Throughout my grandfather's life he had seen our numbers dwindle. If people recovered from tuberculosis, smallpox, and trachoma, and avoided syphilis, they were often too weak and crippled to do the life's work that should have been their contribution to the life of the people. By the time of my childhood, the dread diseases had by no means ceased to scar our life, but our numbers were now growing. Far more of my generation than of my parents' or grandparents' generations lived to see manhood. People who had no sophisticated scientific knowledge experienced this change, and were aware of it, simply by seeing so many of their children come of age. There were fewer children to be buried and more to be fed, clothed, and taught. For the first time in a century it no longer appeared that the Indian peoples of the interior were simply going to die out.

Not only were more people reaching adulthood, there was also more work to do. The generation that was then in their prime of life had developed all the techniques of European farming and already had the skills to hunt and fish and gather crops. Neither way was completely adequate to produce a secure and comfortable life, even materially. But both together could produce to the point of surplus.

The growing towns made it at least thinkable that some of that surplus might be sold for cash. Other sources of cash were becoming common as well. There was a strong fur market for trappers. Some of the men took winter jobs as loggers.

There was hard work to do, but doing it brought rewards. The same leaders who decided when the fishing or hunting should begin now took on the additional task of leading the people into the fields to work.

This was a time when it was still possible for Indian people to believe that the government and the church could teach us new ways that would make us strong. Not too many people worried about losing their culture. Our culture was just naturally a part of us; we could learn the white man's ways and still retain our own ways. These people were not wrong. They were betrayed. If the government had allowed the people of that time to explore the different paths of life, Indian societies would have found ways to retain the best of our own culture while at the same time adopting the best that European culture had to offer. That moment of discovery was never allowed to happen. It was aborted by the medicine of the new regime.

There actually was a moment in our history when we had conquered the old diseases, and the new diseases of alcoholism, prostitution, and welfare had not yet arrived. The new diseases followed on the footsteps of the Indian agents who were making

53

their presence felt more and more during these years. It was the job of these new white chiefs to displace our traditional leaders in their care over our day-to-day lives in order to bring our way of life into line with the policies that had been decreed in Ottawa.

The agents were armed with three laws that made them, for the moment, the stronger party in the contest for power. The new enforcement of provincial game laws was used to destroy the base of our traditional economy. We would no longer be permitted to use the skills we had developed in gathering the fruit of nature. If you were seen with a freshly killed animal—or even sometimes just carrying a rifle in the forest—you were liable to imprisonment.

You were not much freer in farming than in hunting. The agent had the authority to regulate all sales of farm produce by Indian people.

But what really made the agent more powerful than the chiefs was that he was now empowered to dispense welfare to anyone who could not make a living while their neck was within this noose woven by foreign laws.

The deliberate destruction of the buffalo herds in order to starve the plains Indians into submission is well known. The Indians of the interior were now being starved into submission by laws and regulations that combined to destroy the economic base on which we had survived for thousands of years, at the very time when all the forces of nature were combining to give us a strength we had not known since the arrival of European settlement.

Many of these laws were not new. The game laws and hunting and fishing regulations of the province had been on the books for some time. The federal Migratory Birds Convention became law before World War I. If you follow the records of the reserve commissions, the land registries, and Indian Affairs, the destruction was complete long before the period I am recalling. Well before the First Great European War, the Canadian government had developed a sophisticated and all-encompassing program designed to destroy any pretensions of self-determination among the Indian nations of Canada. The demands of the war coupled with our remoteness delayed the full effect of the system until a decade after the war. If you follow the lives of our people rather than the

54

Word that was handed down at Ottawa or Victoria, this is the time when the system took hold.

Within a traditional society, the economy is an accurate reflection of the environment. It has a plan, in the sense that it is highly organized. At the same time it is not something that must be continually reconstructed in your mind in order for it to go on working. It is something that you simply live with, like your own body. Nonetheless, economic organization is just as much a part of the total environment as in the most highly industrialized societies. If people in a traditional society do not think about questions of economic organization in great detail it is because the economy is the total environment. The organization of the economy has grown naturally over the centuries out of the relationship between the people and their environment.

Our traditional forms of government were not overthrown because they were inadequate to the society for which they cared. Indian societies could very well have continued to govern themselves while other cultures grew up around them. So long as we could actively possess and use our land base, we were capable of survival and strength. Our traditional political and religious systems were attacked because they regulated and celebrated a certain kind of economic structure which the European powers in Canada wanted to destroy.

"The earth...and every living thing that walketh upon the earth."

What was happening to the Shuswap and other Indian peoples of the interior plateau when I was coming of age was the same process that had confronted almost every other Indian society in North America up to that time, except those that were even more remote than we are. They are the ones who are under attack today, the Inuit and Indians in the northern parts of Canada. The differences in the way in which the process has been carried on from time to time, however interesting and important they may appear, are matters of detail.

The land is ours, by every natural right and every principle of international law recognized in relations among European powers. The land that is ours by every natural right was coveted by European powers. Seizure of our land for the use of their own

55

people could not be justified by the law of nations or the principles of international law that regulate relations among European powers. So it became necessary to concoct a theory that would justify the theft of land.

It was not easy to design such a theory. At one time or another the best minds of Europe and European America were summoned to contribute to the idea that crime had its proper place. The result of the collected work of these many minds was a series of racial and cultural myths: that we were savage and uncivilized; that we were war-like and had no respect for human life; that we are, therefore, unworthy of respect; that our lives are not European lives, and our property is not to be valued in the way that Europeans value property until it is firmly held in European hands.

The development of this thought was not perfected by men who could be called typical racists. Many brilliant minds who justly deserve to be remembered as the most staunch Euro-American defenders of Indian rights gave official blessing to the belief in our racial and cultural inferiority.

Chief Justice Marshall of the United States Supreme Court is best remembered for his judicial statements recognizing the sovereignty of the Indian nations. He hedged his statement with severe limitations and called us "domestic, dependent nations." But he did it at a time when even that much recognition brought the severest disapproval down upon his head. When he passed a judgement that recognized at least the limited sovereignty of the Cherokee Nation, the President of the United States at that time, Andrew Jackson, commented, "Mr. Marshall has made the law. Now let him enforce it."

But Chief Justice Marshall, for all his wisdom and courage, is still quoted in the courts to this day, for what is perhaps the ultimate expression of the theory of our inherent savagery and racial inferiority. In 1810, he said:

> Although we do not mean to engage in the defence of those principles which Europeans have applied to Indian title, they may, we think, find some excuse if not justification, in the character and habits of the people whose rights have been wrested from them.
>
> The title by conquest is acquired and maintained by force.

The conqueror prescribes its limits. *Humanity, however, acting on public opinion, has established, as a general rule, that the conquered shall not be wantonly oppressed, and that their condition shall remain as eligible as is compatible with the objects of the conquest.*

Most usually, they are incorporated with the victorious nation, and become subjects or citizens of the government with which they are connected . . . *and a wise policy requires that the rights of the conquered to property should remain unimpaired* ; that the new subjects should be governed as equitably as the old, and that confidence in their security should gradually banish the painful sense of being separated from their ancient connexions and united by force to strangers.

But the tribes of Indians inhabiting this country were fierce savages, whose occupation was war, and whose subsistence was drawn chiefly from the forest. To leave them in possession of their country was to leave the country in a wilderness; to govern them as a distinct people, was impossible, because they were as brave and as high spirited as they were fierce, and were ready to repel by arms every attempt on their independence.[13] (emphasis added)

Mr. Justice Norris, of the Supreme Court of British Columbia, quotes, in *Bob and White,* this statement of the American Chief Justice with approval in a recent case in which he finds in favour of the right of Indians on Vancouver Island to hunt.[14] He adds that his judgement is "entirely consistent with the opinion of the Privy Council" in the leading cases on native rights in Canada.

The argument in favour of property rights and against the oppression of conquered peoples is founded in "wise policy" designed to secure the "confidence [of the conquered peoples] in their security" under the new regime. So widely spread is this principle that "humanity . . . has established it as a general rule" as though it were a part of the Law of Nations.

Indians, however, are an exception to this general consideration of humanity because we are "fierce savages, whose occupation was war."

The Cherokees and Creeks about whom Marshall was commenting had an agriculture that was probably better developed than that of Marshall's own ancestors when they arrived in North

America. They were among the first Indian peoples to learn to read English and develop their own school system. The Cherokees already had an alphabet and a written language before Europeans arrived.

The prairie people, against whom the longest and cruelest wars were fought, and who have become the imaginary stereotype for the white myth of the Indian, rarely made the concerted effort that is an essential ingredient for warfare.

The peoples of the northwest coast had produced the most highly sophisticated of Indian cultures. Because of the very complexity of their economic resources, they had created highly elaborate ceremonies and rituals that substituted giving for killing. When the charge of being too "war-like" could not be applied to these people, they were condemned for the fact that they had succeeded in institutionalizing warfare, through the potlatch, and reducing violence. They were now guilty of being both too warlike and insufficiently violent.

My own people had also created or adopted ceremonies, games, and rituals that translated the desire for power into constructive action rather than the violence of war. Many other Indian peoples, who did not need to be totally preoccupied with feeding, clothing, and sheltering themselves had done the same.

There is no need to recite the entire list of North American Nations simply to say that there was no place on this continent where Marshall's classic European description of North American peoples could be accurately applied. When our own history is contrasted with the cultures that fostered the myth—Spain, France, and England—and their tendency to make warfare a major occupation, the accusations against us hardly deserve the dignity of such a serious reply.

The myth that Marshall blessed was already far older than his Court when he sat on the bench. It carries on to this day. It was never meant to be a statement of historical truth. Like any great myth, it was meant only to be believed.

If wars were fought to extend the sovereignty of one nation over the land of another, but the leader of the conquering nation was not concerned with whether the newly acquired lands were used and occupied by his new subjects or his old ones, then it would make sense to say with Marshall, "the rights of the conquered to property should remain unimpaired."

Perhaps some European wars were fought that way. I do not know. But if the object of the war is to acquire land for the king's present subjects or the nation's present citizens, there is no real room for the rights of the conquered. The object of the conquest is to destroy those rights. The continued resistance is a struggle to preserve them.

It was the intent of the founding fathers of both great Euro-American Empires, the United States and Canada, to make us guilty of something or other that would give them excuse to do what they desired to do. So whatever we might do that was different from their customs would be considered savage, evil, primitive, or otherwise unacceptable.

The conflict between our civilization and theirs has often been represented by the story of the big fish eating the little fish who has eaten one that is smaller than he. This story forgets to mention that when we were the big fish, we lived with the Europeans in a state of mutual dependence. Such a way of understanding the world has been a far greater plague upon our houses than all the diseases that have visited us. They have caused the diseases to be spread in the name of God, Christ, love, civilization, and humanity.

For colonialism to be fully effective it is necessary that the leaders who propagate the myths about those whom they have conquered must not only convince themselves of what they say—it need hardly be said that they must convince their followers down to the humblest peasant and foot soldier—they must also convince the conquered. The conquered will only submit to the theft of everything they hold when they can be convinced that it has been done for their own good. Conquest only becomes colonialism when the conquerors try to convince the conquered that the rape of his mother was committed for the sake of some higher good.

Colonialism may deprive and oppress the people it colonizes through looting and pillage of their homes, starvation of their children, the spread of disease. It may go to the extremes of generosity in the promises it makes in return for what is taken. It may even fulfil some considerable part of those promises. However personally we may experience one course or another—and the particular course may indeed change our lives for generations to come—it is still a matter of detail within a common pattern. The colonial system is always a way of gaining control over another people for the sake of what the colonial power has determined to be "the common good." People can only become convinced of the common good when their own capacity to imagine ways in which they can govern themselves has been destroyed.

There was only one way that a new economic system could have been introduced into the Shuswap at that time. First, a shortage of essential goods had to be created where there had never really been one. Secondly, a new source of supply had to be created, one that was entirely outside the common frame of reference so that it would not be well understood, one that would in no way be as plentiful as the old supply. Thus only a select few would have their needs satisfied. This, in turn, would create a new set of leaders who were always indebted to the outside source of supply.

Most of all, the new economic system had to be made to appear legitimate. A way had to be found to make its decisions about the distribution of scarce food and clothing and houses acceptable in the minds of the overwhelming majority of the people.

This was the role of the church. It was not only our chiefs and wise men who had to contend for power. Our Mother the Earth had to contend with Holy Mother the Church.

Among some Indian peoples the church was accepted the moment it arrived and began to give out the Word in the fashion it had chosen to receive it. Almost every people that accepted the church that readily had already had a prolonged and unhappy contact with European culture. When a whole people are so sorely crippled that they can hardly support one another they seek a collective saviour, a messiah. People can even reach such depths of despair that if their own religion fails to produce such a saviour, they will turn to another if it presents itself.

Many Indian religious societies did produce great prophets during their times of strife: Handsome Lake among the Seneca and other Iroquois Nations, Sitting Bull many years later on the plains.

It takes time for genuine religious insight to arise out of the depths of a people's experience. Where the church was already present, or where it moved in before a natural growth could develop, the missionaries were able to present themselves as the agents of the Saviour. They said all the things that need to be said to people who have joined the wretched of the earth.

"Repent your sins and come unto the Lord."

"You must be born again."

On the plateau, Christianity had come in slowly over the preceding century. Whether our own rituals, dancing, and ceremonies were kept alive depended on our economic strength from time to time. It was not a matter of religious commitment. People took on Christianity to the exclusion of Indian customs during the famine years. The famine, death, and disease came more and more often. But just as people tried to maintain one economy while they developed another in the hope that each could support and strengthen the other, so people tried to absorb Christian custom and belief into our way of life, rather than being absorbed into its way.

For a long time, becoming a Christian meant going to church on Sunday and accepting the services of the priest at births, deaths, and marriages. It did not mean giving up the traditional understanding of the world that shaped our day-to-day lives. It did not interrupt our relations with the land or with one another.

Even as our people became deeply involved in the life of the church, they brought with them our own ways. The death ritual, for instance, was transferred from a traditional to a Catholic expression. Where there used to be a ceremony twice a year for bringing new provisions to the dead, people would now go to the cemetery to repair the fences, pull out the dead flowers, and in season put new ones in their places.

Many people believed that it was possible to take on the ways of the church without dishonouring the ways of our grandfathers. They hoped that the Mother Earth and the Mother Church would be sisters and friends.

The people liked the comfort and security and the sense of hope and strength that the church had to offer. The church, in turn, recognized that the giving that was the foundation of Indian religious beliefs was a field of strength that was worth their while to cultivate.

Potlatching is a two-way process. Within this present world you give, and sooner or later, you receive in turn. The priests attempted to replace potlatching with the practice of giving wordly goods to the church in exchange for an everlasting life. Many old people have told me they used to compete to see who could give the most to the church. When they gave, the priest would promise that it would all be returned in the next world. The poverty that they took on for the sake of the church, the reverend father would assure them, would be returned to them by the Father in Heaven. By the time I was old enough to ask questions of these old people, they had nothing to look forward to but the Great Accounting.

When the church first became strong in the plateau, Indian people would give in the same way that we were accustomed to give to one another. But the church wanted cash, not swaddling blankets for the Baby Jesus. So the devout learned to turn their goods into cash.

The economic organization that was symbolized in the potlatch worked among local, regional, and national communities. It was the fact that it was fairly localized that allowed the two-way flow to continue generation after generation. When goods were turned into cash which flowed across the seas and upward toward the heavens, the cycle that had perpetuated itself for so long was broken. The Imperial chain was complete.

So long as the ills of the people were strictly spiritual, the church had strong medicine. But the priest was not curing anybody of the pains he had to live with every day on this earth. And when a European doctor was available at all to Indian people, his medicine was not any more reliable than my grandparents'. And there were many people, like my grandmother, who would not go to a European doctor because they could not believe in his way of doing things.

Whether or not the talents of the European doctor were available or effective, the priest was determined to create a place for him. I remember the priest coming on his monthly round to preach against my grandfather. He would hold up pictures of people burning in hell. "You're going to burn like that for ever and ever and ever, if you go to see that man."

As more and more of our people went to church, they found themselves faced with a dilemma. As the priest sowed increasing hatred against my grandfather, fewer and fewer of our people would come to see him. People who had gone to church in the morning would sneak around to see my grandfather in the dark of the night. There was always a group who were more committed to the old ways who continued to come, but the older committed ones were dying off while the younger ones experienced the agony of being caught between the two ways, our heaven, their hell.

My grandfather would have preferred to let people go wherever they could find strength. He would be there when they needed him. The priest proclaimed him to be in league with the devil and banished his followers out of God's house.

So God was left alone with the priest while my grandfather went back to the woods, the songs and chants, and the sick people who needed curing and comforting. Until his last days he refused to contest the priest for power.

"That's not the way you win the people," he used to tell me. "First you learn to live with yourself. Then people will see your strength and come to you when they need it."

"It's you, you have to work within life," he would add. "Don't ever go to confession. As soon as you do that you are caught in the trap of lying to yourself. The minute you lie to yourself you're not a man. You have to learn to live with yourself whatever you do."

In his last days there were very few people who came to see my grandfather. He had lost virtually all the support and status that had been his for so many years, a status similar to that of any country doctor in his home town.

All areas of our life that were not occupied by the Indian agent were governed by the priest. Their roles were in every way parallel paths, the more they fed off one another and made each other strong. Looking back on it, it is easy to see that the whole structure of the church and the government as they relate to Indian people are almost identical. The greatest gift the Dominion of Canada made to the church was the control over education. The residential schools were the laboratory and the production line of the colonial system.

Three things stand out in my mind from my years at school: hunger; speaking English; and being called a heathen because of my grandfather. On the day we arrived at the school, each new boy was assigned an interpreter, who was a senior student. All the teachers were monks, or devout lay Catholics. We called them

63

brothers. In my first meeting with the brother, he showed me a long black leather strap and told me, through my interpreter, "If you are ever caught speaking Indian this is what you will get across your hands."

I still cannot remember how I learned to speak English. I can only suppose it was through the fear of that strap, although we were soon into enough other trouble that caused the wrath of the Almighty to be visited upon our hands or backsides or whatever and whenever pleased the brothers.

I remember one young boy who came in for the first time the year after I did. The brother, through the interpreter, asked him his name.

"Mosquito," he answered while he still had a note of pride left in his voice.

The brother led the class in ridiculing him. This was the name the boy had been taught to use until he would be old enough to earn his own name. So far as he knew he did not have another name. The priests finally determined that Mosquito had once been baptized Robert.

Boys who came from families who were known to practice Indian religion were a special subject of ridicule by the brothers. They would teach the other boys that we were heathens and devils and instruct them in ways to belittle us. I came in for a special share of this ridicule because the brothers were very aware of my grandfather's work as a medicine man.

We spent very little time in the classroom. We were in the classroom from nine o'clock in the morning until noon. Another shift came into the classroom at one o'clock in the afternoon and stayed until three. The longer half of our day was spent in what the brothers called "industrial training." Industrial training consisted of doing all the kinds of manual labour that are commonly done around a farm, except that we did not have the use of the equipment that even an Indian farmer of those days would have been using.

We would pack fifty pounds of green cord wood by foot from where it was tied up in a boom by the river up to the buildings, a distance of a mile and a half. Brothers or helpers were stationed along the trail. If we stopped they had whips to get us moving again.

When we would come back from holidays the weeds would be

about four feet high, and had roots, it seemed, that were half that far into the ground, they were so hard to pull. Our first task when we returned from summer holidays at ten years of age was to pull these weeds and pile them for burning.

Of course, we milked the cows, fed the pigs, slaughtered the animals, pitched hay. Normal farm chores for nine- or ten-year-old boys became light work after you had been at that school for a few months.

There was a derrick fork on the outside of the barn that was used for hoisting hay up into the loft. The load of hay would come in on a wagon and the derrick fork would be swung into the load and take half of it away into the loft. Farmers all over the valley used horses to swing that fork around. Some of the up-to-date European farmers had tractors. But the brothers at the school used Indian boys to hoist those tons of hay. The team of horses were out grazing quietly in the field. The truck was parked in the shed.

Hunger is both the first and the last thing I can remember about that school. I was hungry from the day I went into the school until they took me to the hospital two and a half years later. Not just me. Every Indian student smelled of hunger.

After we came from the fields or finished the barn chores, we went to the dining hall. For supper each boy got one ladle full of mulligan and a piece of bread. For breakfast the next morning the same ladle was your measure of porridge and there was another piece of bread. Lunch was another ladle of mulligan and another slice of bread. You could not have a second helping because there was no such thing.

Kids learned to become experts at picking locks to get into the potato or carrot bins in the cellar. Some senior students succeeded in breaking into the priests' wine cellar. When we were pulling weeds around the potato patches we would pile them as high as we could for burning. If we thought it was safe we would throw a potato in with the weeds. By the time the leaves and weeds had burned, the potato would be half-cooked. You tried to stick around the same weed pile, or get back to it, to dig out your potato.

When the brother on duty suspected we were doing this he would allow us to stay in the field until the fire had almost burned itself out. Then he would suddenly order us all to march back to school.

We learned to eat raw fish. If the priests would get in some fish from the fishery, we would steal some of them if there was any way open. With luck we could half cook it over an open fire without getting caught.

We learned to dry and eat dandelion roots, the buds from rose bushes, the green leaves from the trees. These were not part of our diet as Indian people. We learned at the school that we had to find ways to keep our stomachs full, or at least something else than empty.

We learned to steal not only from the priests and monks, but from our own brothers. We reached the point where we would do anything to deal the other guy out of a slice of bread. The stealing among ourselves was kept in line by the creation of a debt system. Somebody who was unbearably hungry would borrow a quarter-slice from another boy. He would then owe him two or three "bread"—that was how we referred to a single slice—very much in the manner that credit works at a general store for people who are on welfare. There was no escaping once you fell into that system. There were boys there who owed five hundred bread.

That was industrial training.

The only time I did not feel hunger during those two years was when my grandparents came. It was thirty-five miles to our home, a full day's ride by horse and wagon. And another day back. They came at Christmas and Easter. When they came they brought deer meat and bannock and other real food you could get full on. Nobody thought to want candy when we had not seen meat for so long.

For weeks before they would come I could not think of anything besides the food they would bring with them. The food always crowded out the people. It was not my grandfather who was coming. It was meat, dried fruit, and roots. Hunger like that numbs your mind.

That was industrial training.

There was a rule at that time that Indians could not go past Grade Eight. I do not recall many boys staying around long enough to protest the education that was being denied us.

Nothing else contributed so much to the destruction of the Indian people as a nation as the school system run by the churches and supported by the government. It was the perfect instrument for undermining both our values and our economic base. The residential school (not just the one I went to—they were the common form of Indian education all across Canada) was the perfect system for instilling a strong sense of inferiority.

When we came back home for summer holidays, or when we simply left school, we were equally unfit to live in an Indian world or a European world. We had lost time learning our own skills. The agricultural skills we were being taught were already obsolete.

Our values were as confused and warped as our skills. The priests had taught us to respect them by whipping us until we did what we were told. Now we would not move unless we were threatened with a whip. We came home to relatives who had never struck a child in their lives. These people, our mothers and fathers, aunts and uncles and grandparents, failed to represent themselves as a threat, when that was the only thing we had been taught to understand. Worse than that, they spoke an uncivilized and savage language and were filled with superstitions.

After a year spent learning to see and hear only what the priests and brothers wanted you to see and hear, even the people we loved came to look ugly.

Before we went away to school we packed wood into any house we visited. Just in the same way, our mothers, or sisters, or aunts, or grandmothers, or even a neighbour-woman did not ask if we were hungry before they put food in front of us; we did not have to ask if she needed wood to fire her stove or water with which to cook before we went and fetched it. When we came back from school we would not lift a finger, even in our own homes when we were asked. We would storm out and spend the night at some uncle's place, where we would stay until he got tired of seeing us sitting around doing nothing.

It was the kids coming back from residential school who brought the generation gap with them. The colonial system that was designed to make room for European expansion into a vast empty wilderness needed an Indian population that it could describe as lazy, shiftless, and always living off one another. The colonial system required such an Indian for casual labour, and as an object of its charity and pity. Most of all it needed such an Indian to whom it could point to proclaim the superiority of its own kind and their natural right to have

> ... dominion over the fish of the sea, and over the fowl of the air, and over every living thing that moveth upon the earth.

What was most nearly destroyed was the value of a person's labour as a contribution to the life and well-being of the community. It made sense to take on the challenge of hard work, whether it was hunting or fishing or farming, when the work would bring food to the tables of many homes, strength to the community, and glory and honour to the person who did it.

For the same reason, it made sense to endure the hardship of going up into the mountains by yourself when you came of age. It is no hardship to be honest with yourself when you know who you are. The knowledge of yourself that you bring when you come back into the village is as important to the well-being of the community as the food you bring to the table. When the line between mine and thine is clear to you, there is no longer much need to think about it. You can afford to share.

There is a vast difference between that kind of hardship and poverty, a hardship without purpose or benefit to anyone.

So many of the Indian men of my generation have said, in the wee hours of the morning, "My father told me to be white. When he was on his deathbed, forty years later, he said, 'My son, I made a mistake. You raise your children and your grandchildren as Indians.'"

Even my grandfather, when I had come home from school for the last time, said to me, "Things are going to be different from here on in. I don't think it is wise for me to teach you to go up into the mountains. I think it will be a detriment rather than an asset to you."

Perhaps he knew then that I would meet the dark cloud of unknowing on another route than the one he had travelled.

4

~~~~~~~~~~~~~~~~~~~~~~~~~~~~~~~~

We Honour
Our Grandfathers
Who Kept Us Alive

IT IS VERY much a mistake to identify the cultural and political renaissance that is going on among Indian societies today with a *new Indian resistance*. The fact of the matter is that there was never a time since the beginning of colonial conquest when Indian people were not resisting the four destructive forces besetting us: the state through the Indian agent; the church through the priests; the church and state through the schools; the state and industry through the traders.

Today's renaissance can be seen in the resurgence of our languages, in the growth of political institutions both old and new, in the revival of Indian religion in urban Indian centres as well as on the reserves, in the growing number of young people seeking out the wisdom of the grandfathers and finding ways to apply it in their own lives, however different their lives may appear from the old ways. These are the real signs of the renaissance; there is no separation between the cultural artifacts—the drums, totem poles, and moccasins anyone can collect—and the day-to-day life in which the culture is evident, through work, or family life, words of friendship, and music.

The renaissance of today is the fruit of the accumulated labour of our grandfathers. If it appears that we are only now awakening and discovering a new strength, it is because the current climate of political, social, and economic forces is allowing what was always beneath the surface to emerge into the light of day.

Above all, the appearance that we are only now coming alive is an illusion created by the press and public institutions, who have for so long warped, distorted, and falsified the story of our resistance. For so long we were treated in public discussion, school books, Parliament, and the media either as if we did not exist at all, or as if we were an appendage to the Department of Indian Affairs, as airports are an appendage to the Department of Transport. Now that we are occasionally allowed to speak for ourselves, the listener or reader is made aware that the last words he heard directly from an Indian were the speeches of Tecumseh, Red Jacket, Sitting Bull, or Chief Joseph. All these were great men and we honour them, but neither more nor less than we honour their children, who filled the generations between then and now.

We cannot recall to life the great political leaders whose names are still commonplace in their own villages without first recalling that their greatness came from the people whom they led. There were many little housewives and ordinary workmen, whose names are lost to all but their most direct descendants, who carried on the struggle in the way they led their own lives and in the material and spiritual support they lent to make our spokesmen strong. Their strength will be returned to their children three times over.

One very ordinary man stands out in my mind for a single moment of greatness, which the people in his own village did not share until long after the event. Alex Thomas was not a latter-day Sitting Bull filled with prophecies and the magic to communicate them. He was not a man of many words. He was an honest man whose beliefs were embedded in his bones and were just as strong.

One day, in the fall of my third and last year at school, we were packing wood up from the river where it had been floated down in a log boom, a mile and a half up to the school buildings. Alex Thomas came riding along on his horse.

Old Alex sat there in his saddle watching us nine-year-old kids carrying the big stacks of wood. He saw the school's horses grazing in the pasture having a fine feed while we worked. He saw the school disciplinarians standing along the trail with their rods to administer encouragement to us in our labour.

He got off his horse and walked down to the teacher supervising us. He never laid a finger on the teacher, but by the time he had finished telling that man how the scene looked to him, when horses played and children sweated, I think that man must have felt pretty small. A short time after his meeting with Alex Thomas, the students saw that teacher for the last time, walking across the field with his suitcase in his hand.

At that time the school was keeping students until they were eighteen years old. The older students were often bigger and certainly stronger than many of the teachers. Up to the time of Alex Thomas there had never been any sign of outward resistance. Sneaking. Lock-picking. Dominating the younger children. But no direct resistance to the hand that was holding us down. Now the students' confidence began to grow. A teacher would raise his yardstick to strike a student. The student would grab the stick from the teacher's hand and the rest of the class was instantly on top of the man. It was a crude and juvenile way of returning the violence to its source. But it was not submission.

After that year, the school lowered the leaving age to sixteen years, and I remember some fairly big fifteen-year-old boys who were told the next fall that they did not need to come back.

Alex Thomas did not plan to incite a series of rebellions. I am sure that he did not even plan the verbal attack he made on the teacher. He was a simple, honest man capable of an honest and direct gut-level reaction. He did not need profound thoughts and an elaborate plan of many words to distinguish work horses from children. He participated in the human situation as he found it, and brought to the situation what it most lacked; call it what you will—honesty, directness, industrial training, human relations. We honour our grandfather Alex Thomas who brought us in touch with the silver thread to reality. With a single act, with words most of us had never heard, he reversed the cycle of colonialism that was being played out on that farm school.

You say I am making too much of a small thing? This is the way that the cycle so often works in the large as well as the small. Look

71

beyond the Shuswap. Look beyond the Americas. The pattern is the same everywhere I have travelled among people whose souls have been in the shadow of colonialism.

When the visitors, or settlers, for their own reasons decide that they are no longer willing simply to live next door to you, but must also control every aspect of your life, then there begins a period of increasingly bitter struggle. The early part of this struggle is always won by the party with the strongest combination of weapons, number of men, and means of travel. The victory is assured to them because they have the instruments of war. A sharing economy loses out to a taking economy simply because, when the takers have done their thing, there is not much left to share. And it is the cultures that are given to taking which are most likely to dedicate themselves to producing an excess of weapons and boats to the neglect of more basic needs. They become the visiting parties. When the sharing societies tire of sharing with people who do not return the gifts, the visiting societies find a justification for conquest and colonization.

But what appears at first to be a total victory becomes, in the longer cycle of history, an illusion of the moment. The conqueror must find ways to hold down the people whose sovereignty he has stolen. To free his energies for his main purposes he must convince them to submit for their own good. But the teaching of submission runs against the grain of all experience.

The still, small voice that utters the words contained within every silent soul has all the force of the firecracker that splits a glacier or unleashes an avalanche. So much energy accumulated from the day-to-day experience of centuries is held back by inertia. A single rolling stone clears the path for the mountain peak to tumble.

The conqueror cannot lie down to sleep or turn his back to relieve himself for fear that the little people will rise up and conduct their own lives. The fear and irritation give rise to hatred, which soon begins to feed on its own growth.

You think I am talking about the deep south of the United States, or some newly independent African country? It seems unfair to you, or just plain rhetoric, to speak this way about Canada today. Come home with me and I will tell you what I know from my own Indian people here in Canada within the memory of my own lifetime.

The Indian societies of British Columbia began to develop new forms of political organization centred around the issues raised by colonialism from the time that the colonial forces became oppressive. I have already told how the first reserve commissioners found the peoples of the southern interior organized for war when they arrived. The Potlatch Law was first brought in by Proclamation in 1882, and then by statute in 1884:

> 3. Every Indian or other person who engages in celebrating the Indian festival known as the "Potlatch" or in the Indian dance known as the "Tamanawas" is guilty of a misdemeanour, and shall be liable to imprisonment for a term of not more than six nor less than two months in any gaol or other place of confinement; and any Indian or other person who encourages, either directly or indirectly, an Indian or Indians to get up such a festival or dance, or to celebrate the same, or who shall assist in the celebration of same is guilty of a like offence, and shall be liable to the same punishment.

This law was so unenforceable that no arrests were made for the first five years after it was passed, although numerous reports from agents and missionaries complain of the continued practice of the mid-winter ceremonies year after year.

The law was unenforceable legally because it lacked definition. The first test case was made in 1889. Hemasack, a Kwakiutl, was arrested by the Indian Agent Pidcock, who then judged and convicted him and sentenced him to the maximum penalty of six months. Judge Begbie, in overthrowing the conviction, gave the opinion that potlatching was an acceptable practice unless liquor, rioting, and debauchery were involved.

> If the Legislature intended to prohibit any meeting announced by the name of a potlatch they should have said so. But if it be desired to create an offence previously unknown to the law there ought to be some definition of it in a Statute.[15]

Judge Begbie also gives an account of the manner in which Indian agents, who were empowered to act as justices of the peace, were accustomed to exercising their judicial authority. Even in the moderate tones appropriate to a judge's "bench notes," the nature of Canadian justice in its application to Indian people is made clear:

> I have some difficulty here; but I think on the whole the prisoner is entitled to his discharge. It appears that the prisoner was charged on the 1 August for the offence of celebrating the Indian festival known as a potlatch and on the same day committed for trial at Victoria on that charge. Being brought up before me on the Speedy Trials Act, a day was fixed for his trial. But before that time it became known that the J.P. at Alert Bay had already tried and convicted the prisoner of the offence. . . .
>
> Of course it may be said all difficulty is eliminated in the present case where a defendant pleads guilty. But it seems an abuse of the forms of justice to take advantage of that plea against an ignorant Indian who speaks no word of English and allege that he has pleaded guilty to an offence, the facts constituting which we should ourselves be unable to set forth. . . .
>
> A plea of guilty means guilty of the Act forbidden by the Statute.
>
> It is by no means clear that it was fully explained to the defendant what the Statute forbids. It would seem the Statute should set out what acts constitute the forbidden festival. Until a defendant knows what those forbidden acts are, how can he say whether he has committed them or not?

Judge Begbie said he was no more capable of understanding the charge against Hemasack than was the Indian himself. They both suffered from an excessive respect for law, a disease which did not afflict the agent Pidcock or most of his colleagues.

The law was unenforceable administratively because the Indian community in general, even when they were offered money, refused to cooperate in convicting their brothers. Pidcock wrote to Ottawa saying that the Indians wouldn't act as constables, and that only with a jail and a white constable might he be able to enforce the law.

We honour our grandfathers, who refused to persecute their brothers for money. We honour our grandfather Hemasack, who endured Pidcock of whom we will speak no more. We honour Judge Begbie as a fitting grandfather for our European neighbours.

74

Even before Hemasack's case, numerous petitions had been made to the local authorities. Many Indian agents and missionaries were of the opinion that it was better not to enforce the law in the hope that we would see the natural merit of their ways and forsake our own voluntarily. None of these petitions, not even the presence of a proper justice like Judge Begbie, did more than gain a reprieve for us until there was a stronger demand for enforcement.

One petition sent to Sir John A. Macdonald from the Cowichan is especially revealing of the attitude of the petitioners: "We therefore ask you to have the law amended that we may not be breaking it when we follow customs that are dear to us."

An acting Indian agent at Metlakatla, B.C., describes the situation honestly in a letter:

> [the potlatch law] proves a great stumbling block to the Indian Agent . . . inasmuch as a great majority of the tribes express a determination to stick to what they term "the oldest and best of their festivals."
>
> The Indians are ready to give up any other old custom when it is shown to be harmful. They contend that there is but "what is good" in the Potla[t]ch and refuse to give it up. A minority of these Indians led on by certain missionaries clamor for the enforcement of the law against Potlatch and shout shame at the Government and the Agent for having a law and not carrying it out. . . .
>
> I would most respectfully suggest the advisability of repealing that clause of the Act, or else make its enforcement dependent upon the pleasure of a majority of the Indians of any Indian settlement.

It was the Toronto *Empire*, a predecessor of the present *Globe and Mail*, that sparked the renewed public pressure for an enforceable Potlatch Law by an article entitled "The Evil Potlatch." The article ended with an attack on the non-enforcement of the law as it then stood:

> The law remains on the Dominion Statutes, but it is practically a dead letter; and the Indians, instead of being an upright and an industrious people, are a filthy, indolent, degraded set, a disgrace and a curse to our country.

Articles such as this prevailed against further petitions from Indians and more learned and humane articles by a very few European friends of British Columbia Indians, until an amendment to the old act was passed in 1895, making it possible to gain convictions.

In the fall of that year the Nass River Indians petitioned the Commissioner against the actions of a minister who was also the local justice of the peace. Rev. McCullagh had found constables who were willing to arrest other Indians who followed our own ways. The petitioning Indians suggested a compromise: "If the parties who wish to prevent the Potlatch will give to those who have claims for what they have given heretofore then the people will be willing to relinquish the practice." About $5,000 would have been required to pay off the debts that were outstanding, and thereby allow those who were owed the money to care for the elderly and the young. There is no indication that Mr. McCullagh was willing to indulge in such unspiritual concerns.

The Nass River Indians presented another petition, in which they compared the potlatch to the practices they had seen in the growing European towns such as Victoria and Vancouver,

> ... contradictory state of affairs adorning your civilization. Churches are numerous; the theatres are located in the various sections of the town; and saloons multiply in numbers; all of which are in conformity with your laws, consequently we wish to know whether the ministers of the gospel have annihilated the rights of white men in these pleasures leading to heaven and hell exactly in different directions. . . .
>
> We see in your graveyards the white marble and granite monuments which cost money in testimony of your grief for your dead. When our people die we erect a large pole, call our people together, distribute our personal property with them in payment for their sympathy and condolence; comfort to us in the sad hours of our affliction. This is what is called a potlatch—the privilege denied us. *It is a chimera that under the British flag slavery does not exist.* (emphasis added)

Other statements from Indian spokesmen also pointed up the inconsistencies in what the law allowed white men to do in their ceremonies and festivals and what it allowed Indians to do. The

Nootka Chief Maquinna published an article in the Victoria *Daily Colonist* of April 1, 1896, comparing the potlatch to a banking system. Furthermore, he says,

> They say it is the will of the Queen. The Queen knows nothing about our potlatch feasts. She must have been put up to make a law by people who know us. . . .
>
> The potlatch is not a pagan rite; the first Christians used to have their goods in common as a consequence must have given "potlatches", and now I am astonished that Christians persecute us and put us in jail for doing as the first Christians.

We honour grandfather Maquinna and the Nass River spokesmen who learned enough of the European ways to know the difference between what they believed for themselves and the words they put out to steal our minds.

Although the European friends of the Indians were few and far between, those who deserve the name of friend were the ones who were willing to listen and study, and were, therefore, well informed. However often their own brothers may have ignored them, they were also well published. Franz Boas, the father of Canadian anthropology, wrote a letter that appeared in the Vancouver *Daily Province*, and which he later adapted as an article for a British scholarly journal in which he argued the value and legitimacy of the potlatch.

Boas' material was later presented in the form of a letter to the Deputy Minister of Indian Affairs at the time, Dr. Duncan E. Scott. Scott was an outstanding scholar in his own right. He was the first man to publish an English-language version of the Iroquois Constitution. But the traditions of the civil service seem to have held a far greater sway over him than the knowledge he gained through study. In 1923, the Iroquois Confederacy sought to bring its case before the League of Nations and had secured the support of four member nations who would sponsor a resolution referring the matter of *Six Nations vs. Canada*[16] to the World Court. Scott found an eminent lawyer and retired colonel who would write a report saying that since the Six Nations govern themselves with "no written constitution" and by "long established custom" "it is impossible to ascertain the facts [of their

77

constitution] with exactness." Dr. Scott used this report as the text of an order-in-council claiming to overthrow the Confederacy, which the local agent delivered to the chiefs with a force of twenty officers of the R.C.M.P. accompanying him to make his meaning clear. Flexibility was the basis of Dr. Scott's scholarly administration.

That was many years later, and I am getting ahead of my story, but it cannot be said that ignorance played a role in the decisions of the government of Canada about the Indian people in those years. Ignorance of particular details, perhaps. But not ignorance of customs, beliefs, ceremonies, styles of government, methods of inheritance, economic organization, or anything else of substantial and enduring importance. Men of power who plead ignorance perpetuate their own belief in the great lie of their ancestors. Some Indian people have come to think that there are two schools of anthropology: one that brings men knowledge of themselves, and another that replaces the missionaries as the servant of the state.

We honour Franz Boas and those who have truly inherited his gifts.

The efforts of the missionaries and the agents were so unsuccessful that, in his *Annual Report* of 1913, Duncan Scott quoted Agent Halliday from Alert Bay to confess their failure at discouraging Indian customs. He mused about the possibility of education changing the old customs—if the people at Alert Bay did not become extinct, as their death rate was almost double their birth rate.

The same Halliday launched a series of prosecutions against the people he was sent to care for in 1914 and another series in 1920. But by this time, the Indian societies had learned to retain lawyers when they went to court about a serious matter. It is one thing for the Crown to launch a prosecution against an undefended individual. When people organize themselves well enough to seek legal advice, have counsel in court, and learn how to stay out of court, the process becomes both expensive and ineffective from the government's point of view.

The lawyers were useful, not only in court, but in finding ways for us to potlatch that were beyond the arm of the law. One way was to disassemble the potlatch, by holding the different parts—the feast, the dances, the giving—at different times and places. Another was simply to move the feast to a distant place known only to the invited guests, perhaps a distant island. I can remember people passing out oranges with dollar bills stuck in them. As long as the police or agent could not find all the elements of the potlatch present in one place or time, there was no offence. The variations that grew out of the possible loopholes were as numerous as the people who kept the traditions strong.

We honour all those grandfathers whose imaginations rose above those of their oppressors.

> At the first time when God gave land to the people, he gave some to the English, French, Japanese, Chinese, Indians, too. Now the white people change God's work and take our place from us and think we have no place or anything.[17]

Meanwhile, much more widespread and sophisticated political organization was developing on the land question. Whereas organization on the Potlatch Law usually followed tribal lines, bringing together the different bands of the same society, the land question was able to bring together many more Indian societies into a single concerted action under a common umbrella.

The decision to deny the land claim of the Indian peoples of British Columbia began with the first lieutenant-governor of the province, while he was Chief Commissioner of Indian Affairs immediately before Confederation. Commissioner Trutch was asked by the Colonial Secretary to investigate a complaint from a settler:

> That branch of the Shuswap Tribe . . . numbering, I am informed, less than five hundred souls, claim the undisputed possession of all the land on the north side, between the foot of the Great Shuswap Lake and the North River . . . where lie thousands of acres of good arable and pasture land, admirably adapted for settlement. I have heard of one cattle owner who paid their Chief, Nisquaimlth, a monthly rent for the privilege of turning his cattle on these lands . . . .
>
> These Indians do nothing more . . . than cultivate a few small patches of potatoes here and there; they are a vagrant people who live by fishing, hunting and bartering skins; and the cultiva-

tion of their ground contributes no more to their livelihood than a few days digging of wild roots; . . .

In 1866, Trutch introduced a program at the Kamloops and Shuswap Reserves for cutting back the acreage that had been granted under Sir James Douglas. His preferred method for doing this was simple and straightforward. Douglas had appointed a man called McColl with instruction to measure out the reserves according to the wishes of the people living there. Trutch proceeded, in his own words, "to disavow absolutely McColl's authority to make these reserves."

By this process of granting recognition with one hand and taking it away with the other, by the time British Columbia entered Confederation Trutch had created a policy that led to a complete denial of Indian title.

When he became lieutenant-governor of the new province, Trutch wrote to the Prime Minister with his solution to the "Indian problem." First, he proposed that the responsibility be placed in the office of lieutenant-governor. Second, he recommended ordering in naval vessels to control the forty to fifty thousand "utter savages." Above all, he urged the Prime Minister to grant no compensation:

> If you now commence to buy out Indian title to the lands of B.C. you would go back of all that has been done here for 30 years past and would be equitably bound to compensate the tribes who inhabited the districts now settled and farmed by white people equally with those in remote and uncultivated portions.

A totally different view came from the Governor-General of Canada, Earl Dufferin—hardly a man to disturb the sovereignty of the Crown—on his first tour of British Columbia.

> In British Columbia . . . the Provincial Government has always assumed that the [title] to the land, as well as the sovereignty over the land, resided in the Queen. Acting upon this principle, they have granted extensive grazing leases, and otherwise so dealt with various sections of the country as greatly to restrict or interfere with the prescriptive rights of the Queen's Indian subjects. As a consequence, there has come to exist an unsatis-

factory feeling among the Indian population. Intimations of this reached me at Ottawa two or three years ago, and since I have come into the Province, my misgivings have been confirmed. Now I consider that our Indian fellow-subjects are entitled to exactly the same civil rights under the law as are possessed by the white population and that *if an Indian can prove a prescriptive right of way to a fishing station, or a right of way of any other kind, that that right should no more be ignored than if it was the case of a white man.* [18] (emphasis added)

It certainly never hurts to have friends in high places. Sometimes they are just too high. Under the new Confederation, the province, not the Dominion government, claimed the land. The Dominion had an interest in the issue only because they were to control "Indians and lands reserved for the Indians." But the reserves could only be set up where the province agreed to relinquish its claim.

The petition of 1874 from the "chiefs of Douglas Portage, of Lower Fraser, and of the other tribes on the seashore of the mainland to Bute Inlet" is generally taken as the first extensive organizing effort made by the different Indian groups of British Columbia against the policy of ignoring our title to the land. The petitioners had assembled figures on the amount of land granted to each reserve all the way down the Fraser River from Hope to the Pacific Ocean.

Not long after the Fraser River petition, the Nishga began to organize around the land issue, to seek legal advice, and to develop petitions. They went first to Victoria and then to Ottawa, where Sir John A. Macdonald promised that lands that were being claimed by the Anglican Church mission would be returned to the people. But the Church Missionary Society, which had made the claim in the midst of its own internal dispute between the new Bishop Ridley and the well-established missionary Duncan, could promise to deliver votes. The Nishga could only talk of honour, promises from the Queen's personal representative the Governor-General, English common law, and ancient tribal custom—hardly enough to sway a prime minister to turn away from votes.

Petitions and local pressures continued until 1906, when the Salish Indians of the Cowichan on Vancouver Island sent a delegation to present a petition to King Edward VII. The Cowichan petition raised four major points for redress:

1. That the title of their land had never been extinguished;
2. That white men had settled on their land against their wishes;
3. That all appeals to the Candian government had proven vain;
4. That they had no vote and were not consulted with respect to agents.

Another delegation representing twenty tribes visited His Majesty in 1909 after an attempt by the province to dispossess the Skeena Indians, near Prince Rupert, of some land. The same year saw the formation of the first intertribal organizations for the purpose of presenting the land claim, the Indian Tribes of the Province of British Columbia.

The next summer, Prime Minister Sir Wilfrid Laurier promised an Indian meeting at Prince Rupert: "The only way to settle this question that you have agitated for years is by a decision of the Judicial Committee, and I will take steps to help you." Following Laurier's statement, another reserve commission, the Mc-Kenna-McBride Commission, was set up to try to reapportion lands more satisfactorily. But many bands refused to discuss anything but the question of Aboriginal Title with the commissioners, and others refused even to meet with them.

The first comprehensive written record of the British Columbia land claim[19] was a memorandum of the Douglas Portage Chiefs, prepared by their counsel A.E. O'Meara, dated May 3, 1911.

We honour those chiefs for their diligence, and we honour their counsel who suffered the abuse of his brothers at the bar.

Three years later, Duncan Scott, who continued to serve as deputy superintendent general of Indian Affairs for the government of Sir Robert Borden, as he would for William Lyon Mackenzie King, prepared an order-in-council to fulfil Laurier's promise and allow the claim of the Indian Tribes of British Columbia to go to the Privy Council. But not directly to the Privy Council. The case would have to begin in the Exchequer Court of Canada, a court that mainly dealt with highly technical administrative questions and whose bench was traditionally filled with retired civil servants who are highly expert on obscure questions of tax law. But our fathers were told there was no other way to the Privy Council than through an appeal from a lower court. This much could have been accepted.

But there were four other principal conditions:[20]

1. The Chiefs had to agree in advance that if the court upheld our claim to title, we must surrender the title to the Crown for whatever compensation they might choose to give; and, the Chiefs would accept in advance the judgement of the McKenna-McBride Commission as the full allotment of reserved lands;

2. The province, by agreeing to this commission's report—which its own premier had helped to write—would have satisfied all claims against it;

3. The Indians would be represented in court only by lawyers chosen by the Dominion government; and, the case could only go to court if the province also agreed to be represented by lawyers it could choose for itself;

4. If the courts decided that we did not have title, the Dominion government would ever after be the sole authority to decide what was in our interest, without further protest.

"If you win, you lose," was the attitude of the Canadian government. They were saying to our fathers, "Now that you are learning to play the game by our rules, we are going to change the rules with each new play. We will not only see that you are opposed. We will be the judge, the jury, and the God who makes the ultimate law."

Shortly after the First Great European War, in which many Indians served, Duncan Scott offered the Iroquois Confederacy an arbitration about their status and sovereignty under similar conditions. The Confederacy would be allowed to choose one of the arbitrators, but all three members of the arbitration panel would have to be judges of the Supreme Court of Ontario. The Confederacy would also have to be represented before the panel by a "British subject," thereby excluding any member of the Confederacy, as well as any non-British international jurist, such as the lawyers they had already consulted in the United States.

We honour our fathers who turned their backs on a government which was so contemptuous of their own courts, and their justice.

New leaders were emerging at this time, men who had grown up during the years of this struggle, and who had seen the short-comings and pitfalls of local and divided actions based on piecemeal petitions about individual grievances. They made themselves masters both of our own way of knowing the world, and of European ways.

Rev. Peter Kelly, a Haida from the north, and Andrew Paull, a Squamish from the south of the province, brought almost all of the tribes of British Columbia together through their work as the principal organizers of the Allied Tribes of British Columbia. With the support of many of the elder Indian statesmen of the day, the Allied Tribes started to organize in 1915.

Although Peter Kelly's name became a household word in every Indian home on the coast, it was Andy Paull whom we came to know and love in the interior. For the next thirty years, from the time he started to serve the Allied Tribes as secretary, there was never a moment when he was not organizing something. Andy Paull was always a very colourful character, and as he developed years of experience, he became an extremely able politician. The larger political goals were never far from his mind, but his organizing efforts reached into every aspect of Indian community life.

He organized the hop-pickers in Chilliwack. They would come in from all over the province, not just the Fraser Valley area. He would organize a potlatch to bring them all together. Out of that he formed what amounted to an employment agency to match up the workers with the jobs, keep tabs on people who might get lost in an area that was new to them, and see that everyone got home at the end of the season. If there were crops ready to pick in Washington State when there was no work in British Columbia, he found work for us there.

He helped the Indian fishermen to organize as a separate group from the Fishermen's Union. In the 1920's a full third of the coastal fishermen of British Columbia were Indian, and the figures are probably not much different today. The coastal Indians never claimed much land when reserves were being set up, because they claimed their fishing spots as part of their aboriginal title. If the main fishermen's union wanted to strike, the success or failure of the strike depended on the good will of the Pacific Coast Native Fishermen's Association, and later the Native Brotherhood.

He trained many Indian bands and managed their bookings for concerts.

Lacrosse was a major sport at that time. A good Indian team could capture the imagination of an entire town, Indian and non-Indian alike. At one point, Salmon Village of New Westminster was a very big team that everyone looked to as a challenge to Ottawa for the national championship. Andrew developed a team for Salmon Village that brought together the all-star players from both east and west.

He rented a train coach to take them east for the championship game. The only coach they could afford was an old one that had only wooden seats when all the rest of the train was made up of modern coaches with nicely padded seats. But he had gotten the team rolling eastward at just the same speed as anyone else. He got the women to make enough bannock and dried fish to last for the whole trip to Ottawa.

After they had won the first three games, the mayor of Vancouver sent a telegram of support and the money started to roll in—enough to let them move out of their fourth-rate hotel into something you might call respectable. They lost the next four games in a best-of-seven series.

Whenever Andy travelled, which was most of the time for the rest of his life, he would try to take leaders with him from the communities most affected by whatever issue was current.

All the money Andy Paull ever spent in his organizing work was Indian money. Wherever he went, the blanket or the hat was passed to keep Andy travelling and working. Often, on his later trips to Ottawa, when I was old enough to remember and be active, we would raise enough money to just get him to Ottawa. A week or so later we would get a wire from him. It was time to chip in again and help him get back home.

The belief in sharing and giving and mutual support, the tradition of the potlatch, could be moved in many directions. The missionaries had moved it away from the people to serve the heavens. Now two Indian leaders—one ordained as a minister, and another described by a senior Queen's Counsel in British Columbia who knew him well as "very close to being a lawyer"—brought it back to the people to serve a far wider Indian community than it had ever reached before. Without his lawyer-like skills, Andy Paull could never have served the people so ably. Without a belief in the traditions of our people he could never have travelled so far on one-way tickets. It was this belief that made him free of the worry of how he would get home, or where he would eat and sleep along the way. Not only Andy Paull, but many others travelled the same route on the same kind of ticket.

When Andy Paull fell into disgrace with the Native Brother-hood in 1945, it was our dollar-and-cent poverty that brought about the split. Where a ride, a meal, and a bed could always be found for a friend, large amounts of cash just did not exist. People had been sending Andy to Victoria, Vancouver, to meetings with prairie and eastern Indians, and to Ottawa for many years. The sheer difficulty of travel and lack of funds meant that a group who had helped to send him on his way, however generously they had given, unless they lived close by him, simply had to wait until his next time through their area to learn the results of his last trip. It might be six months, a year, even two years before they would see him again.

People had been giving in this way for thirty years. The whole world had just come through six years of European and Asian warfare. Many Indian men had fought in those wars. Suffering, time, and money had taken on new dimensions. People had been made to believe in instant results and reports of victory that came back as quickly as the radio waves.

There developed a resentment against Andy Paull when people no longer remembered how to wait to find out what he had accomplished on his last trip. It no longer made sense to wait two years to hear from this little Squamish man when you heard voices from London, Paris, and Berlin the second that they spoke. People began to say that he was not reporting back because he was pocketing money for himself. If Andy Paull had kept the kind of financial records people say he should have kept in the little office in the corner of his house, the Indian people of British Columbia would still be passing the hat to pay him back. It is hard to believe in the importance of keeping good financial records when fund-raising is a crime.

Fund-raising was made a crime for Indians in Canada in 1927, right after Andy Paull, Peter Kelly, and their lawyer, A.E. O'Meara, succeeded in bringing the Claim of the Allied Tribes of British Columbia before a Joint Committee of the Senate and House of Commons of Canada. But I have gotten ahead of myself again.

When the Allied Tribes rejected the government's offer to surrender our title before we ever got into court, the effort to press the claim continued to mount. In 1920, the Parliament passed an act enabling the implementation of the McKenna-McBride reserve commission report. When the government was preparing an order-in-council to actually implement the report under this act, four years later, the Allied Tribes first presented a memorandum opposing the petition, and later met with the Minister of the Interior, Charles Stewart. He again suggested bringing the matter to the Privy Council and offered his support.

Finally, on June 10, 1926, a petition was presented to the Parliament of Canada by the Allied Tribes of British Columbia, signed by Peter Kelly, as chairman of the Executive Committee. The government agreed to send it to a special joint committee of both houses of Parliament. The petition is an excellent summary of all the negotiations, memoranda, petitions, resolutions, and commission reports from 1875 to the time the petition was drawn up. But the petition did not ask Parliament to act in place of the Privy Council, and decide on the merits of the claim that the Indians of British Columbia continued to hold title to almost all the land presently included within the province. The active part of the petition asked Parliament for four things:

1. to amend the act of 1920 implementing the McKenna-McBride Report so as to safeguard aboriginal rights;
2. that steps be taken to define and settle the outstanding issues between the Allied Tribes; the province and the Dominion; (what was most important about defining the issues was a recognition that the Allied Tribes were a party to negotiations that up to that time had always taken place as a two-way action between the Dominion and the province);
3. *"that steps be taken* for facilitating the independent proceedings of the Allied Tribes and enabling them by

securing reference of the Petition now in His Majesty's Privy Council and such other independent judicial action as shall be found necessary *to secure judgement of the Judicial Committee of His Majesty's Privy Council deciding all issues involved";* (emphasis added)

4. "that this Petition and all related matters be referred to a Special Committee for full consideration."[21]

The value of going before a joint parliamentary committee lay in the opportunity to present to an official public forum the case that had so often been made to the Crown or ministers of the Crown in private or at Indian meetings. It was an opportunity to demonstrate the just and reasonable nature of the claim and the need to make the legal arguments before the Privy Council, which at that time served as the highest court of the whole British Empire. It was, I think, clear to most of those concerned that Parliament was not being asked to act in place of the Privy Council. It was being asked only to make it possible for the courts to be opened to the Indian people.

Any pretense of a judicial proceeding broke down within the first thirty seconds of the discussion. Some members of the committee had already been on record for ten years or more as being opposed to giving any serious consideration to the claim. The minister was also an active member of the committee—if this was Canadian justice it had not yet learned to distinguish the prosecutor from the jury—in fact, he was a little more active than the chairman.

After the chairman, Senator Hewitt Bostock, then Speaker of the Senate, had cleared away some procedural matters such as the hours of sitting and introducing the petitioners, he said:[22]

I understand Mr. O'Meara is to appear as counsel. I presume the right way would be to allow the Indians to present their case first.

Hon. Mr. Stevens, the Minister:

I have a suggestion I should like to make in that regard; I might say I have been fairly familiar with this controversy since Mr. O'Meara took it up in 1910. I think the Committee would get a better grasp of the situation if we had Dr. Scott before us first, and let him give us the background of the whole business. You will then get, in a short time, a grasp of the general situation. Then we can have Mr. O'Meara.

Mr. O'Meara and everyone he represented were soon to be had indeed. The province had refused to appear, and now the minister was directing the chairman to call his deputy as the first witness. If the committee had any pretense of a judicial proceeding, Charles Stewart, Duncan Scott, and the government they represented would have been in the role of defendants. Instead, their innocence had to be established as the first point of procedure before any petitioners would be heard.

Other members of the committee were not much more devoted to normal procedure than the minister. As soon as he had spoken Hon. Mr. Belcourt chimed in:

> What authority has Mr. O'Meara to speak for anybody? If he has no authority, I, for one, do not propose to listen to him.

Duncan Scott repeated much of the history of the claim, but the real point that runs throughout the many pages of his testimony is the one that Lieutenant-Governor Trutch had made so many years before: he, as deputy-superintendent general, was the man in the best position to decide what was in the best interests of the Indians. He analyzed the annuity payments and land grants given to prairie Indians and told the committee how much better off we were under the care and guidance of his department, at his discretion, than under treaties that would establish (1) a legal right to our existence; and (2) a minimum level of land and compensation.

> The important question to be decided by the Dominion Government, guardian of the Indians, is whether the claim of aboriginal title is to be referred to the courts, and if not, what course is to be adopted in the future treatment of the question, and what motive or policy is to prevail in our future relationship with our wards. *It is our duty to consider what advantage is to be gained by the Indians from this reference. If successful, will their position in British Columbia be improved, or will any advantage follow, financial or otherwise?* Or is all that is favourable in their

relations with the British Columbia government to be jeopardized. (emphasis added)

He threatened the committee with what might happen if they upset the agreement with the province which had been made without the participation of the Indians and enacted over the protest of the Allied Tribes.

> We must, I think, consider the effect of a reference to the Courts by the Dominion Government upon the confirmed agreement between the Governments [of the Province and the Dominion]....
>
> A review of the present Indian policy of the Dominion Government in British Columbia [will show it] not to differ in any respect from the general Indian policy, and the British Columbia Indians will appear as recipients of like benefits to other Indians.

We were all being cut to the same mould under the uniform cookie-cutter of Dominion policy, a policy that judges all acres to be equal soil even if one is mountain top and one is river bottom.

Dr. Scott even quoted Governor Trutch with approval when he asked the Committee to make a comparison between:

> the character and condition of the British Columbia Indians described by Hon. Mr. Trutch in 1872, and the Indians who have appeared before the Government urging their claims, the result will be striking. Mr. Trutch states that *"by far the larger proportion of them are utter savages"*; *the deputation of the present day have been headed by an Indian who is a Minister of the United Church. His companions speak and write English and are self-supporting members of society.* (emphasis added)

Finally, Dr. Scott told the committee that education is the key to the aboriginal title claim:

> [At the time of Union] the British Columbia Government had no very well developed policy, yet they had established or were thinking of establishing schools for the Indians and were looking forward to the time when they would become self-supporting members of the community....

90

A complete building programme totalling $1,310,000 would suffice to establish all necessary Indian schools within the province. When it is completed, the annual maintenance would cost $468,000, and 4,415 Indians will be under training. . . .

If instruction is provided in agriculture and fruit-growing in districts where it is applicable. . . . the needs of the British Columbia Indians will be provided for, and by such an expenditure not only would the supposed Indian title be amply satisfied, but the obligation which the Dominion overtook at the time British Columbia came into the Union will be met most fully and comprehensively.

Industrial training!
When Andy Paull got up to testify, he was asked to swear an oath. Dr. Scott was not asked to swear.

Andy Paull first asked for permission to question Dr. Scott. He hoped to show that the Indian people had spent large amounts of money themselves on education, medical care, and maintenance of law and order. Dr. Scott was saved by an intervention from his minister:

> Mr. Paull, we only have twenty minutes; will you deal with that
> very important matter, the question of aboriginal title, first.

When Andy Paull began to give a basic introduction to the claim he was told that he had to give evidence, not present an argument. Questions were coming at him from a variety of committee members at once. Mr. Stewart explained that Mr. Paull should present evidence, not to support his petition, but "in rebuttal on the constitutional question." Everybody but his own lawyer seemed to be allowed to ask Andy Paull questions. And when the several members asked at once, others complained that their own procedure was unclear. Finally, the committee made a decision. They decided to begin hearing testimony from the petitioners the next day at 10:00 A.M.

A good night's sleep did not seem to improve the humour of the committee. When Mr. O'Meara, whose own personality seems to have been a little abrasive, attempted to give an oral summary of the documentary evidence, he was repeatedly shouted down by the committee members. Some referred to him as a witness.

Others remembered that he was appearing before them as legal counsel. There was even a motion carried that "if this witness has no evidence to offer, we proceed with some witness who has evidence."

Andy Paull was then recalled to answer questions put by the members. He did manage to use the questions to present a comprehensive history of the land claim, including the various promises that had been made by British and Canadian authorities and to read into the record what seemed to him to be important portions of the documents from which Dr. Scott had quoted at length, which Dr. Scott had forgotten to mention. How differently the practice of reading documents into the record is received according to who the reader is.

Many of the members' questions tried to reduce the fundamental constitutional and legal issues to a list of grievances that could be resolved within the existing framework. Andy Paull tried to answer these questions by showing how many specific hardships were being caused by a lack of either a treaty or a recognition of title, without at the same time losing sight of the basic question. Occasionally, sympathy was expressed by members for some of the problems, but consideration of possible remedies was avoided.

When Mr. Stevens pointed out that twenty acres per family had been the allotment in 1875, it was now 132 acres — a situation that arose not from an increase in acreage but from a decline in population — Andy Paull replied by showing that the 47,000 acres removed by the reserve commission were worth $1,522,704 while the 87,292 acres added were worth only $444,853.

When Andy Paull tried to document the hardship that was being worked in many different areas by restrictions on the right to hunt and fish for food, members would reply that:

> If you pass a statute as you suggest, to give a certain thing there will be an abuse of it. . . . How would you suggest we can control your people from abusing that privilege, if it were given to them?

Or later,

> Of course you recognize, or ought to recognize and I hope the Committee will recognize, that that is impossible . . . it will

result in the game being more or less destroyed in a very short time.

A delegation from the Interior Tribes, from the central and northern interior of the province, also came before the committee to testify. Their lawyer, Mr. McIntyre, was at least as gruff and abrasive as Mr. O'Meara. Although he agreed that the Allied Tribes had focused their case on the experience of the people they represented from the southern interior and the coast, Mr. McIntyre was determined to attack the integrity of the Allied Tribes. So long as he continued in that vein he was heard respectfully.

Mr. McIntyre, like the members of the committee, tried to narrow the discussion down to a list of grievances that could be remedied by specific administrative actions. But his two witnesses, Chief Johnny Chilihitza and Chief Basil David—who each spoke in their own Indian languages through an interpreter—dealt squarely with the constitutional issues. Unfortunately, neither of them was equipped to make the detailed and documented case that Andy Paull had presented. So long as they dealt with the issue in grand and large terms that were not made concrete with the kind of detailed historical evidence that demands a substantial reply, they were also allowed to speak freely.

The case that Johnny Chilihitza made, just because it was put in an unlettered but simple and straightforward way, was probably the most pertinent and relevant testimony, as well as the most eloquent, that the Committee heard:

> Long ago the Indians had laws, but since the white people came, the Indian laws are cast aside by the white people, and they impose their white man's law on the Indians. . . . Sproat came as a messenger from the Queen, and he said: . . . "The Queen has learned of your country, and it is a big country, and the Queen wants to keep your reserves, and put them in four posts. . . . If you believe in the Queen, and take her as your sovereign, she will take care of you always. . . . If in any way you have trouble in your country, you will speak to the Queen and she will send word over and have the trouble fixed up for you Indians."
>
> The Indians did not seem to agree to have their lands in four posts, and then Sproat told the Indians that if they consented to have their reserves posted . . . the Queen will send another messenger. "When the messenger comes again you will speak

about your country; it is a big country, and all what is in it, and you Indians and the Queen will make an agreement"....

The Indians killed both deer and fowls, but still there was always plenty of game. Now the white people have made laws concerning the deer and they have told the Indians not to kill any more deer. They say to the Indians: "It is you Indians that exterminate the deer, and the fowl by killing them off in such numbers; now, we will not allow you to kill any more deer; if any of you Indians is found out killing the fowl or the deer, you will be sent to prison."

On the 11th of April, 1927, the Committee brought down a report stating:

> It is the unanimous opinion of the members...that the petitioners have not established any claim to the lands of British Columbia based on aboriginal or other title.

The Joint Parliamentary Committee had saved the judicial committee of the Privy Council a great deal of detailed legal work, in response to a petition that primarily asked for the right to plead before the courts. After congratulating themselves on the fairness of their hearing, the committee's report reviews the history of the matter again, concurs in Dr. Scott's testimony about the excellence of the work of his department, and makes some concessions in favour of lenient application of hunting and fishing regulations. The report concludes:

> Your Committee would recommend that the decision arrived at should be made known as completely as possible to the Indians of British Columbia by direction of the Superintendent General of Indian Affairs *in order that they may become aware of the finality of the findings and advised that no funds should be contributed by them to continue further presentation of a claim that has been disallowed.* (emphasis added)

Even before the report was tabled Parliament had already acted to see that no further funds should be contributed. On March 31, 1927, the Parliament of Canada passed an act to amend the Indian Act which made it an offence to raise funds for the purpose of pressing any Indian claim:

149A. Every person who, solicits or requests from any Indian any payment or contribution or promise of any payment or contribution for the purpose of raising a fund for the prosecution of any claim which the tribe or band of Indians to which such Indian belongs . . . shall be guilty of an offence and liable upon summary conviction for each such offence to a penalty not exceeding two hundred dollars and not less than fifty dollars or to imprisonment for any term not exceeding two months.[23]

I do not know if this was the darkest hour in the history of the Parliament of Canada. If there were other moments when the forces of law and order were so warped and distorted I will let others speak of their own suffering.

If in any way you have trouble in your country you will speak to the Queen and she will send word over and have the trouble fixed for you Indians.

We honour our grandfather Johnny Chilihitza, who knew the meaning of law, and our grandfather Basil David, who travelled with him so far.

We honour our great grandfather Peter Kelly, who returned in charity two-fold the learning he took from all cultures.

We honour our great grandfather Andrew Paull, whose scholarship and diligence combined with humour and humility to strengthen him for the work for which he was raised.

The land claim did not die when Parliament declared the finality of its own judgement. But the central focus of organizing activity on the part of the Indian people of British Columbia did change from the question of aboriginal title to the more immediate causes of poverty with the onset of the Great Depression: welfare, employment opportunities, the local application of hunting and fishing regulations. These were the issues that had brought people together in the very earliest intertribal organizing efforts. But there was no surrender in the struggle for survival. There was only a strategic change in direction in the face of heavy fire which was essential to carry on the struggle.

In 1931, a meeting of Haida and Tsimshian people at Fort Simpson, inspired by the work of the Alaska Native Brotherhood in which many of those people had relatives, founded the Native

Brotherhood of British Columbia. Meanwhile, farther south on the coast, the Kwakiutl fishermen were getting involved in labour-union types of organization and were becoming more aware of their distinct role as Indian people within the fishing industry. In the early 1940's, the Kwakiutl Pacific Coast Native Fishermen's Association and the Native Brotherhood merged under the name of the Native Brotherhood of British Columbia.

The Depression and the increased vigilance of the Indian agents had forced attention to the day-to-day issues. The Second Great European War brought about a reunion of the surface issues of poverty and the underlying question of aboriginal rights. Income tax had only been introduced in Canada as a wartime necessity in the First European War. Like so many temporary measures it continued long after its original purpose was served. But Indian people had always been exempt from taxation of any kind so long as the money was earned on our own land. Indians across Canada have always considered that this exemption came from our right to the lands reserved to us. So long as these lands are unsurrendered, they are reserved for the "use and benefit of the Indian people" who live on them. This matter of principle takes on a highly practical aspect when so much has already been lost, and so many disabilities imposed on our attempts to support ourselves.

Indian people supported the war effort in far more substantial ways than paying a part of what little income we had in taxes. More Indian people enrolled, in proportion to our actual numbers, in the armed forces than any other group in Canada. Because we lacked European education, most of our men served in the infantry. We were among the first to see action and the last to come home. The objection to paying income tax for the duration of the war was not an objection to the war effort but only to a further abrogation of our aboriginal rights. And, when you consider how little cash income we had to contribute, and how the government survived without our cash in the first war, it seems that the government's desire to impose the tax also flowed more from a desire to prosecute our aboriginal rights than from a need to enhance the war effort. Perhaps the leaders of the day knew what happened when "temporary taxes" are imposed.

Andy Paull, Peter Kelly, and Guy Williams, today a Senator from British Columbia, developed the Native Brotherhood of

British Columbia into the strongest Indian voice in the province around this issue, while continuing a concern with the day-to-day matters of the coastal Indians as fishermen.

The Native Brotherhood never did become as strong in the interior as the Allied Tribes had been because of their identification with commercial fishing and with Protestantism. While our ways of life continued to differ according to the kinds of land we lived on, and according to our ancient customs and beliefs, it was not tribalism but the differences in our relations with European institutions that continually kept us apart.

When Andy Paull left the Native Brotherhood in 1945 he formed the North American Indian Brotherhood. Although his strongest support was to come from the southern coast and the interior of British Columbia, Andy did succeed in gaining membership, including moral and financial support, from Indian leaders in all corners of Canada, and the eastern United States. Still, there was no doubt that the North American Brotherhood was always a support group for Andy Paull's own powerful and unique personality.

Whenever there was a political discussion among British Columbia Indians, so long as Andy Paull lived after that, the password was that the Native Brotherhood of British Columbia was a body without a head, while the North American Indian Brotherhood was a head without a body. Like every political joke, it was an exaggeration based on a certain kernel of truth.

The North American Brotherhood, like the Native Brotherhood, began with a focus on matters of general interest: voting rights without loss of Indian rights, liquor rights as a way of ending most of the criminal charges facing Indian people, and pensions and welfare on the same level enjoyed by the Canadian population.

The demand for voting rights without loss of aboriginal rights and Indian status reflects, perhaps more clearly than any other issue, the central concern of most Indian people today, as well as the constant nature of our basic goals throughout this century of struggle.

If the Canadian claim to establish a Dominion with sovereignty from sea to sea was based on any element of natural justice, or if Canada was in any way touched by the Great Law that must to some extent govern all nations, there must be a basis on which the Indians of Canada can participate in the larger society of Canada while we continue to be Indian.

Progress, wherever I have lived or travelled in North America, has meant to native people the wedding of our own traditions and values with the methods, knowledge, and technology of the global civilization throughout our lifetime. Few, if any, Indian people have ever shared the belief that seems so common among European leaders that moral progress is a secondary by-product of the development of new techniques. You have to be very strongly in the driver's seat to convince yourself of a thing like that. I know that there are many white people today who have come to reject this idea of an inevitable moral progress. Perhaps there were always some who saw that industry and technology produce nothing more than tools. However good and useful those tools may be to human welfare, there is nothing inevitable about the parallel development of the wisdom to use those tools well. That is the wisdom of the Fourth World, and I believe that the grandfathers whom I have recalled here, including the many whose names I have not mentioned, shared, if not always the wisdom itself, at least the vision of the wisdom, and the knowledge that its day must come.

Before Andy Paull and the other leaders of his generation died, they saw at least some small sign of victory. Their presentations to the Joint Parliamentary Committee in 1948 led to the revision of the Indian Act in 1951, repealing the Potlatch Law and the 1927 ban on organizing. Indians were no longer to be defined in Canadian law by saying that "a person is any other individual than an Indian." But the surest sign that the lives of our fathers had meaning did not lie in convincing the Parliament of Canada of our humanity. It lay in the fact that the tradition of the potlatch never died. The organizing and coming together of people to work for our common goals never stopped.

5

~~~~~~~~~~~~~~~~~~~~~~~~~~~~~~~~~~~~

Scratching
for a Start

IN ANY MAN'S life, and any people's history, there are far more "if's" than actual events. It is impractical to consider these "if's" in depth, because they are shrouded in the darkness of uncertainty. But it is not unseemly to know what might have been.

Perhaps my grandfather would have taught me the ways to go up into the mountains if the decision had not been taken out of his hands as well as mine. The old people still tell me today that I would not have made much of myself if I had continued to go to that school.

Christmas and the parcels of food that would soon come to deliver us from hunger were just beginning to preoccupy the minds of the younger students. Perhaps the first snow of winter had fallen on the plateau, but there were still no swirling drifts to cover the fences. Hardly enough snow had fallen for a good snowball fight when I was taken to the hospital for the first time, and left the school for the last time. This would have been my third year at school. I had just turned twelve.

I was in that hospital almost continuously for the next three years, and in and out of one hospital or another for six more years after that. I had tuberculosis of the hip; today it is called osteomylitis. I hope the new name has brought a better understanding and an improved treatment.

There was an excellent sanitorium in British Columbia, but in those years it did not accept Indian patients; provincial policy at that time was to ignore the existence of Indians in providing public services. Federal policy was not likely to cover the costs of such an institution. The time I did spend in the Royal Inland Hospital in Kamloops and the Coqualeetza Indian Hospital at Sardis covered the greater part of the next eight years of my life.

There were four European people in my early life who showed me the best that their society had to offer by way of understanding and generosity. Each one taught me a new skill. The nurses in that hospital, and one in particular, gave me the first of the four great lessons I was to receive from European people.

The hundreds of simple acts of care and kindness which a nurse might do for any number of patients every day can be "just a job to be done." These same acts can also become the foundations on which two people learn to understand and to touch each other deeply.

The nurses I remember brought me all the books and games we never saw at a school for industrial training. They taught me to read, and to use my enforced quiet to my own advantage. Is it too much to think that the many hours of solitude, and the time those nurses spent showing me how to enjoy and make the best of those books was another way of receiving a snam?

Far better than I remember the baths and towels, meals, and beds, which were all warm and plentiful, I recall the nurses who brought me those books, and who sat with me those many hours. At some point, when my leg had grown numb from lack of exercise, they taught me to walk again. But I recall them rekindling the imagination of my childhood, which had grown numb the same way.

I honour those women who kept me alive as though they were grandmothers of our own nation.

When I began to spend more time at home again and visit around our village, I was already in my mid-teens. It was hard to put your finger on at first, but anybody could see how much things

100

had changed for the worse. You did not have to have an advanced political consciousness to realize how wretched and despised our people were in the eyes of the white men who held the power in the area. And in our own eyes.

When I had gone to town with my grandfather years before, I had seen people drunk in the streets. But I had never seen such a sight in our own village. Now people were drinking more and more.

People were starting to resist the church—silently, but so as to be heard—by not attending on the Sundays when the priest would come around, by drinking on Sunday. In a small community those are pretty loud actions. The odd person would get sufficiently drunk on a Sunday morning to walk into church and show his feelings in a less passive way.

The resistance was there, but it lacked the leadership that could crystallize it.

A trip to the movies in those days, or even now, involved finding a ride into Chase or Kamloops. As my leg grew stronger I found it was faster to walk unless I knew somebody with a car or wagon who was going to town. Either way, just the going and coming was a whole adventure.

When a bunch of Indians would get to the movie house, we were never allowed our choice of seats; there was a small corner of the theatre where they always put us. For a long time this seemed to me just a part of the way things were, like the distance to town or the rain that soaked you on the way home. It was only as I grew older that I developed a resentment and realized that this movie-house reservation was not as fixed and certain as the Creator's will.

If you had the money for Cokes and chips after the movie, you sought out the lowest-grade restaurants in town, so low that their white patrons did not feel themselves too good to be eating in the same room with Indians.

Of course, when a boy first went to town he simply followed the route laid down by the older boys, who no doubt learned it from the ones who were a couple of years older than they were. The novelty of a trip to town can last a long time with country boys. Besides, this was where you might find a ride home, or at least company to shorten the distance of the long walk. So the cycle of isolation and the symbols that point to discrimination and low esteem become absorbed into the daily custom and life style of the wretched of the earth, until we come to believe what is said about us. If those of us who had been taught better than that in our early years felt a conflict, it was the immediate reality that held sway in our teen-age years.

The one experience that weighs against the dominant impression of that time after I came home and before I began a regular job was Andy Paull coming around to speak.

I'm not sure how I came to be the one to make fire for Andy Paull when he came to our area. But I know that I had that job by the time I was fifteen. By this time Andy Paull was heading the North American Indian Brotherhood, which had its strength in the coastal and interior peoples of British Columbia. He would come around as often as six times a year. We would meet in the community hall at ten o'clock on a Saturday morning. Several hours before that I would be firing up the old pot-belly stoves so that it would be good and warm by the time the people had begun to gather.

I doubt that I understood very much of what the older people were talking about at those meetings. Maybe it's just that I do not recall any of the discussions, but if any of Paull's message sank in at that age it was at a very low level of consciousness.

My first job was at the sanitorium at Tranquille. My own doctor had agreed to release me on condition that I not work and that I have a good, healthy house in which to live. Our own house was good in many ways, but a one-room house with neither central heating nor running water was not what the doctor had in mind. After two years and seven months in an institution, I was willing to promise anything; I promised to find a proper and healthy house to live in and not to work.

Fortunately, there was a shortage of labour in 1941 with all the able-bodied men off in the war. When I finally managed to see the supervisor of the sanitorium, a Dr. Stalker, he understood my needs right away. I was to get room and board and a few dollars in return for cleaning trays for two hours after each daily meal. Officially, I was an employee. In fact, I was like another walking patient who paid for his services in labour rather than in cash.

When the war ended and the men were coming home, the sanitorium let me go. By then I had regained my strength and was ready to see the world, so I joined the migrant Indian workers on their way to pick apples in the orchards of Washington state. When I came back from my second season in the orchards I decided it was time to stay home for a while.

My first job at home was at the lumber mill across the river from our reserve. When I started work there I became determined to get on as a boom man, working on the big log booms that came down the river—bringing them into the quiet water above the mill where they formed a jam until they were needed, and opening up the boom to shoot them into the mill. This work was both skilled and dangerous. Boom men were paid better than yard men. But more important to me at that time was that a good boom man was always in demand. The job offered security.

Security, or rather the search for security, came to dominate my working life in my choice of jobs, my style of work, and my attitude to work. When my work was frustrated by the conditions around me, I saw those conditions as a barrier and my desire for security led me into political activity. It was not a grand vision or a keen sense of history that caused me to become politically involved. It was a series of small but important frustrations that stood in the way of both personal and community security which forced me to confront my own stubbornness.

While I was working as a boom man at the mill I began to farm our old family land. Our fields had lain fallow for a number of years, and they would not be brought back under cultivation without a struggle. The first season's work taught me that there was no way to run a farm on a haphazard or casual basis. But it was also pretty difficult to keep up the booming job while putting the necessary work into the farm.

When I became serious about farming, I found a prairie farmer who had moved into the Shuswap and bought the local general store and the farm that went with it. I began to work for him so I could gain experience and enough cash to keep my own farm going. I never asked him how much he was going to pay me, but as long as I worked for him I was never broke for seed money or anything really important. Later, when I had my own farm running for a number of years, he started coming over to help me when we were bringing the crops in, and we just helped each other. He was the second European who helped me on my way.

The only community or political matter that interested me during the years I was farming was the irrigation ditches. There is plenty of water in the Thompson and Fraser Rivers and the lakes that feed into them, but no farmer on the plateau can rely on the rainfall to bring home a good crop. You either develop an irrigation system that is reliable or you pack it in. The skeleton of an irrigation system is the ditches, and nothing short of hard labour is going to keep them clear enough so that the water flows throughout the growing season.

Even in my early teens, ditch-cleaning used to be a lively sort of activity, where all the families on the reserve got into their wagons with the horses hitched up and went to the ditches. The women cooked, the children gathered firewood and cooking water, and the men cleaned the ditches from seven in the morning until maybe six in the evening.

By the time I was working my own farm, if somebody showed up at that hour he would work by himself until a few others showed up at ten o'clock or ten-thirty. The department had declared our ditches to be public works and was paying us two or three dollars lunch money. People would show up early enough to claim their lunch money, but no earlier.

Oftentimes the lunch money did not come, and a few of us would work hungry. If it did not come for two or three days, these men stopped coming too.

Under these conditions the work lost any of the natural rhythm that is needed to get things done. It became an agony for all concerned. The ditches had filled in with dirt, leaves, and sediment from the collapse of our own internal organization, and the level of commitment from the government was never enough to clean them out.

It was this more than any other issue that got me going to meetings of the band council. In the past it had been our old chiefs who had taken the responsibility for seeing that important community work was done; it was their successors who would have to get the water flowing through the fields again. Besides, where else was there to turn?

But it was the agent who now held power. The council could only move in the directions toward which he pointed. There had been a generation of councillors and chiefs who had been selected by the agent who stood between the older tradition and the present reality. It was not that the chiefs and councillors of that day did not mean well. But it had been so long since they had taken a position independent of the Department's initiative, based on their own way of seeing the people's needs, that they had forgotten how to be leaders of men. The authority of a chief had fallen so low that people almost snickered at the man who held the office. Any pretense at dignity would have made the chief like the king without any clothes; everyone knew that his robes of office were woven of imaginary thread by a fraudulent tailor, but only the innocent child knew enough to laugh at him leading the parade in all his finery.

Unlike the fairy-tale king, these chiefs had not become ridiculous because of their own foolish pride and vanity. They had been made to look ridiculous because it was impossible to give leadership to a community when any effort to raise the aspirations of the people would have been taken as a hostile action against the government.

During those years when I was farming I was no more successful at breaking that cycle than anyone else. When there was a meeting of the council, especially for the more important meetings that were held jointly with the council of the neighbouring reserve, I would go around to the homes of the other young men and try to get a group to see just what went on at those meetings. If I had invited all the young men of the village to a dance with a colony of advanced lepers I would have had a better response.

What really launched me into politics was the effort of the Department, through the local agent, to make us pay our own medical bills.

By this time I had been working in the lumber mill for ten years and had developed a fairly steady income. I had been working there long enough to get on the medical insurance program the company had set up for its permanent staff. I had made an application to the medical fund, and it was only a matter of months before the policy would go into effect.

I had come out of the hospital for the last time when I was twenty-one and had never been back. But the importance of good medical care had been firmly impressed upon me, from more than my personal experience. Even for less serious illnesses that required only a visit to the doctor's office the difference in treatment for an Indian and a European was obvious to anyone who sat in the waiting room. Indian Affairs paid only a fraction of the standard fee to the local doctors and had no real staff of its own. If you sat in most doctors' waiting rooms at that time, you did not need to look at the patients' faces to see who were the Indians. You just had to time the length of each patient's visit in the examining room. Half a fee, half a visit.

One of the few doctors who ran his office on a different basis was Dr. James Treloar. My second youngest son needed to have his tonsils removed, and it was Dr. Treloar who was to do the operation. My medical insurance had not yet taken effect.

One day, Dr. Treloar drove over to my house on the reserve. I remember being very surprised when he drove up; it was the first time a European doctor had ever come to our house. He had come to show me the letter from the Department of Indian Affairs telling him that the department would not be paying for the operation, his fees, or the hospital costs. It was the new policy of the Department that any Indian with a job should pay his own medical expenses.

I had developed a pretty independent attitude. I told Dr. Treloar I did not care what the Department did. I had a good job and I would see that his bill was paid and that all the other costs were covered; even if it took a little while, I assured him he would get his money.

"That's not why I came," he objected. "There is no doubt in my mind that you can pay for it. Your reputation is pretty outstanding all through this valley. The reason I came to visit you is that, while you can afford to pay for it, you should think how many other Indians in this valley can do that.

"There's not more than five other families outside of your own in this whole area that can pay for medical services. The other thousand Indians around here could not pay if they saved a lifetime.

"Once you pay, they will start to compel others to pay. Once they start to make them pay, you know what will happen to the Indian people. Because they can't pay they will stop seeking medical care. And they've pretty well forgotten how to treat themselves with their own medicine.

106

"The mortality rate is going to shoot right back up where it was twenty years ago," he warned me.

"You're a fighter but most of your people aren't fighters. They'll treat hospitals and doctors as they treat the church when they're not happy with it. They'll just turn their back on us and not come around when they are sick."

I told him that was none of my business.

"Aren't you concerned that people will die?" he asked me.

We tossed the matter back and forth for maybe two hours. I think I was still naïve enough at that time to be afraid of going to jail if I did not pay my bills.

"I'll submit my bills to you each month," he promised me. "That's the normal practice of our office. But don't pay them—until such time as you're sure your people have lost this fight."

Lost! We had hardly begun to fight.

We honour Dr. James Treloar who practiced his medicine with the same love my grandfather practiced his.

After reflecting on Dr. Treloar's words for the rest of that day I sat down and wrote to Andy Paull. I had had no contact with him up to that time other than lighting fires in the meeting hall when he came to speak many years before. I had no official capacity, either on the reserve or in any organization. I spoke only for myself.

Andy Paull must have replied to my letter the day that it arrived. I had explained the problem to him and asked, "Should I pay or not?"

"If you pay," he told me, "you will be fighting me on this issue, because I have already taken the government up on it."

When the word got out that I was not paying my bill, people started to come around to see me with their bills in hand. What the doctor had said was coming true. The poorest people, who had not had a cash-paying job in years, came around with bills in their hands and the most worried looks on their faces.

I just told them what Dr. Treloar had told me. "Don't pay."

The Indian agent was obliged to get the consent of the band councils on the different reserves. At that time the Indian agent in Kamloops, Fred Clark, had given verbal notice to the chiefs and received a passive agreement from them that there would be no interference if he imposed this plan. But he had not yet put a formal resolution before them. I was able to find a few councillors who agreed that there should be no resolution adopted without a public discussion. Nothing would be done behind closed doors. The agent kept postponing the meeting to consider his resolution until he felt an auspicious moment was at hand.

At that time boom men in the mill were making about sixteen dollars a day. In the season just before Christmas, a good Christmas-tree cutter could make a hundred dollars a day bringing in Christmas trees. The only problem was that you had to travel as far as Athelmere, five hundred miles, to get a good Christmas tree harvest. Fortunately, I was on good enough terms with my boss that he gave me a leave of absence to go to Athelmere for a month.

I had just arrived at the work camp near Athelmere when I got the telegram from my wife that the Indian agent had called a joint meeting of our Neskonlith Band and the neighbouring Adam's Lake Band on the question of medical costs. I don't think I ever got my bags out of my car.

The car I was driving at that time was a 1929 Chrysler. It was not as old as I was but it sure had trouble on those mountain roads. Up and down. The only gear that got it up those roads was reverse. I suppose the brakes had been replaced since I had bought it, but the next set were going to come out of all that money I had gone to Athelmere to earn. Luckily, not too many other drivers would go on those roads at all in that season. Coming down those hills I relied on the gears and my prayers to see me around each corner.

I arrived at the Council House on the Adam's Lake Reserve, just as the people were gathering for the meeting. When I spotted the agent's brand new Departmental car outside the hall after nursing that old tortoise-shell around those mountains, I knew what I wanted to say.

It was unusual at that time, even for a joint meeting of the two reserves' councils, to attract six people besides the councillors, so I was surprised to see the hall packed. Here was an issue that touched the heart of every person who was concerned for the health of his children. I had tripped across a lesson that I hope has stayed with me to this day. Leaders who call their people apathetic because there is too little response to their leadership are likely pointing in the wrong direction. Since that day, I have never met people who are apathetic in their response to a leader who speaks about a matter of real concern and in a language that they can understand.

At that time, the agent still used to chair the meeting. The chiefs sat around him on the benches, agreeing or disagreeing with his initiatives, but without exerting much control. As I walked in, Mr. Clark was sitting in the middle of the council table ready to call the meeting to order.

As soon as he had called the meeting to order he said, "There's somebody in this room from another reserve who really does not belong here and is a troublemaker. And the band council should get him out of this room." There was not much doubt who he had in mind.

I stood up, walked to the council table and slammed my hand on that table. "Mr. Clark, you're a gutless son of a bitch. You haven't got the guts to speak out and say who you mean. You beat around the bush and try to make my people kick me out. I belong here a far sight more than you belong here.

"Even if this is not my reserve, it's still Indian land. You're a white man. You have no right here. I know why you want me kicked out of here. It's because you want to compel these people to pay their medical bills.

"You've used me as a guinea pig. There's no way I'll ever pay my doctor bills. No way. Never. We're going to fight this as a people. Furthermore, I'll tell you something else. I'm going to organize all the Indians of British Columbia."

I said a lot of things in that speech I had to live up to later on. This was one I had not thought out until I found myself speaking. It was a commitment born from the fury of seeing this man trying to squeeze money out of my people that they just did not have. When he began the meeting in that way, he had become for me a living symbol of everything that had impoverished and divided my people. To see him have the gall to ask us to lay out cash after superintending us into the most extreme destitution was the worst sick joke I could imagine. Up to this point I was certainly not aware of having any political ambitions. That man had made me angry—so angry I was not content merely to tell him I would organize all the Indians of British Columbia.

"You know that I am the spokesman here. These chiefs have appointed me to be the spokesman."

When I said that I would organize all the Indians of British

I stood up, walked to the council table and slammed my hand on that table.

Columbia, the agent had had a big smirk on his face. Now he began to take me seriously. "Is it true," he asked the chiefs, "that you have asked this man to speak for you?"

After a long silence, the chief from the Adam's Lake Reserve nodded his head in agreement. All the other chiefs followed his lead. That was the first time I was ever elected to speak for a group. Most people start by getting their feet wet. I started with a total immersion course.

Once Mr. Clark saw that he had to deal with me as the spokesman for the two reserves, the meeting was terminated fairly quickly. He did allow me to elaborate my views, but I think he was already aware of what I would say before I spoke.

Once I had spoken out, making all those threats and promises, there was no going back. I had challenged the reputation of the Indian agent with my own reputation. Now I had to carry through. The problem was that I was not the least bit sure which way was forward. So I explored every organizational channel I could find. Over the next few years I became involved in every kind of organizing activity that was available in that part of the country.

The possibility of running for councillor from one district on the reserve never appealed to me. If I stood for election it was going to be for chief. After I was defeated in my first attempt, I began organizing every kind of activity anybody expressed a desire for.

Our baseball team had been getting together on a fairly haphazard basis. Whatever funds were raised for equipment were simply scrounged. The baseball team was in worse shape than I remembered it in my early teens. In those days nobody on the reserve had a truck. The team contracted with a white farmer to provide him with so many loads of hay in return for which he transported the team to the surrounding reserves for Sunday afternoon games.

The ball players themselves did not fill the truck. So anyone else could hop a ride for a nickel or a dime. Our team was always assured of a good turnout, so it always had the support of the community if it needed something.

Now the team organized dances. We rented the community hall and charged admission. People objected at first to being charged admission to come into their own hall. But everyone was profiting. The band got the rental money. The team made enough to outfit itself with new equipment. And at the dance, a good time was had by all.

Being partly crippled had a lot to do with my success. I never coached a team because I was not much of a player. But I was free to concentrate my energies on organizing and managing the team when no one else was tending to those less dramatic tasks.

Many of the activities with which I became involved had nothing directly to do with specifically Indian concerns. Often one activity had no real connection with the next. I became involved in church groups as well as with different clubs and associations in town. I wanted to find out more about how white men generated their power base.

At one point I found myself elected president of the Legion of Mary Society, a Catholic lay society, even before I understood its role. I went around door-to-door on the reserve selling. I think I hoped that the outreach this would provide into every corner of the community, combined with the respectability of presiding over a church-sponsored society, would help me in the next election.

Then one day I went to see the priest to discuss the problems of a family I had visited the night before. This elderly couple, whose pension barely gave them food and clothing, needed a tank of fuel oil to see them through to the end of the month. The reverend gentleman assured me that the Legion of Mary Society dealt only with spiritual matters. We were there to warm the soul and overlook the body.

Another dead end. I threw my spiritual presidency in the ditch with the autumn leaves and looked around for other avenues.

I attended the local equivalent of the parent-teachers' association until I felt assured that they had very little to teach me about the uses of power.

Then I discovered the Chamber of Commerce. The secretary of the local Chamber in Chase was the owner of the pool hall. When he saw the interest I had in developing organizational skills he began to invite me to meetings. He would spend time with me explaining how they went about organizing for things their members wanted, and he would introduce me to his friends.

We maintained a close working relationship for many years. When I did begin to achieve some success in developing local and later regional activities, I could always count on his support. If it was equipment for a ball team that we needed he was the man who helped us open the doors.

We honour Paul Paulson for his friendship and loyalty.

As the resistance to the new regulations requiring us to pay for our own medical care spread throughout the reserves in the Kamloops district, I began to travel further and further through the interior. A carload of us would make the trip into the Okanagan, the Thompsons, or up into the northern parts of British Columbia.

Out of these travels came the idea of bringing together representatives from all the tribes of the interior. It was one thing for a few of us to visit each group separately, and quite another for people to meet each other face to face and express their own concern. Indian Affairs had consulted with each group separately for all these years, and succeeded in keeping our people weak and divided. If people were ever to gain control of their own affairs it would only be through coming together and making a common cause. We also had to develop a method of organizing that did not put all the focus of the community's hopes on a single leader who would then be open to attack from both sides—from the government when he succeeded, from his own people when he failed.

The first gathering I undertook to organize took me well beyond the beautiful but small and isolated world around Kamloops. Lance Kelton, secretary-manager of the Kamloops Chamber of Commerce, helped me to organize the meeting and secure the Elks' Hall. He even brought the Indian cadet corps he commanded at Lytton into Kamloops and we had a big parade.

Long before any of us had ever heard the phrase "community development" he had the good manners to stay in the background. He would tell us who to see and what procedure to follow. He was always at our disposal, but he never attempted to do things for us or to take special credit for having been a good neighbour.

I have always felt that his friendship with me led to his early retirement as secretary-manager of the Kamloops Chamber of Commerce and his decision to move to Vancouver.

We honour Lance Kelton for his gentle humour and the insight into the human condition that it gave to him.

It was largely through the inspiration of Andy Paull that I had been able to carry on the fight on the medical bills issue, and develop it to the point of a meeting of all the interior tribes.

We had begun to correspond with each other as a result of this issue. While the medical issue was continuing, a group of us organized a local support group to help raise funds to keep Andy Paull going. Whenever he came around, he was in dire need of funds and we would have to pass the hat.

We formed an Indian dance troupe that performed at festivals of all kinds and for special events. If a family lost their house through fire or suffered some other personal tragedy, we would hold a dance outside their house and give the funds to them. This was still passing the hat, but it was a way of assuring a large and congenial crowd through which to pass it. The money we raised at public occasions went into a trust account for the North American Indian Brotherhood. After that when Andy Paull would write to us we could send him a cheque without leaving ourselves short for local emergencies.

Andy Paull also began to invite me down to his home periodically. His health was already beginning to decline, and he was limiting his travel to the most essential trips. But he could still talk late into the night and recall with the most vivid detail every important project he had undertaken. On occasion we would go the short distance into Vancouver and he would show me the big city. It was on a visit to Andy Paull's that I toured the harbour and the airport for the first time.

All this time I was still working on the booming grounds. I would work until the ice closed the river and all the boom men were laid off. When the winter had settled in, I went on the road hitch-hiking from one reserve to the next. The old Chrysler had finally died. There were enough other Indians with cars on the road now that it was almost as fast to hitch-hike as to keep coaxing such an ancient beast up the mountain roads in reverse.

I have always suspected that Andy Paull had an unseen hand in my discovering an entirely new kind of work that was to take me away from the booming grounds and keep me criss-crossing the interior of British Columbia and commuting to Vancouver.

By 1958, Andy Paull's health had failed to the point where he rarely travelled at all. He now began to concentrate on the one aspect of his work that he had neglected throughout the last half of

114

his career. He contacted a great many of the elder leaders with whom he had worked to ask them to carry on the struggle he had led for so many years.

The need for new leadership was underlined by another consideration. The Diefenbaker government had won its second election, and for the first time had the support of a majority of members in the House of Commons. Before the new session was called together, the word was already out that there would be a Joint Committee of the Senate and Commons on Indian Affairs.

There had at first been talk of Andy Paull going to Ottawa on a stretcher to appear one more time before a Parliamentary Committee. His own organizing efforts had led to the creation of the first committee in 1927. His presentation had propelled him into national prominence at the very moment when the first attempts at intertribal organizing in two generations were being repressed. The sheer stamina that kept him going until the next committee, which sat from 1947 to 1949, had made him worthy of admiration throughout the Indian community across North America. The submissions made to this committee gave rise to the new Indian Act of 1951 which, however much the servants in the Indian Affairs Branch perpetuated the paternalistic traditions, did lay the foundation for change and flexibility in Indian-Government relations. It repealed the prohibitions against potlatching, and fundraising, and disposed of most of the other disabilities Canadian tradition and law had imposed on Indian people. It seemed right and proper for Andy Paull to be allowed one last word before he went out. But by the time the first planning meetings were being held, everyone who cared for him knew the time for his last public appearance had passed.

The change of governments with the elections of 1957 and 1958 meant that the change of membership on the committee would be as sweeping as the change in the delegation we would send to Ottawa. Mackenzie King had been prime minister from 1921, when the land claim had been received after the First Great European War until 1948, halfway through the proceedings of the second committee. Now King's successor at Ottawa, Louis St. Laurent, had been defeated and a new Government had taken office. More than a hundred seats had changed hands in the two elections. So great was the change of membership in the House of

Commons that the average age dropped from fifty-five years to forty years as a result of those elections.

There was no partisan consciousness among Indian people so far as federal politics was concerned. Mackenzie King always maintained that we could only have the vote by giving up our rights as Indian people. So long as we were not involved in the electoral process, party differences didn't seem to matter. The Liberal regime had formed an almost unbroken chain through the century. Now we at least had a new jury before whom we could plead our case. And John Diefenbaker's reputation for defending Indians in court had spread across the prairies into British Columbia. There were just the right ingredients to make a major effort seem worthwhile.

One of our first meetings was at Chilliwack, where I met Henry Castilliou. Henry had already served for some years as legal advisor to the North American Indian Brotherhood. When Andy Paull had summoned his closest political colleagues to see that his work continued, Henry Castilliou was the one non-Indian whom he asked to share this burden.

Henry's grandfather must have been one of the first Europeans to settle in the interior. He had moved north from Mexico and developed a ranch on the plateau. His father was a judge for many years, and was still on the bench when I met him. Henry had inherited both the legal tradition and the love of the land. He had studied and worked as a forester and only later went into law.

Henry was one of the very few lawyers of that day who was willing to work seriously with the full range of legal problems besetting Indian people. He did not restrict himself to the comforts of a Vancouver law office. Nor did he restrict his studies to the law library. It seemed to me as I came to know them that he and his father had probably read every important book written on the Indian history of British Columbia.

Henry received no money for his work as counsel to Indian organizations. But he was able to get paid for representing Indian people in murder trials. This was the only charge on which the federal government was willing to provide legal aid. There were perhaps eight such cases a year in British Columbia. There were also Indian clients who paid their own way when even this much help was not forthcoming. Henry tells of a client who was living on pensions of $100 a month who borrowed a down payment from

116

friends and relatives and paid the balance off at $90 a month without ever being asked for such a stiff share of his modest income. Mind you, the man lived off the land during that time, but he made those payments every month for a year.

When I met Henry at the Chilliwack meeting, he took the opportunity to talk to me at some length. Not long afterward he offered me a job as an investigator and translator for his criminal law practice. When he had a case on which he wanted me to work he would call me from his Vancouver office to give me the particulars and send the money to send me on my way. My main job was to gather all the possible background information that might be useful—every possible version of the events surrounding the charge, the character and background of the accused, finding credible witnesses and learning as much about their background as about the defendant's. When I had all this together I would catch a bus to Vancouver and go over my notes with Henry.

When a case would come up in court we drove together. We slept together in the car. We sometimes got lost together and many times got stuck in the spring mud of a back road together.

I learned a lot about the court system, its concept of justice, and the idea of truth. Many evenings when I was staying at Henry's house, the judge would call me into his den to talk about the law, or history, or sometimes just the lighter sides of life. Once, when I had been working for them only a short time, the judge was trying to explain the different kinds of truth. Soon I found him saying there were different kinds of lies. It seemed strange to me then to think that the wrong of a lie depended on what difference it made to make a false statement. I suppose I was still at the stage of thinking that the truth was the truth and a lie was anything else. The idea of a "little white lie" just did not make any sense at all.

As I faced the realities of a courtroom in case after case——perhaps eight in the first year—I found that words carried as full and varied a range of truth as the judge had said.

I recall one woman who was a witness for the Crown. It was very important to discredit her testimony if we were to establish any kind of reasonable doubt on behalf of our client. After the Crown had finished its case there was a recess of two or three weeks. I went back to the village where she was from to dig up every possible fact that might be of use.

Two matters came out. One was the circumstances under which

her earlier marriage had ended. The other was her membership in a secret spiritual society.

When the potlatch had been outlawed, the Indian spiritual societies that maintained our traditions had largely gone underground in order to carry on their work. The social function that these societies serve is not really different from the function of traditional European mutual benefit societies. But the mutual benefit function takes the form of carrying on the potlatch celebrations. When they went underground they became known by names different from their traditional names so that they could not be identified with ceremonies that had been declared a criminal offence.

When court resumed Henry called her to the stand again. He did not need to have her elaborate on her membership in the secret society. He had only to make the most passing reference to it to shatter the poor woman's confidence so thoroughly that she could no longer say that she was certain of anything she had seen at the time of the fight that gave rise to the matter before the court. Even though she had already given complete testimony only a couple of weeks before as to what she had witnessed she was no longer sure that her own words had been true.

For me, this whole matter represented a cruel dilemma. The charge of murder had arisen out of a fight in front of a hotel between a very drunk and dissolute Indian and an equally drunk and dissolute white man. Neither man had benefited in any visible way from the finer things that his society had to offer. On being struck by the Indian, the white man had fallen to the cement sidewalk and struck his head. The concussion he suffered led to his death.

There is nothing in me that says that he deserved to die. Neither is there anything that tells me that the accused deserved to die. But the suffering we inflicted on that woman on the witness stand was not any less offensive to me than the vision of the defendant hanging from a rope. His crime lay in losing touch with the traditions that would have made him strong. Her crime lay in maintaining the traditions and speaking with the strength that they gave to her.

The dilemma was between truth and consequences. The truth may well have been what she told the court during the Crown's examination of her. But the question with which a defence counsel and his staff have to deal is whether there is a reasonable doubt that can be raised about the defendant's role in the events at trial. The consequence of raising no reasonable doubt would be either hanging or many years in prison. The court has the duty not only to decide guilt or innocence but also to determine punishment.

Were there any real alternatives—rehabilitation of the man's basic problem, instead of retribution by a society that never really cared in the first place—there is at least an even chance that a man would plead guilty or not guilty according to his own honest view of his actions. The need for trials would not be lessened. But a great many trials where the underlying issues are never allowed to surface might be resolved in ways far more beneficial to both the accused and the society at large. And certainly, the need to damage the public reputation of a witness by raising matters completely incidental to her testimony might never arise.

There are many truths.

We honour Judge Castilliou for his patience and wisdom.

Henry taught me as much through examples quite unrelated to our court work as he did in the most dramatic moments before the jury. Although I had a stubborn streak going back farther than I can remember, I was never outspoken or verbally aggressive. There were exceptions when I was well and truly angered at an Indian agent, but anger has its own price. My stubbornness would lead me to explore every possible channel. But if a channel was closed, it was simply closed.

One day when we were driving up to a trial in northern British Columbia, Henry decided that the tires on his car were getting pretty thin. We found a gas station advertising tires just as we were getting ready for coffee. He instructed the attendant to install a complete set of tires.

When the car was back down off the hoist with the work completed, he asked to see the written warranty that had been promised. He stood there silently while he read the complete paper. Then he bellowed, "That's not worth the paper it's written on!"

We came away with the old tires and the same assurance of a safe journey that the paper offered. What struck me was that he would challenge a man's word just because he knew it was worthless. There were many men I talked to without trusting what they told me. I would listen carefully and then discard their words like waste. Provoked, I would walk away before they finished. But he had told the man just how he should dispose of the warranty himself. That was another matter.

It was not long before he called on me to exert the same force in a more serious way. The Vancouver *Sun* had written an editorial that was pretty disparaging of the Indian community in British Columbia. Henry had taken it upon himself to write a reply.

When I walked into the office the next morning he handed me his reply and told me to take it to the editor of the *Sun* . I was to see nobody less than the editor. And I was not to return until I had gotten his promise to print it.

I had never seen the inside of a newspaper office in my life.

First, the editor's secretary told me to leave the letter with her. I told her I would wait. I waited and I waited. Half way through the afternoon the editor announced he would give me thirty seconds. When I blurted out my message he laughed at me and told me to tell Mr. Castilliou he would not print his reply. I felt I had done my job. When I got back to the office Henry turned me around and sent me out the door. I had not gotten a commitment from the editor. By the end of the day he had let me back into the office long enough to tell me he would not print the article Henry had written but he would write an editorial retracting his disparaging remarks.

Henry taught me how to gather information, and to sort out the facts and honest beliefs from the half-truths and deceptions. He also taught me to assert myself once I knew that I was on firm ground. Of all the lessons that he and his father taught me, if these two were learned well the rest would have come no matter what course was followed.

During my first three years of political organizing, Henry Castilliou was both my teacher and my main source of a livelihood. I honour him as a blood brother.

Our second major meeting to prepare a submission to the Joint Committee on Indian Affairs was at Hope on the edge of the interior at the top of the Fraser Valley. Clarence Joe from Sechelt, Chief Bill Walkem from Spence's Bridge, Charlie Brown from Lytton, Chief Oscar Peters from Hope, and Chief Genevieve Mussell brought together between two and three hundred people.

Two critical decisions came out of the Hope meeting. First was the recognition of the absolute need to develop the direct involvement of the people in each local community, an involvement that had always somewhat eluded Andy Paull despite his best intentions. Travel conditions had improved. Those of us who had jobs were enjoying a significant though small cash income. There had always been a need to make representation with an effective claim to speak for the people. Now there was the physical possibility of doing so.

The second decision was that our submission to the Parliamentary Committee would be made under a new name, the Aboriginal Native Rights Committee of the Interior Tribes of British Columbia. Many of us wanted to continue the North American Indian Brotherhood, not only from our admiration for Andy Paull but from a desire for a strong national and international organization. But that same desire for strength and unity made us realize that if we were ever going to bring Indian people together in our own province, we must do so under a banner that had not yet become identified with any leader, faction, or position. The NAIB had become so much a part of Andy Paull that while he lived, even if he was too close to death to play an active role, it seemed neither morally right nor politically sensible to operate under that umbrella.

Shortly after Andy Paull died, many of the same people who had breathed life into the Native Aboriginal Rights Committee called a conference to draw up a new constitution for the NAIB. At the same time Telford Adams, from Six Nations near Brantford, Ontario, and other eastern colleagues of Andy Paull were trying to reformulate the NAIB at the other end of the country.

Although our limited resources forced us to concentrate on our own region of the country, the constitution we adopted clearly spelled out our aspirations for a national and international body that would unite Indian people in every corner of the continent. What we could not have known in 1960 was just how fast the winds of change were going to blow through both the Indian world and the general political geography of North America in the decade ahead.

For the meantime we had postponed any revival of the NAIB for an indefinite period and had still before us the task of meeting with every Indian band we could reach in the interior.

We travelled throughout the area twice. Once to hear peoples' words and gather together all the points that they raised and prepare a draft of the brief. On the second tour we took the draft back to the people for their response. This was the first time in the history of intertribal organizing in British Columbia that such effort had gone into creating a direct involvement of every interested member of each local community. We met with people at the reserves near Chilliwack, Chehalis, Lytton, Lillooet, Kamloops, Cranbrook, Penticton, Williams' Lake, and Stellaco. The Allied Tribes had taken great care, as far back as 1915, to bring together chiefs from as many bands as possible. The medical issue had brought out not only chiefs and councillors but hundreds of concerned parents. The internal traditions of every tribe had always required the direct involvement of the people. The chief was there to speak the mind of the people, but not to be the mind. Even in those nations where the chief's title was hereditary, his authority was limited to speaking the people's mind, unless he also established himself as a leader in hunting, defence, or other areas of special skill.

If our approach represented a change at all, it lay in extending this commonly shared internal tradition to intertribal matters for the sake of dealing with Ottawa. This was an adaptation of the technology of the global society to our own values and traditions.

The Land Claim was still the issue most often and most strongly raised in our community meetings despite the many years since it had been actively pursued. Perhaps people's memory of the Land Claim had been reinforced by economic forces. The farms on which interior Indians were trying to gain a living were never more than fifty acres, and sometimes as small as two acres. In the one or two areas where farming had brought some measure of prosperity, the band had to pay rent to the province for grazing land it had never surrendered. From our travels we were able to document the situation on each reserve and show the relationship between the lack of a land base and the present poverty.

The thought of abolishing the protected status of reserve lands would not be proposed as official government policy in Canada until 1969, a year after the election of Pierre Trudeau. But it had been official policy in the United States since 1951 and the rumble of approval from Ottawa bureaucrats had been heard all the way to the west coast. We told the Parliamentary Committee that:

Poor as [some reserves] may appear to others, they are rich in memories and traditions for us. We wish to leave them to our children as we received them from our parents. We will not willingly surrender them. We should not be required to surrender them or the privileges attached to them.

A very common item observed by the Indians is the matter of enfranchisement, where the Indians become enfranchised, and then come back to live on the reserves time and time again, showing that they would rather live with their peoples, or that they are not ready to compete alone as citizens in the non-Indian world.

The communal living pattern and the reserve system has helped to keep the Indian away from the larger metropolitan areas, and if the reserve privileges were taken away from our peoples; we would still live together and be a burden on larger communities. The Seattle Indian ghetto which consists mainly of Canadian Indians is an example.[24]

One essential step to making reserve life more socially viable was to remove the remaining disabilities imposed on Indians who maintained their status under the Indian Act. The main value of the Act from our point of view was that it was the one legal protection of our lands, and spelled out the basic rights and privileges of living on the reserve. But it also included a price tag. Indian people who remained under the Indian Act and lived on a reserve could not bring liquor into their homes, and any non-Indian who bought an Indian a drink was guilty of an offence. Under provincial law an Indian could not go into a beer parlour. (After I bought my first good suit for going to court, I found that no liquor store attendant ever turned me away if my collar was tucked in and my tie done up correctly.) The result was that the only legal way that an Indian could drink was by not getting caught.

The government's own Hawthorn Report[25] would later document how much of the abuse of liquor was directly related to the prohibitions imposed. The excessive drinking in turn gave rise to further abuses of the law. An Indian who was invited to a non-Indian social event was immediately segregated by the fact that he could not accept a drink. The abuse of alcohol by depressed people, of any culture, is a far more complex problem than can ever be dealt with by a prohibition law. The effect of the law was to ensure that the maximum number of people would be caught up in the vicious cycle, and, because an offence had been committed, the opportunities for any constructive way of dealing with the problem were minimized. As a first step in a much longer process, we asked that the disabilities be removed.

The other disability that we wanted removed was the denial of the federal vote. Mackenzie King had taken the position followed by Laurier, the earlier Mackenzie, and John A. Macdonald, that Indians could vote only on condition that we stopped being Indians. Enfranchisement under the Indian Act means that an Indian has demonstrated to the satisfaction of the minister that he can support himself, and that he no longer desires to remain a member of his band. We suggested that, if ever Indian people were to become part of the general community in Canada, it would be when the representatives of that community in Ottawa decided to accept us as Indian people. We wanted a vote as Indians, and not by becoming brown white men.

The government was now changing its policy on Indian education from one favouring residential schools to one favouring provincial schools. We found that this was a change from one form of discrimination to another. For migrant and semi-nomadic Indian families there was a continuing need for residential schools at the senior levels. But Indian parents should have the same kind of voice in the education of their children, through a local school authority, as European parents enjoy through their school board. It should also be possible, we thought, to adapt the school year to the needs of these families as well as to develop a curriculum based on the actual social and economic needs of the people in that school district.

The whole issue of medical costs and the extent of services provided by the Indian Health Service was raised.

We suggested that law enforcement on the reserve should be carried out by an Indian police force under the supervision of the local council.

We suggested a number of ways in which more authority could be transferred to the local council in each Indian community to carry on its own administration, and to develop its own policies and programs. Indian superintendents could become resource persons in band management and self-government. Chiefs and councillors who made a full-time job of serving their community should receive enough compensation for their work that they would not suffer hardship for their services. Several sections of the 1951 Act, the first to completely replace the Indian Act of 1875, while appearing to remove disabilities had, according to the courts, placed our lands in certain situations under provincial jurisdiction. Other sections had merely replaced oppression with ambiguity. So long as the new law was interpreted by the old personnel there was little change. We asked for a favourable clarification.

Reviewing the position that was formulated by the interior tribes thirteen years ago I am struck by the similarity to the position taken by other Indian groups across Canada and the United States. Even more striking is how little change has occurred in the substance of the relationship between government and the local Indian community as it impinges on the daily lives of people.

The government adopted much of the rhetoric Indian people used in our submissions to that committee of Parliament. But the words came to sound as hollow as a gutted rabbit. The Diefenbaker government did agree that Indian people could vote in Canadian elections without threatening our status as Indians. They also repealed the liquor prohibitions. Beyond that, the condition of the Indian people has worsened on almost every count.

Many words were spoken in the next decade about "community development," "self-government," and "full consultation." Many of these fine words were recorded by a whole series of regional, provincial, and national advisory councils, and later by a governmental task force.

While these words were being spoken the urban ghettoes that had been predicted by scholars and medicine men alike were being spawned in almost every Canadian city. The poverty of Indian communities continued to flourish. Band councils continued to be denied the right to sit at the negotiating table when education and other public services were being purchased for them by the federal government. "Participation" was defined as a band council resolution approving of the facts, after they had been accomplished. Band administration continued to be based on budgets prepared primarily in Ottawa.

A Commons Committee studying Indian education ten years later reached the conclusions that had been written for our submission ten years earlier by the first woman chief in Canada. The parliamentarians were finally learning what Indian mothers had known for a century. Their report was tabled on June 30, 1971. On September 18 the Minister addressed a meeting of the Catholic School Trustees Association and told them that it was only through provincial schools that Indian children would ever achieve equality. He was rejecting a report that had been approved by four political parties and endorsed by eleven provincial and territorial Indian organizations. He made this speech on the fifth day of a school boycott by three reserves in northern Alberta in support of demands for Indian control of Indian education.

Two years before, the government had brought down a statement on Indian policy that had all the markings of the U.S. policy of termination, dressed up with all the right talk of equality. Treaties were described as an "anomaly." The idea of aboriginal rights was rejected as too vague a concept on which to base government policy. "Prove to me," Mr. Trudeau was heard to say, "that such a thing as aboriginal rights exists." The whole history of British colonial rule, however great its faults, demands a recognition of such rights. And children starve or swarm into ghettoes while he demands proof that we are human beings entitled to the same protection under law for our property and communities as anyone else.

The Trudeau-Chrétien Policy of June 1969 brought the Indian leadership across Canada to complete unanimity in declaring that it was a return to the Mackenzie King policy, which said, in effect, "Indian or Canadian, and never the two shall meet." When the previous administration of the National Indian Brotherhood described the policy as a statement of "cultural genocide," nobody disagreed.

This was the fruit of the decade of consultation that was to follow the hearings of the Joint Parliamentary Committee. But within the Indian world there was another kind of growth going on. The new generation of leadership that was born for the interior tribes in 1958 with the founding of the Aboriginal Native Rights Committee was paralleled by the rebirth and rapid growth of regional and provincial organizations, and traditional Indian bodies in other parts of the country. A new generation of young people was also coming of age — young people whose energies had not been sapped by disease, depression, and political disabilities.

6

~~~~~~

Becoming
a Fisher of Men

As long as there is somebody around the community keeping everybody's mind moving toward a goal then there is community development happening. Once you get into a state in which you begin to accept the way things are then change begins to appear impossible. You stay like that until somebody comes along who has the capacity to get the minds of the people moving again.

"Is this where you really want to be?"

"Do you want to do something about it?"

These are the questions that the community development worker gets people to think about. It is not always necessary that he say very much himself or even put these questions directly to people. He only needs to get people to ask these questions about themselves, in terms of their whole community.

When we talk about whether a community development worker is needed, we are not asking whether the work needs to be done.... The question is really whether there is a vacuum—a space not being filled by a person local to the community—that therefore needs to be filled by someone from outside.[26]

WESLEY MODESTE, a young leader of the Cowichan people, gave me these thoughts when I returned to Vancouver Island to collect my own thoughts for this book. Hearing his words was like hearing a voice from the past. When I first went to the Cowichan, Wesley was a young man, respected by his peers, secure in his own identity, but not a person who was likely to theorize about the broader social and political implications of that identity. I knew then the same good feeling a teacher must know when his students exceed him in his own teachings and accomplishments.

Community development was first introduced as a program of the Department of Indian Affairs at the time when the War on Poverty was catching the popular political imagination of North America. John F. Kennedy had sponsored the Peace Corps and VISTA program in the United States. People were becoming excited about involving the so-called underprivileged, underdeveloped, and disadvantaged peoples in the solution of their own problems. Canada had to do something.

Lester Pearson created the Special Planning Secretariat of the Privy Council to plan and coordinate poverty programs (as well as other ill-starred happenings, such as the Company of Young Canadians.) It also gave rise within the old Department of Indian Affairs to a new approach to the Indian, "that of entering a relationship with Indian people as human beings." This was the central goal of those few idealistic members of the public service who developed the concept of the Department's Community Development Program, which the government bought.

The Department had sponsored other programs in the past that were sold to the government, Parliament, and the small portion of the Canadian taxpayers who interest themselves in these matters as the cure-all for the "Indian problem." "Education," and "integration" were earlier cure-alls. When the full moon of community development began to wane, "self-determination" became the new rallying cry. Someday, when numbered years have become too numerous to be meaningful, archaeologists will find it useful to date government relations with Indians according to the cure-all in fashion from time to time. "The Year When the Winds of Change were Noticed" is much more helpful than 1962. Nineteen sixty-nine might be recalled as "The Year of the White Paper," and 1970 as "The Year of the Red Paper."

The trouble with these programs is that they are all good. It is easy to challenge the tonics sold by a road-show doctor, but today even penicillin invites immunity. The Community Development Program was not designed or intended to be a magic elixir, but there soon grew to be a strong suspicion among its participants that the politicians and bureaucrats bought the idea with just that hope in mind.

There was, I believe, a genuine misunderstanding from the very beginning. Those who designed the program and trained the field workers truly desired to see people take power into their own hands, and said so in the papers they prepared. The bureaucrats and politicians reading those identical words within their own frame of reference found hope for the solution of their problems. Put another way, every field worker who was sent out had to decide whether he was there to sell his Indian community on the solutions for which the government wanted to find acceptance, or whether he was there to serve the community, and help it find ways to give voice to its own felt needs.

Throughout the three years in which the Joint Committee of Parliament had sat, the Department had come under very severe attack, not only within the hearings but from every corner of the country. Local and provincial Indian organizations were beginning to find their feet. The Canadian Association for Adult Education had given rise some years before to the Indian-Eskimo Association as an urban-based, non-Indian support group. The anti-poverty craze produced spokesmen of every political stripe within the non-Indian community who were labelling Indian reserves, based on last summer's visit or a canoe trip in their camping days, as Canada's Apartheid Policy. Indians had always been complaining. Now there were sophisticated, organized urban voters, whose view of the matter may have been entirely different from ours, but who were, nonetheless, pointing at the same problems and the same administration. Indian Affairs needed a corps of field workers who would be skilled in getting Indian people to solve the problems Indian Affairs had defined in a manner that was acceptable to the Department. What happened was something else.

I was one of the first Indians to be hired by the program, and the program was on its way out when I left two and a half years later.

Farrel Toombs was the man the Department hired to train its

staff in community development. Farrel proved to be a man with an amazing insight, and one who would not allow himself to be swayed by pressure of politics and yet was always open to the needs of the group he was animating. In the three months he worked with us at quarters in Laval University in Quebec, he impressed me as a person with a high degree of humanity, the kind of humanity that seems to transcend every situation. If there is any one man outside the Indian community in Canada who has inspired human development within our community it is Farrel Toombs.

The Department was hiring two kinds of people, both to be given the same kind of training before being placed in the field. Those with degrees would be community development officers. Each officer would have a junior colleague who would be an Indian, without a degree, and usually from a tribe other than that of the community in which they were working.

From the practical viewpoint of field-work, the chief difference between officers and workers was that officers received four to five hundred dollars more in salary. If there had been more Indians with degrees available, the Department would gladly have made them officers. Inevitably, the teams that were sent out must have looked a little like cut-outs from a Lone Ranger set. Certainly, when later I was posted to the Cowichan, many of the people there were quite convinced I had shown up at the wrong camp.

The Department had agreed that, in addition to having the CD staff undergo the training program, its whole staff—Indian agents, headquarters and regional administrators—would have to be retrained so that they would know about CD. This meant that the training session which I attended at Laval, which was the first of a series, was made up of roughly equal numbers of Indian superintendents or other seasoned civil service officers, professional social workers with academic degrees who were trying to break into the new field of CD, and people like me, who were just plain Indians, though some of us had played some leadership role in our own community.

Farrel Toombs had a strange way of teaching a course. The last thing he would ever do is to stand in front of the class and give instruction or lecture us. Instead, he would wait for us to make some demands on him, or preferably on ourselves as a group.

He was always the first to arrive in the morning—at least until a group of superintendents who thought this was some trick they had already learned made a point of arriving earlier, no matter what time he arrived. When others would begin to arrive, or if some were already there, he would chat simply as one of the group.

If there had been an agreement that we would begin at nine o'clock in the morning, about five minutes after the hour someone would look around the room, as if to take attendance, another would clear his throat, and a third person would say, "When are we going to start?"

"It's up to you. Whenever you want to start." And Farrel would sit there with the rest of us, waiting for somebody to start something. Something. Anything.

When too many days had started this way, and discussion carried on throughout the day in what seemed a totally disconnected way, confusion began to build up in all of us, a confusion shared equally by all three groups. What differed was the way the civil servants, the academics, and the Indians each expressed it. The civil servants allowed their confusion to grow into resentment against the one they decided was not delivering the goods they had ordered. The academics withdrew when there was nothing put before them worthy of their attention. The Indians had never felt certain what our role within the departmental framework was. The new level of our uncertainty only lowered our desire to act. We sat there as we have sat for so long.

Finally, there was a series of outbursts from superintendents who thought the whole thing a waste of taxpayers' money.

"When are you really going to start teaching us something?" they demanded.

"Whenever you're ready."

The academics were also beginning to find that their feelings of uncertainty were becoming more than they could control. At first they demonstrated this by going skiing, instead of attending group sessions. Then they decided to take an initiative. Some of them suggested that they knew of social animators of very high reputation in the United States. Could these American animators be invited to come up and set us straight?

"When do you want them?" Farrel asked.

He arranged for them to come on exactly the week that was suggested. And this time he went off skiing or attending to other matters.

The three men who had now replaced Farrel had been described to us by our academic colleagues as men who had been recognized by industry, government, and organizations of every type in the United States as the top men in their field. Now we really expected performance.

The first morning they walked into the room and chatted amiably. A few minutes after the hour, someone cast his eyes about the room, another cleared his throat, and a third asked, "When are we going to start?"

"Whenever you're ready," the reply came back.

By the second day with this new leadership, the tension had simply become too great. Within the first hour someone jumped up and said, "You're supposed to be high-priced help. The Canadian government is paying you big money. When are you going to start to teach the course?"

"Any time you want to get started."

Now even I could not stand this any longer. "You sonofabitch! You're no better than Farrel Toombs. We may as well as have had Farrel Toombs here!"

Then people really began to speak their minds. Disciplined civil servants and sophisticated academics cried like children when they began to tell of the frustration that had built up in them when nobody had laid down a clear-cut agenda for them to follow.

Learning, for all of us, had become a strict set of rules, a curriculum laid down by people who had never met the class, a teacher whose orders were to wade through the course outline he had been handed, and a class filled with students who dutifully made notes, read the texts, counted the footnotes, and were prepared to respond with the correct references whenever asked.

Farrel Toombs had refused to fulfil our expectations. He believed that this kind of teaching produced people who saw life, and work, and their place in the community in pretty much the same terms that had been set down for them in the classroom. He described the typical classroom situation as one in which "a system of unilateral dependence is imposed." Dr. Toombs had carefully constructed a course for us designed, first, to destroy that unilateral dependence, and then to replace it with an experience of mutual dependence. For him, the classroom was always a model of society. The only question was, "Which model?"

When the group was prepared to discuss and define its own goals, to break down the barriers that stood between each faction so that a consensus could be reached and experience could be shared, only then did it become possible for him to teach us. Teaching meant putting at our disposal whatever information and access to resources he might have. It meant helping to draw out of each individual the things that might be hardest to express, yet most important to say. It meant helping the group listen to what each person meant as well as what he said. Although we all spoke English, the manners, and style, the value we placed on words were so different in each of the three classes of people that we had to set about learning a common language. Farrel Toombs taught us to do that. It was like a total immersion course. Three months was not an underestimate of the time required.

For me personally, and no doubt for a great many of the others, this meant a tremendous change in style and attitude. When I spent some time at home people said I had become a different person because I never talked very much. I was becoming less concerned, in my political activities, with generating an issue under my own control, and more concerned with trying to find the unspoken focus of the community and the person best suited to articulate that concern. I began to feel that, however much the political activities of my recent past had demonstrated an authentic concern for the needs of the people, there had been a tendency for political leadership to become a matter of a few friends developing a platform and selling it to potential supporters.

More important than the political activities in themselves was the way they were the most conspicuous symbols of style and attitude in everyday life. The few Indians in Canada who were getting ahead were people, like myself, who were following the example of individual development without much conscious consideration one way or another for the needs of the community. We were following the model we saw in the surrounding white world. I don't think Farrel Toombs' own philosophy stressed either group or individual development. He simply healed the rift between the two so that a person no longer had to decide, "Me or them?"

Nor was his course just a discussion of philosophy. Farrel Toombs is a psychiatrist, a social scientist, and a sound academic. He would not hesitate to cite references, authorities, and experiments to justify his conclusions. In his written work he did this very often. But in conversation he was capable of explaining the most complex ideas in the most lucid manner, and waiting until someone asked for authorities or background material. I have met only one or two other academics who did not make me feel incapable of understanding the sophistication of their thought just by their roundabout way of using words.

When we left, many of us wished we were just beginning. We felt prepared to start to learn. Now we had to play his role, and share our experience of mutual dependence with others.

Sometime later, when I was just beginning to find my way around the Cowichan community, the thought came to me that Farrel Toombs, and the many scholars whose writings he had assembled, had provided a scientific basis for the view of the world, and the individual's relationship with the community and the universe, that my grandfather had tried to teach me before I was twelve.

The Cowichan Reserve is on a deep cove on the inland shore of Vancouver Island, not quite halfway from Victoria at the southern tip of the Island to Nanaimo. It is the one part of British Columbia that dips far to the south of the main international boundary at the forty-ninth parallel. Coming from the interior plateau of the province via Ottawa and Quebec City, the difference in the climate stayed with me throughout my first winter.

Cowichan Reserve adjoins the town of Duncan, named for the missionary who tried to harmonize an unorthodox version of the Anglican liturgy with a traditional Indian economy in his model community at Metlakatla, which is nowhere near the present town of Duncan. By the time Duncan had a loyal Indian following, the church found he was no longer useful for its ends. If it was not an omen specifically for my time there, it was certainly ominous for the century that followed him.

The Cowichan is just outside that very small area in which Governor Douglas had succeeded in negotiating treaties, which is still the major area of European settlement on Vancouver Island. Although the Cowichan people have been a primary target of every assault on traditional culture, they have succeeded in resisting all attempts to destroy their own way of life. At one point I was told by a civil servant that none of the white administrators who went there had ever been able to understand where the people's strength came from.

A good deal of help in maintaining a separate identity came from the townsfolk of Duncan, whose own leaders were generally retired colonial officers from the British army who had brought with them the class system that had been the ladder of their success, and which automatically ostracized the Indian people. Any ghost of Douglas's dream that two communities would integrate simply by living side-by-side should be laid to rest at Duncan. If 99 per cent of the citizens of that town had never seen Vancouver Island, the separation between the European and Indian communities would not have been any greater.

Indian traditions would not have been destroyed by a healthy integration. They would have had to adapt to a new and voluntary association with a neighbouring culture which, in turn, would also have had to adapt. The community would have kept most of its own ceremonies and its annual life-cycle because they were an expression of a relationship with that land and sea that had supported the people since long before Moses led his people into the desert. The mere presence of new neighbours need not have destroyed that relationship. There is a difference between the pressure of numbers and the demand for power.

When I first began to understand the source of their strength, having already been told that nobody from outside had ever understood it before, I thought perhaps it should be treated like a state secret of the Salish people. Or rather, like a piece of sacred knowledge that is spoken only under the most sanctified conditions. Now I am convinced that the best way to keep the secret is to shout it out. The few people outside the Indian community who will listen carefully enough to understand it are already well enough down the road to changing their own values and standards.

I was concerned about how people would accept me at the Cowichan for several reasons. First, I was a stranger. The major defence of any small community against invasion by outsiders is to isolate them. Their size alone prevents any other defence. Indian and non-Indian alike, village-folk have learned through the ages to extend a courteous distrust to an outsider until they are content that his wares are genuine. It is a healthy defence on their part, but something only the most foolish and insensitive outsider could fail to take into account.

Secondly, the advantage of my being an Indian could almost be offset by the fact that I was from the interior. Coastal Indian people have traditionally taken such a pride in their own culture that they tend to look down on interior Indians, whose way of life is a good deal less elaborate. When the commercial fishing industry developed in British Columbia, the coastal Indians played a leading role from the beginning. Whatever their standing in relation to the surrounding European communities, they were wealthy compared to the interior tribes. Whenever there were efforts to organize the Indian peoples of British Columbia as a whole, the coastal people would express strong doubts about how much the interior people had to contribute.

The most serious disadvantage was being an employee of the Department of Indian Affairs. Whatever fine words might have been spoken in Ottawa or Quebec City, the worker's independence and freedom to serve the community would have to be demonstrated before it would be believed; and, it would have to be believed before a community development worker would be accepted.

For some time I simply wandered around, making mental notes and meeting people in every corner of the community. I noticed that there was no single family that dominated the band, as sometimes happens in a village of only 1,400 people. Only a quarter of the work force were permanently employed; but, that is twice the average of the national Indian community. Many of those who worked had to travel to logging camps or to the city and came home only on holidays and long weekends. But there were also those who worked at logging in the area; and others who continued to fish. Many of the women earned extra money by knitting sweaters, the most popular traditional craft of the region.

I also got to meet the non-Indians who were supposed to be servicing the community. Besides the agency staff, and such townpeople as the doctors and nurses at the hospital, there were the missionaries.

On my first meeting with the missionaries they had my work cut out for me. Their request was that I discourage the traditional Indian religions and stay away from any associations with their leaders. They told me that the religious ceremonies were harming the people because they lasted late into the night and made the children unfit for school the next day. I restrained myself from any comment about midnight masses.

That discussion focused my attention just that much sooner on the fact that there were five different religious bodies operating within a community of 1,400 souls. None of them was ever going to become strong enough to truly serve the community as a whole. All of them were too deeply entrenched in their own approach to offer anything but the offering they had brought with them generations before.

Two of the five religious groups were distinctly Indian. One was the traditional Indian community, centred around the Big House. The other, Indian Shaker Church, mixed many traditional practices with Christian religious thought. All its ministers, bishops, and members were Indian. At the Cowichan, it was second only to the Catholic Church in strength of numbers; its membership extends all along the west coast of the continent. Two of the strongest traditional features it had maintained were the practices of feasts and of mutual help. It had extended the ban on alcohol from the mid-winter ceremonies to the entire year.

These two groups were the ones that so distressed the missionaries, and were the ones which, at the height of their ceremonies, came closest to uniting the entire community.

The three European churches were the Catholic, Pentecostal, and United. They spent a great deal of their energy condemning the two Indian religions, who respected each other's differences because neither one believed in proselytizing. Seeing the Indian religions in their full strength, I came to admire them, and I wondered then if they would not have gained in numbers if they had sought converts. The Shakers never actually discouraged interest on the part of potential converts. It is necessary to be invited to be initiated into the Big House. Part of the ritual of initiation into the secret society that was the centre of the spiritual life of the Big House includes taking the person, often without his prior consent, into the society's seclusion. The two kinds of people most often taken are those who express a traditional value in their lives or those who show an interest through extreme hostility to the Big House. A person who occupied himself with hostility was seen in the larger context to be resisting the greater powers, as though he felt in danger of being touched by them. Perhaps both groups would lose in spiritual strength what they gained in numbers if they actively went out to sell their wares to every wayward soul.

The demands put upon the people by the mere presence of five religious factions, three of whom could not abide any but themselves, created such a serious division as to guarantee the prevention of any significant social change.

The other deep underlying conflict was personal status. During raiding parties, coastal Indians used to take hostages, who became part of their own community. The people who were captured in this way are often referred to, in English, as slaves, but they were too often adopted or married into the family of their captors for this term to be accurate with the meaning it has come to have in the last four hundred years. Still, there was no doubt that neither they nor their descendants had the social status of a true Salish.

This difference of hereditary social class was not apparent most of the time. But, for example, if there were a family quarrel, especially in the presence of alcohol, a Salish woman married to the descendant of a captive might just throw up her husband's ancestry to him.

There was one religious situation in which people not only crossed conventional lines, but completely forsook any barriers between them. Regardless of what faction or religious denomination a person belonged to, when he died there was a real coming together.

Most Indian nations have a special religious society that not only sees to the burial of the dead, but more important, makes provision for the bereaved family. The clan to which the person belonged also plays a major role in lending strength to its weakened members. Although it no longer may have followed a strictly traditional structure, the practice of maintaining a form of social insurance that was very close to the potlatch belief persisted and transcended any other religious belief.

As soon as the word went out that someone had died, one person became responsible for taking up a collection at every house in the community. If that person was away, he would still be notified so that he might name another to act in his place. It was such a consistent thing that you could have charted a graph of the factors determining the generosity with which people gave. Generosity was influenced very largely by the esteem in which the dead person was held, not on a religious or family basis, but according to how well he had given in his own lifetime. It did not hurt him to have had great wealth or personal prestige, but neither was that essential to stir other people to give generously to his widow and children.

There were other giving-practices that carried over into the funeral ceremony itself. When the body was buried people would begin to gather near the grave and make speeches about the many virtues of the dead man or woman. This was a part of the condolence ceremony that in some Indian societies reaches its high point with clowns breaking into the wake to force people to laugh and enable them to endure the realities of this world.

It is a sign of modesty, as well as of mourning, not to make the speech yourself. Instead, you hand a dollar or five dollars, according to your means, to someone who you want to speak for you. It is not likely that you have asked him in advance. The giving is the asking. Part of this money finds its way back into the fund that will be distributed among the family of the dead person.

The other occasion on which people crossed religious lines was during the mid-winter ceremonies at the traditional Big House. Only the members themselves could attend the more sacred religious ceremonies. But on open days many of the uninitiated came to watch. People gathered from every Indian village and every town and city on the coast of Washington and British Columbia. The ceremonies moved through January to March from one community to another, so that every reserve had the chance to host the whole nation once a year. Although the planning mechanism did not appear complex, the possibility of a conflict of dates never arose. If only the initiated attended, the gatherings would have brought hundreds of people together. On open days, the number ran close to a thousand.

After some time, I managed to get permission from the band council to do a survey. They agreed that it would be good to know how many people had to travel to the States to find work, how many women knit sweaters for sale, how many families had running water, and other information that would be basic to a portrait of the community.

I wanted to do the survey and have their blessing for it, because I was still meeting mainly with the leadership of the community, although the occasional outgoing and curious person would ask what I was doing at the Cowichan and chat about his own concerns. Once I could tell people, when I knocked on their doors, "The chief sent me," I was able to get into every house in the reserve but one.

This was one area where I disagreed with many of my colleagues in the Community Development program. There was a tendency, especially among the officers, to sit and wait for the people to come to them, and it is important to be receptive when the people do come. But they rarely come; they have gotten along without me, or any number of other strangers, for many centuries.

It took no computer to read the results of that survey. Despite all the religious divisions that kept the people apart and had succeeded in preventing coherent social action for so many years, almost all the people with whom I spoke—and I visited every house on that reserve—shared a single vision of how they wanted to change their lives. The vision was of a sound, well-constructed home with the sort of comforts, such as running water and central heating, they had seen their own wealthier people and even the poor white people of Duncan enjoying. The dream of a good house was as much a part of the spiritual life of the Cowichan as any dance or hymn, and as interdenominational as birth and death.

If you talked about knitting sweaters for a living, women would tell you that they would like a nice house to work in. If you talked about the price of food, people came back with comments on the price of lumber. If you talked about the condition of the migrant workers, people talked about the living conditions at home. If you talked about spring flooding, people talked about foundations. All signs pointed toward one path, the need for better housing.

Unconsciously at first, I began to look for the one person who could give public voice to what all were saying in the privacy of their own homes. It was the toughest job I had ever had, to restrain myself for the first time from giving leadership, and instead to wait until I could assist a local person in discovering the necessary skills. I had been a respected leader in my own community. I had never in my life sat in the waiting room of an Indian agent. Unless he was meeting with another Indian person on a private matter, I took it for granted that his door was open for me. Even if it were closed. Now I had to learn not to kick doors open, but to move other people to believe that the same doors were open to them.

I had met Abraham Joe before. Often when we met he asked me what I was doing there. He had sat on the council when they passed the resolution giving me permission to do the survey. Now he was still questioning me to find out what I was about. He knew I was working for the government, but that did not satisfy him.

Abraham Joe had seen most of the berry fields of the west coast, and a good many logging camps as well. On a quiet social evening he enjoyed letting you know the number and variety of scraps he had won in his lifetime. He was also a member of the band council—the only member who would tell the agent where to file his ideas of what was good for the community. He was quite capable of elevating words and principles into action.

One day he asked me again what I was doing there.

I told him, "I'm like a leader. I'm here to help the Indian people."

He was not satisfied, but he left it at that for a few days, then came over to see me.

"Look," he said to me this time, "I want you to help me. I'm the chairman of the public works committee. I can't get anyone to work on my committee. Everyone tells me they're not interested. I'm a one-man show and I don't know what to do with a public works committee if nobody is interested."

"Abe, the trouble is you've gotten into a field nobody is interested in. Public works is for roads and running water and the like. Not too many people have cars. They don't need paved roads to walk on.

"If you talked about running water you might get a response but you don't talk about those things. The reason you're not getting a response is that the people can't relate your committee to anything that will benefit them. You've got to get involved in something that is of interest to the people."

"Well, what do I do?"

"Well," I said, getting ready to take the plunge, "you should really get involved in the housing."

I did not mention our research survey and the signs I had seen that the housing issue was burning throughout the Cowichan.

"There is already a chairman of the housing committee."

We must both have had the same estimate of the number of houses that would be built under the direction of that committee, because he said to me, "You know what I think? I think you're a troublemaker. I don't want to talk to you again."

During the next month we kept doing our survey, and I kept hoping to meet another person with Abraham Joe's abilities. Finally, one Sunday morning he called me and asked if I had ever gone salt-water fishing.

"No, I never have."

"Would you like to go?"

So off we went in his cabin covered boat. We had our lines all set up and the boat set on its course before he said very much to me.

Several miles from shore, he began, in a quiet voice, "Now I've been giving what you had to say a lot of thought. I've mulled it over in my mind, and I've decided that I want to hear more about it."

This was about one o'clock in the afternoon. Abe forgot to turn the boat around for shore until it was getting dark. This time I did explain how strongly the survey reflected one consistent demand throughout the community. We also talked about the ethical aspects of leadership. I told him then what I still tell myself today: it is the people who make or break a leader. If he is giving voice to their souls they endow him with that status; if he fails to speak their minds he is forced out; if he encircles the people with confused zeal by running after every concern but their own, he may be tolerated, but never respected or admired.

As the sun was setting down into the sea, he picked up a pencil and paper and started to draw a seating plan of the council.

"I have one more question. Here is the council, with the chief at the head, and the councillors all around him. Here I sit." Making another x in the row. "If I pursue what we're saying here, what will this guy do to me?" Making another dot. "And what will this one think of me?" Making still another. "And the Indian agent, what will he do to me?"

I took his paper with the diagram of the council at their table headed by the chief and the agent, and made little dots all over it. "The thing you have to ask yourself is who put you there? Did this man at the agency office put you there? Or this man who represents the other end of the reserve? Or this chairman of another committee? Or the people who so desperately need those houses?

"Pick a small crew of people you can trust to share your ideas with at first. Start planning with them. They're the ones who will convince the people they can get their houses. The only thing you must never do is hesitate."

"I'm going to do it," he said, "We're away." I don't even remember what fish we caught that day.

I did not hear from him again until he phoned ten days later.

"George, I'm in serious trouble. The chief phoned me. The agent phoned me. They're all accusing me of having secret meetings behind their backs. They're going to bring me before the council for disciplinary action for having secret meetings. What do I do now?"

"We've got to prevent their meeting from taking place," I told him. "The only way to do that is to call a mass meeting."

It was already eight o'clock at night. I told him to gather his committee together right away and go to as many houses as possible that very night.

"Go to the poorest ones first, and work up from there. Tell every person that if they come to the meeting tomorrow night they will get their house. Don't hesitate. If they ask how they will get their house, tell them they will find out at the meeting."

That was the biggest meeting that had ever taken place at the Cowichan. The chief began by making a motion that it was not the business of the meeting to deal with housing. That was a council matter, and the council had appointed a housing committee to deal with the matter. The issue was just confused enough that a motion to refer the matter of housing back to a committee that had not yet been able to deal with the problem might just pass without a heavy intervention.

I was an outsider with no particular right to speak. The chief had every right to throw me out of the meeting, and out of the community. It would take a bright star to let me steer my way through the waves of feeling going around that hall.

I said that I had visited every one of their homes. That every mother and father present had told me how unhappy they were with the way their children had to live.

"Many of you are living in one-bedroom houses. Your kids have no water for bathing. Your wives have no water for washing. It's very difficult for you. You told me that. I did not make it up, but I saw it with my own eyes.

"I happen to know that there is money to build a house for every one of you. The money is there. All you have to do is to tap it. But only you can get it.

"There is an office of Indian Affairs in Ottawa that has this money. But they won't give it to you unless you fight for it. What have they done for you when you did not fight? There is an office in Vancouver! What have they done for you? For years you've lived that way. And you'll continue to live that way. There is an agency office right in this town. You have a superintendent. He's not prepared to do anything for you. If he was, you would not be living the way you do now.

"Even your chief and the housing chairman. They can't get to that money without your fighting with them. They aren't strong enough by themselves. Besides, they have fairly good houses themselves. It is only people like yourself who can fight hard enough for your own housing needs. The agent cannot feel your needs in his gut.

"You are the ones who need your houses. History has shown that only people in need can fight the hardest for the things they need. And only when they get together.

"You're together now. Your chief has been fighting for years. But he has not gotten you that house. Your housing chairman has been fighting for years. He has not gotten you that house. If you fight, and stick together, I promise you, every one of you will get a house. But you have to make up your mind to fight!

"It's not the business of your council any longer. If they could have provided your houses by themselves they would have done it a long time ago."

As quickly as that motion was defeated, the chief moved to set up a grievance committee, responsible directly to the band council. I did not think that was much of an improvement over the previous motion, but I had blown my load. Whatever little credit I had in that community was about to be exhausted. I sat still.

A lot of young people who had never been involved before got on that grievance committee. I still don't know whether they were elected in hopes of tying up their energies and putting a lid on the matter, or whether their elders wanted the youth to keep the issue burning in a way that would leave the council responsible indirectly. Not too responsible, and not too indirectly. Abraham Joe was made chairman, and another councillor was put on the committee. Everyone else was a young person, not yet married, or if they were, with only one or two children. A lot of those young people are still active in Indian political matters today.

That very night the grievance committee held its first meeting as soon as the general community meeting adjourned. People decided that, if they were going to make a public fight of it, they had better have the press in. We started making lists of newspapers, radio stations, television programs. Basically, an agenda took shape for the first two weeks of action.

My own position had been fixed by two thoughts. I knew that the day they fired me I could make more money in a lumber camp than I was making with the Community Development program. And, in the time that I had spent in the Cowichan I had come to believe in the hidden strength of the people there, and in the central concern they had revealed to me. I felt free of my civil service constraints, both financially and morally.

After we had drafted a press release, the loggers left directly for work from that meeting. It was already five o'clock.

It was left to Abraham Joe to contact the press. He was to invite them to meet in a restaurant in town so that he could take them on a tour of the reserve to see the housing conditions. At ten o'clock he phoned me to say that there were too many reporters to fit into the restaurant. We needed a bigger place to meet. Abe did not have a key to the community hall, but he did have the good sense to see that this was not the occasion to go to the agency office to ask for a key. It was quicker to remove the lock.

When the national news that night showed pictures of children sleeping on the floor, and old men with heart conditions wheeling water to their houses from a mile away, the word came from Ottawa for the regional director in Vancouver to get out of his office and see what was going on.

I doubt that the same issues could be so easily publicized today.

145

Living conditions on the vast majority of reserves now are the same as were common then at Cowichan, but there are limits to the number of times the same problem can be publicized in a way that commands headlines. Government today is learning to weather the storm in the knowledge that the far-away urban voter soon becomes numb to anything. A wide-open tour of Indian living conditions was still news then—if there was resistance tied into it.

Abraham Joe was the only person who spoke to the press. He was the man elected chairman of the grievance committee; our role was to help out as much as possible but remain in the background. And the press cooperated in accepting that role on our part.

When the regional superintendent, Mr. Boyce, arrived the following week, the press all returned for the public discussion. Mr. Boyce assured the Cowichan people that there was no way he would authorize the building of another house at Cowichan. He stood up and told the people that they were too lazy to take care of themselves.

The whole meeting was filled with doubt when the regional superintendent said there was no way. He was sitting up on the stage with the chiefs and councillors, and the local agent. Abraham Joe was sitting up there, too. He was wearing the first suit I had ever seen him wear. He had bought it just for this occasion.

Abraham Joe got up, after Mr. Boyce had spoken, and walked right to the edge of that platform in his new suit.

"You've heard what the regional director said. We're not going to get one house. He called us lazy. I want to know what you have to say."

You could have heard a needle drop in the silence that came back to his demand. He called for a reply to Mr. Boyce a second time. Still no needle dropped. Finally, he shouted, "I know what you're thinking. I know what you're thinking! We're going to march!"

That silent, passive crowd just broke out into a mass of cheers, and shouts, and hats flying into the air. The regional superintendent gave up on any further attempt at discussion. Nobody had ever said a word to Abraham Joe about organizing a march. He had spoken from his own gut and a thousand other souls rose up to join him.

Abraham Joe held a meeting of his grievance committee every night for a week until the members felt ready to march. Then they began going around to every house, raising money, and getting commitments from people to march with them. I think he must still have been getting a rough time from some of his colleagues on council, because a couple of weeks later, Abe's morale began to sag.

The fall rains had started. Everything outside was grey and damp and soggy. Inside was often not much better. It was beginning to get to all of us. Abraham Joe called me down to his house one day and said he was throwing it all in. I talked to him until it was too plain for words that we were getting nowhere. He was the spark that had set the fire going. If the dampness got to him, it would smother everything. But I could not find a way to get him going again. I was just getting into my car to leave him, when I turned around and went back where he was standing.

"Abe, I knew right along you would quit along the way. It's no surprise to me."

"What do you mean?"

"I always knew you were a quitter. All those stories you're always telling about being a fighter are just bullshit. I'm glad you're quitting. I knew you would anyway. Now somebody else can step in and do a proper job of it."

"You sonofabitch," he said, "I'll show you I'm not a coward! I'll show you how to make this thing go."

"Bullshit," I said, and wheeled my car away.

He made that grievance committee go until Arthur Laing, who was then the minister, came down and took the same tour the press had made before him. Mr. Laing promised the Cowichan people they would get every house they were asking for over a five-year period.

In the next few months a housing authority was set up and a manpower-training program was introduced to train Indian workers to do most of the work. Most of the grievance committee members became involved with the housing authority, and showed that constructive action could follow from protest where the opportunity existed.

Now that the five years have passed, there is a need for more houses. Families have grown and children who were beginning high school then are now beginning their own families. Whenever

I go and visit the Cowichan these days, members of the housing authority tell me of one problem or another. And all of them are real problems. No home-making program is ever complete. But a good deal of the money, the skills, and the political structure within which those problems can be resolved have been put at the disposal of the people. It is this ability to act on your own problems that is the goal of community development. It is also a dictionary definition of power.

The measure of success was not in the number of houses that came to be built. Although people need to experience success to believe in themselves, it is at least thinkable that they could have experienced it in some totally different form. The measure of success was the extent of human development that took place—the development of skills of every sort from excavation and carpentry to management.

The most important goal could not be measured. Throughout the housing fight people had crossed and recrossed social and religious barriers they had not crossed in generations. The community as a whole had come together and experienced its wholeness in life as it had so often done in death. The Cowichan people had found the strength of which they were capable.

There were a great many other matters simpler than housing that were dealt with during that time, and which, in fact, occupied far more of my time than did the great drama that had become the centre of life for many of us.

We were only thirty-five miles from Victoria, but hardly anyone had ever been to the Legislature. If I was going to town to shop or dig up some information, I would invite anyone who was interested to come along. People became exposed to conferences and meetings of the social work organizations, the police commission, and public health groups. They developed ideas through this exposure that they could bring to bear on their own situations.

It was found that the community colleges, which were already geared to fashion their courses to local demands, were receptive to requests from the Indian community.

There was a pulp and paper mill a few miles from the reserve that had public tours. Nobody had ever taken such a tour. The mill was known to have a policy of requiring a high school diploma for the most menial jobs. After we did make the tour, some of the men went to see the manager, who decided that an advanced knowledge of French verbs and European history was not essential to working in his mill.

Both provincial and federal departments of agriculture were more than willing to respond with the same services they had already created for the general farm population when a group began to make enquiries about starting a cooperative farm to make better use of the reserve lands.

Each of these experiences was shared by a number of people who learned more about themselves than they did about feed grains, mills, police commissions, and legislatures. There is no doubt that each of these experiences had a certain value. But the central concerns of the community on the Cowichan Reserve could only be dealt with through the channel of Indian Affairs for a number of reasons.

The most superficial reason is that at present this is where the administrative responsibility for Indian people and Indian lands lies. A few years ago the government proposed to transfer this responsibility to the provinces. The Indian world saw this cure as far worse than the disease. The housing question is a good example of the practical side to the objections.

Housing is inseparably tied to land use and raises the whole question of the status of the land and the aboriginal rights of the people to that land. Transfer to provincial jurisdiction would destroy the limited security that a destitute people still retain in their land.

Housing is also an extremely costly matter. Our demands on one central government were not strongly enough felt. The same pressure divided among ten provincial and two territorial governments, who must still rely on the federal government for the capital for their housing programs, would be totally futile. Neither had people lost sight of the goal of financing their own homes. However humble they may have been, this is exactly how most Indian homes were built until housing programs were made available.

There was still no economic development program for Indian communities. Indian Affairs preached the virtues of self-help, regular working habits, independence, and the development of local government through self-support. All these things are possible only through economic development.

Indian Affairs sent placement officers to reserves all over the country. This was the job for which I had originally applied, and was offered a position in community development instead; although I had worked for thirty years without ever going on welfare, I was told I lacked the academic qualifications to be a placement officer. The employment officer who came to the Cowichan was always looking for the purity of a consistent work record that would reflect all the virtues the Department praised. If he could only find such a person, he would tell us, there are lots of jobs to be had. When the people who really did live there came to him, he never seemed to be able to find very much. Perhaps Manpower counsellors in the city are no different. Then why go to the city? Why transfer counselling for Indians from one department that does nothing to another department that does the same?

What happened to the Community Development program at the Cowichan is not really any different from what happened at a hundred other Indian reserves across Canada. There was no money for economic development. Whether the demand came in the specific form of jobs, houses, schools, a local voice in budget-making, most of the needs of which people began to speak when they were animated through the CD program were going to cost money.

About the same time as the Community Development program was getting under way, the government commissioned a report on the "Economic, Political, Education Needs and Policies of the Contemporary Indians of Canada," the Hawthorn Report. It gathered together all the popular and scholarly material that pointed to the same conclusions that every Indian leader and most community development workers had reached from their own local experience. Any serious attempt to relieve the oppression of the Indian people would be a very expensive undertaking. Large amounts of money would have to be poured in during the initial stages. But the reward would be a self-sustaining community that would contribute to the total productivity of Canada. Until that commitment of capital is made, no government will ever solve the problem of communities whose own indigenous resources have been undermined.

If the problem were strictly economic, our problem as Indian people would not appear that different from the situation of fishing communities that have suffered a depletion of stock through over-fishing by foreign trawlers, or by pollution from neighbouring mills and smelters. It is not economically different from the situation of such communities as Elliot Lake. And when we read of demands for a local voice for planning programs under DREE in non-Indian communities, that rings a familiar bell for us.

There is no doubt that the Hawthorn Report is absolutely correct when it says that nothing very much is going to change without economic development. Real community development can never take place without economic development. But economic development without full local control is only another form of imperial conquest.

Countless numbers of Indian communities have rejected proposals offered to them under the guise of economic development that promised an uncertain number of menial jobs with no specified opportunities for advancement, in return for ninety-nine-year leases and unpredicted amounts of pollution. This is not a cruel dilemma between moving in one direction or another. It is a choice between one kind of stagnating poverty and another.

Whether the course of development is toward assimilation, local autonomy, or the integration of a self-supporting community will not significantly alter the total amount of money required. Two businesses with totally different purposes may still require the same size office, the same staff, and the same equipment. Neither community control nor foreign control affects the depth of the mine shaft or the size of the factory. They may well affect the design of both the physical and the social structure, and the range of wages.

One community development worker wrote a paper in which he stated that if the common goal of the people was to learn how to build a better bootleg still it would be his job to help them gain the means to accomplish their goal. If housing, jobs, and schools appear to be more admirable goals than a still, it is because most communities have a sound sense of their own needs.

It did not require such a flagrant violation of the tax laws as building a better still for the government to decide that community development was too much of a good thing—communities developing their own internal strength, people taking power into their own hands through democratic decision-making. At that rate, Indian peoples would soon have more freedom than city-living European Canadians.

The question to which my colleague with the would-be still was pointing soon confronted every staff person in the program. It was the question of whether we were to serve the community in which we found ourselves or to serve the government. Were we community servants or civil servants?

The question had been there from the beginning. At staff meetings, in bull sessions, and in community groups, the question was raised endlessly. Underlying any theory of social change, human relations, or economic development was a basic conflict between those community development workers who found their first loyalty was to the community, and the entrenched upper echelons of the civil service in Ottawa.

There was an implicit threat to the traditional civil servant-Indian relationship in the earliest stated goals of the CD program. How can you end the "unilateral dependence," as Farrel Toombs had described it, without threatening the people who had become addicted to the exercise of authority?

As Gerry Piper, a community development officer who resigned in frustration, describes it,

> One doesn't tell a group of battle-scarred, dedicated, overworked and underpaid old vets that their work has been in vain, especially when the group-doing-the-telling is relatively new to the battlefield. Nor does one tell the underworked and overpaid, pension-calculating civil servant that he's about to lose his soft touch. That is political naïveté beyond comprehension.[27]

The naïveté springs partly from a failure of everyone involved to appreciate that there is a certain kind of interdependence even in the most one-way relationship. Corporal Ramsay, the officer who resigned from the R.C.M.P. and wrote his story for *Maclean's* magazine, said that when he helped to create a situation in which far fewer people were getting drunk on a Saturday night in a certain town, he was reprimanded for the decrease in the number of arrests being made. The patrolman who accepts that standard learns to chart his career in terms of fulfilling the expectations of his superiors. Even the drunk learns to be a part of the system after a while, until being driven home, instead of to jail, can be as disappointing as being cut off the bottle. The chief difference between the drunk and the superior officer is that the drunk has no illusion of success associated with his addiction. This is what makes him so much easier to rehabilitate. The same psychology exists within Indian Affairs without the arrest chart for an easy indicator of success.

Piper goes on to say,

> In the second place, and perhaps this is basically a philosophical problem, the idea of minimum or no commitment to an employer, coupled with a need for a working matrix [situation] which demands a maximum of operational freedom, together set out the very anti-thesis [opposite] of the traditional bureaucratic structure and function. The idea that a civil servant would even expect to operate within such a framework is incomprehensible to the responsibility-conscious administrator, and small wonder. At this point, it should be apparent why the classical community development officer is a potential loser.

The crunch came in British Columbia in the form of a directive, telling us of the need to be more versatile and responsive to direction from the agent in the future. Versatile, according to the directive, meant that in the future community development workers would take their direction from the district superintendents. The clamps had already been put on the program in Ontario. Now the Department was hurrying to extend equal opportunity to the west. The program had lasted a year and a half to this point.

The staff of the Community Development program responded to the directive by demanding a meeting with the regional superintendent. Most of those who came to the meeting were officers with high academic qualifications. The depression hung so heavily in that room that you could feel it, as though you were trying to walk quickly when you were up to your neck in a bog. Perhaps it was the tension that made people lose sight of the main objection to the new directives. The protests that were made drove a wedge between the officers and the workers within the program at least as deep as any difference between the program staff and the superintendent.

"How can I," one officer argued, "take direction from someone who is not academically qualified to give direction?"

Mr. Boyce had a pretty quick and valid answer for that when he pointed out that his whole staff had more academic qualifications than he did. His job was not to compete with their expertise but to coordinate the experts and see that they pooled their information. For once I agreed wholeheartedly with his position.

When nobody else had raised what was on my mind and the meeting seemed about to break up, I rose to speak.

"Community development to me is acting as a resource person for the people of the band. So my real boss is the chief, the council and the people. I am at their service. When they need me I move. That is the way I interpreted my terms of reference.

"With your new directives what has really happened is that you have transferred me from the Indian people's direct supervision to the Department's supervision. This program is the first time the government has ever given this kind of generous support for Indian people. Now you are pulling out.

"If I am loyal and committed to the principles of community development then I must resign. If this directive is a government order, there is no room for a committed community development worker within this term of reference."

Eight months later, I did resign. Fortunately I had been offered a position doing the same work I had been doing at the Cowichan under the direction of the Alberta Indian Association.

Harold Cardinal, the president of the Alberta Association, had succeeded in getting funding through the provincial department of agriculture under the Agricultural Rehabilitation Development Act (ARDA). This was the first time that an Indian organization had been faced with the possibility of more than passing-the-hat funding. Later, the Alberta Association was able to persuade the federal Department to fund their community development program through the province, who in turn transferred the funds to them. This was not the most straightforward way to allow Indian people to run their own programs; it was the only avenue open at that time.

Here was at least a partial solution to the conflict of loyalties that Gerry Piper had so aptly described. Indian workers working for Indian communities under the supervision of the executive of an Indian organization elected by the communities in which we were working. There were still questions to be asked: Why should a British Columbia Indian go to Alberta? How real was the local control? Those questions remained to be answered. At least all the lines of authority were drawn within a framework of common interest.

Within three years the Community Development program had gone from a dream of human involvement and social animation to a scheme for building roads, sewers, and schools with the permission of the local council. Participation began as a way of helping people to take a local initiative and was redefined to mean gaining the consent of the band council for Ottawa-desired projects.

The program had been gutted. On paper, the traditional lines of authority within Indian Affairs were re-established. Indians were to Indian Affairs what runways are to the Department of Transport.

Whatever happened to the program, the experience it had given to people, and the knowledge that they gained from that experience, could not be taken away. Those who went to meetings for the first time found how widely shared were their own most personal dreams. Leaders learned that some public services were genuinely open to their participation as Indian people; and where they were welcomed they could contribute to the design of a program as ably as many high-priced experts. The people who had crossed the barriers separating factions within their own communities experienced the wholeness and strength of their community.

On every reserve where the Community Development program had a measure of success, people had a new measure of their own individual and collective capacities, and a new yardstick by which to measure would-be friends. That could not be taken away.

7

The Decade
of Consultation

THE DECADE OF the sixties has come to mean many things to many people in North America. The Vietnam War. The peace movement. Hippies. Draft resistance. Rebirth. Death. Despair. The baby-boom of the forties coming of age, experiencing a collective identity crisis, getting turned off, turned on, toned down, married, employed, unemployed, caught up with the same day-to-day problems that perplexed their elders all the time we were raising them.

Indian people experienced all those things that make the sixties stand out like a mountain rising above the quiet mists of the fifties and the dark uncertainty of the seventies. But there was something more that Indian people experienced during the same years. It was the decade in which we were rediscovered.

As in the earlier discoveries of European history, we knew where we were all the time. It was the explorer who was lost. This time there were major differences on both sides. From our point of view there was the distinct feeling that we had seen this movie before. And we knew how it turned out. From the explorer's point

156

of view it was different because this time some at least knew that they were lost.

The explorers of the sixties came to the Indian world in three different guises.

There were the youth who had lost their way into their own world amidst the civil strife and continuing westward expansion of the United States. They were probably the first European people ever to come to Indian reserves with nothing to sell. In fact, they were often poorer than we were. They looked at first like a new breed of beggars. While they had strong political convictions they had no definite "final solution to the Indian problem" to offer us. That was nice. We knew by now what came from Final Solutions. They had a strong spiritual sense that had led them on the search in which they discovered us. They were so in dread of their own salvation that they never thought to tell us how to save our souls. That was also nice.

While they did not want to possess our souls the way the missionaries had, they wanted us to possess their souls. This was a new and unique problem. They protested that they had been colonized and exploited spiritually much the same way that we had been by their own elders. You could see that this was true. They protested too much. If every Indian spiritual leader in the Americas had joined hands and every little housewife on her reserve had offered up her surplus strength, we would not have calmed the souls of some of those good people.

The best of our own thinkers told them to continue their search and tried to lend them some strength to continue the journey. They told them it was forbidden for any man to give his song to another man until he was preparing to die. They would have to carry on their quest, and discover their own relationship with the land, the water, and the animals until the Creator gave them their own song. But it would have to be a song that they could sing to their own people. They would have to do more than discover their own song. They would have to discover a ceremonial situation in which the song could be given and received within the same spirit. If they were to do that they would have to find the roots of their own tradition. Perhaps they are the same roots as our own, but they have taken such a different direction that their own people will not recognize them. And if you do not share your song with

157

your brothers and sisters, grandparents and grandchildren, it is decreased in value by every generation you omit.

Each people must find its own way of thanking the same Creator for the same gifts. Otherwise, the gifts have not been shared and the language of those people has no meaning.

I hope they carry on their search, so that the bitter frustration and gritting of teeth that they have known will not be passed on to their children not yet born.

I hope they carry on because there were many lasting friendships born of their "discovery," many minds met on our early contacts. When their songs are listened to by their own people it will lend as much to our own strength as to theirs.

The second group of discoverers were the anthropologists. They were not a new breed. They had been slipping singly into the Indian world in a slow but steady trickle for eighty years or more. Now they came in hordes, until it became a commonplace among Indian people that the average Indian family consisted of a man, a woman, two children, and an anthropologist on summer vacation.

Anthropologists, like the youth, did not come to sell, only to take. If the youth were after our souls, the anthropologists were after our minds. There were exceptions, of course, to the selling rule. There were those who stood in our kitchens and our Long Houses and said that we were not drying the fish, or cooking the corn soup, or doing the dances according to the reference books with which they had prepared themselves for this expedition. Sometimes they even offered to show us how it was done.

The largest body of anthropologists were more like vultures—pecking away at our minds, our clothes, our houses, and our graves until we threatened to shatter if they broke rhythm. One reason that they came in hordes was that government, universities, and foundations had set aside large sums of money to satisfy the intellectual curiosity of these travellers into inner space.

Where the youth came in sandals or barefoot, the anthropologists came in Buicks, Toyotas, Jeeps, and Mercury station wagons. They were bedecked with cameras, tape recorders, notebooks, and expense accounts. The weight of their paraphernalia alone threatened to break them from the tradition of the early scholars. Franz Boas, James Tate, and others had come to live

158

among our people without checking into the nearest Holiday Inn and without a tourist's guide to good eating. They had eaten and slept as we eat and sleep. They did not take a helicopter to catch up with our canoes.

Indian scholars have estimated that our poverty "problem" could have been "solved" if all the money spent on anthropologists and sociologists of poverty were given in grants to the Indian tribes they studied. The great Sioux lawyer and philosopher, Vine Deloria, has suggested that Indian communities charge a fee for interviews or permission to study the skulls of our children and grandparents sufficient to cover the cost of the time involved in preparing to become someone else's information. Spread over the number of subsidized scholars now in circulation, this would only mean that they were bringing gifts to their adoptive families.

Many tribes are now insisting that the information gathered be returned to the people for their use. During my term as chief there were two anthropologists who did studies on the Neskonlith Reserve and the neighbouring Adam's Lake Reserve. We asked both to provide us with written copies of anything they wrote, copies of tape recordings of songs and stories, and the return of any artifacts after they had had an opportunity of applying a preservative to stop further deterioration and of making a mould for their own use. The most valuable of the artifacts that had been found was a mask. To the scholar it was definitive proof of the trade carried on between our people and the coast in ancient times. That was also valuable knowledge for us. But the mask was more than information. It was part of an ancestor's grave. Study and preservation could be seen as a three-way process among our grandfathers, ourselves, and the scholar. But to permanently disturb the grave by removing the mask to a distant place without returning it would be like digging up the graves under St. Paul's Cathedral to study the English monarchy. Both anthropologists agreed. One fulfilled his promise. It might be said that fifty-fifty odds are the best that most human groupings can be given. My suspicion is that in our dealings with anthropologists our two reserves fared much better than the Canadian or North American averages.

What distinguished Wilson Duff, the scholar who shared his

The third group of discoverers were government consultants.

findings with us, from many of his colleagues and identified him with the older and finer academic tradition was mainly his willingness to share what he found. His concern was to see that his work found its way into whatever hands would treasure it. So we were as assured by his manner and style as by his words that we would be as high on his list of loyalties as any sponsoring agency. Coupled with that willingness to share was a desire only to go where he was invited, and so to draw a line between honest enquiry and prying into other people's lives. Our people honoured Wilson's efforts by giving him an Indian name.

Some Indian tribes have learned that promises are to be taken seriously only when they are signed and sworn. They are asking scholars, broadcasters, film-makers, and feature writers to sign a contract stating that the material they gather belongs to the Indian nation or some agent of the nation and cannot be released for publication without their consent. Consent is only given on return of artifacts, or on receiving copies of the materials to be published. Whether a fee is involved depends on the financial means of the enquirer.

We have as great a need for scholarship that will provide knowledge and understanding as any other people. We want more of our own people to learn to gather the information as well as to put it out. But race is not a barrier to the scholar who is also a sharer, a teacher, and a friend.

The third group of discoverers were government consultants. If the money granted to anthropologists would have relieved our poverty for this generation, the money spent on consultation proceedings would support all the generations still unborn on the interest alone—with some set aside for inflation.

Official enquirers are a far older breed than anthropologists. They are far more selective about both their food and their intellectual diet. And, in terms of taking without sharing, they are without equal.

British, Canadian, and colonial governments have been setting up Official Inquiries, Royal Commissions, Parliamentary Committees, and internal task forces to study their "Indian problem" since time immemorial. By now they might even claim an aboriginal right to carry on these safaris. The very thought of cutting them off threatens to disrupt the way of life of a substantial part of their population. Unfortunately, the supply of novel testimony has become so depleted that we have had to ask the government to declare not only Indian witnesses but even anthropologists to be endangered species.

The Official Inquiry Problem (OIP) for native people is that it is as difficult to live with official inquirers as without. Throughout the nineteenth century these enquiries typically predicted our extinction. While they bemoaned and bewailed what they saw, and often pointed to helpful ways to arrest our declining numbers their total impact on government was more often to aid in a self-fulfilling prophecy.

A Committee of the English House of Commons in 1837 stressed the need to keep Indian Affairs under strict Imperial control. They observed that the chief exploitation of Indians came from neighbouring land-hungry colonists who also controlled local and provincial governments. Only an Imperial intervention in favour of the Indians could help maintain the balance and keep the peace.

The Earl of Elgin, in 1854, while he was Governor-General of Upper Canada made an eloquent plea for self-determination by Indian people:

> If the civilizing process to which the Indians have been subject for so many years has been accompanied by success, they have surely by this time arrived at a sufficiently enlightened condition to be emancipated from this state of pupilage in which they have been maintained; if on the other hand, the process has been inadequate to achieve the desired end, it has been long enough in unsuccessful operation to warrant the adoption of some other method of procuring this result.[28]

Whether or not we all share his views on what an "enlightened condition" might be, we certainly share His Excellency's scepticism about the effectiveness of his government's programs. Even friends in high places cannot always help you.

It seems that Indian Affairs' centennial project was to gather together all the contemporary evidence that would support Lord Elgin's conclusion. The Joint Parliamentary Committee that began its hearings in 1958 gave rise to one enquiry after another without interruption, until the tabling of the statement entitled *Indian Policy*, in June 1969.

Following the Final Report of the Joint Parliamentary Committee in 1961, the Diefenbaker government seemed satisfied for the moment with the evidence it had officially acquired.

In 1964, the Hawthorne-Tremblay Survey was set up by the new Minister of Indian Affairs and Northern Development, Arthur Laing.

Of all the enquiries that have been conducted, this survey probably worked with the least fanfare and the greatest diligence and produced the most useful collection of information. For the first time a public enquiry seriously considered what kind of public commitment, financial and moral, would be required in relieving the poverty and suffering of Indian people. It comprehended the difference between the goals and aspirations of Indian people and the cost of attaining a decent standard of living that must be met regardless of particular values. By showing that the cost must be met jointly, by the Indian people through our labour, and by the Canadian public through government financial assistance, it demonstrated in a documented analysis, but with a quiet voice, the falsehood of the standard government assumption, "He who pays the piper calls the tune."

While the Hawthorne-Tremblay Survey was still carrying on its work, rumours began to circulate that the government was considering establishing a National Indian Advisory Council. This was to be the first time that Indian people would actually participate in an official enquiry into Indian matters. There was finally to be a distinction made within government between the way Indian Affairs related to Indian people and the way Transport related to trains, planes and ships. So as not to be unfair it should be mentioned that Fisheries had for years been studying the behaviour patterns of fish, and regulating the ways in which human waste and garbage was dumped into the waters reserved for their use, without in any way trying to control the structure of their schools. Indian Affairs was now going to give us our chance — at a price.

The National Indian Advisory Council was to have provincial and regional councils under it. Bands would send representatives to the regions, which would then be represented at the provincial level. The provinces would carry the ball into the national forum.

By a coincidence, the rumours of a national advisory council reached Kamloops about the time that a group of us were trying to organize a district council that would allow the bands in our area to have a single, united voice on matters of common concern. The founding meeting of our district council decided that it would hold an election for the delegates to the regional and provincial advisory councils. Those elections would be held strictly under our own supervision without the advice of any government officials. Whoever won those elections would be returned by acclamation when the official elections were held. This was how I came to be on the regional advisory council, and later became deputy to the Indian co-chairman of the national council.

The National Indian Advisory Council had two co-chairmen, the assistant deputy minister and an Indian elected by the council. When Wilfred Bellgard lost his seat on the council as a result of the local election at home, under the adopted procedure I was to inherit his chair. The Ontario delegation felt that this was unfair because the series of local elections had produced a number of new delegates. I occupied the chair long enough to call an election, in which I won the chairmanship in my own right.

As deputy chairman, and later co-chairman, I was present at almost every sitting of every session of the National Indian Advisory Council. Most of our conferences were discussions of the Indian Act.

In the fifties, there had been a widespread feeling, which I shared to some extent at that time, that the Act itself was the source of all our frustration. When some reserves in British Columbia began to develop very rapidly, many of us began to see that the Act was written in such general terms that it could be interpreted either in ways that would be oppressive or in ways that would be supportive. I think that in the fifties, although we were living under the new Act of 1951, we were still too close in our minds to the old Act, which had included so many restrictions. It had not only been Indian minds that were too close to the old law. The same style of interpretation continued down to the time of our meetings, and in many ways continues to this day.

In fact, the Indian Affairs people who sat with us in those conferences tended to blame the Act itself for the lack of development on reserves and for the control it held over Indian lives. The Indian consensus went very much the other way. There were very strong debates about the directions in which the Act should be revised. Each section was discussed clause by clause. Many ideas were put forward for making the Act more workable, for ridding it of the ambiguities that had been put into the 1951 version, and for making it clear that it should be interpreted as supportive legislation.

The consensus that we did reach was by no means an easy one arising out of any mythical affinity of one Indian for another from thousands of miles away. In fact, the conferences of the advisory councils were the first time that there was enough money available for large numbers of Indian delegates to travel about the country meeting one another. Although a few of the delegates had had some travelling experience and had moved about the country visiting other reserves and crossing traditional lines, many were outside their own territory for the first time. We met as strangers, motivated by a belief that we had common bonds worth discovering and exploring. But in the first meetings those bonds needed very much to be discovered and explored.

The greatest single value that the meetings of the National Indian Advisory Council offered was that the Indian leadership from all across Canada got to know one another, and to discover where our common interests lay.

The consensus that did emerge from those meetings favoured a few small but important revisions. There was a common belief among us that the primary problems lay with Indian Affairs, and the relations the bureaucracy maintained with our people. None of that is prescribed in the Act. The source of the problem lies mostly in the attitude that no legislation can change so long as the present staff continues in the traditional structure, so long as the traditional structure of civil service roles is passed on from one generation to another, like an hereditary title, and the relationship between bureaucrat and Indian never becomes a relationship between man and man.

There was never a point in all those discussions when the Indian delegates recommended that the Indian Act be repealed.

There was no doubt that the delegates from across the land believed that their people wanted to retain their legal identity as Indians. We had begun to discover that, when the disabilities that had been imposed upon us were removed, there was a basis for what the All Chiefs' Conference of Alberta was later to call *Citizens Plus*.[29] We were not yet ready to articulate such a clear and positive philosophy, but we had renewed our contact with the roots from which it could grow. We repeatedly stated that our views were subject to band-council approval.

Perhaps many of the delegates were aware of how the U.S. policy of Termination of Indian Reserves, introduced in the 1950's, had brought instant poverty to some of the most prosperous reserves south of the border.

The Menominees of Wisconsin once counted themselves second in the nation in terms of tribal wealth. When their reserve was terminated it became the Menominee County of Wisconsin, with no different legal status than the other counties of that state. The day on which termination took effect was May 1, 1961, the same day on which county real estate tax bills were due.

"Most of the more than $1 million we had in the bank was gone immediately," according to a statement from Theodore S. Boyd, vice-president of the county's Menominee Enterprises, Inc. Today their county relief rolls are among the highest in the state. The only base they have for economic development is their sawmill and their forest. One possibility for new wealth is the sale of land to a developer who is proposing to flood the nine natural Menominee Lakes to create a single large Legend Lake.

This kind of economic development project has split the Menominees into two camps: those who insist that it is an economic must for survival; and those who insist that you cannot assure your survival by selling your homeland and economic base. Neither faction wants either the lakes or the lands of the Menominees reduced or flooded to the status of a mere legend. Yet, faced with a false choice that has grown out of a policy that was foisted on them by the U.S. government, both sides become more insistent on their own views. A community that needs the support and strength of every member becomes more and more deeply divided by a question that should never have been posed.

Those who want to retain their lands have formed a counter-organization to Menominee Enterprises to give voice to the opposition to economic development that does not provide jobs or security for the Menominee people, Determination of Rights and Unity of Menominee Stockholders (DRUMS). While on the surface it may appear that there is a strong case on both sides, the sides have formed on either side of a barrier that need never have been put up.[30] Economic development that failed to include the aboriginal and human rights of the people and the general good of the community has been experienced on many reserves without being prompted by termination. Termination simply assures that this will be the general rule rather than a constant danger.

The U.S. policy of termination, which President Nixon has opposed but which some officials of the Bureau of Indian Affairs say is still a possibility, had been in effect for about ten years when the National Advisory Council was meeting. It was applied to the Menominees while the Joint Parliamentary Committee was still sitting in Ottawa. There was no doubt that this was not what the delegates wanted.

One hidden price that was paid for the National Advisory Council became revealed only through the experience of its operation. Once the Advisory Council had discussed the Indian Act and received reports from the local and provincial councils, there was a dilemma about where to go next. Because it was merely an advisory council with an agenda set jointly by an Indian co-chairman and the assistant deputy minister, it was too closely tied to the government to become a significant national Indian organization.

Harold Cardinal, who was by then the youngest leader of a provincial organization, said what we were all coming to feel when he attacked the council for detracting from the role of the provincial organizations. Both the finances and the human resources were just too limited to be spread in that many directions. More important, it was creating a situation in which the government could play off one body against another. By receiving advice from a multitude of different sources, the advisory councils, the provincial organizations, the band councils, its own departmental staff, the government had maintained a divide-and-rule situation. It accepted the advice that was convenient to it, and always had an authority to which it could point for justification.

By the third year the Advisory Council had outlived its usefulness. The I.A.A. took over an Alberta Regional Council meeting with the leadership of Harold Cardinal and ended the life of the Council. We simply stopped calling meetings.

The following year, 1967, the government announced the crea-

167

tion of a Task Force under the chairmanship of the Hon. Robert Andras, then a minister without portfolio, to gather again Indian sentiment and expert opinion from across the country. This time it was rumoured that a major policy statement would result from the Andras hearings. So the play was repeated with enough changes in scenery and decoration to make it appear like a new creation.

Where the Parliamentary Committee had held hearings in Ottawa, and the advisory councils were provincially and regionally based, the Andras hearings travelled. Where the Parliamentary Committee had held hearings, and the Advisory Council had held debates, the Task Force would enter into dialogue.

Mr. Andras did enter into dialogue. The sessions took on a sufficiently informal atmosphere that people spoke freely and he often replied in kind. This was followed, first, by reports that he was expressing sympathy with the position being taken by Indian spokesmen, and then by reports of a growing rift between Mr. Andras's stand and Mr. Chrétien's.

The stand that was most repeatedly taken by Indian spokesmen was that no negotiations of sections of the Indian Act, or on such policy matters as education and economic development, could take place until treaty rights and native title were recognized by the government.

This was a change. We had tried the piecemeal, clause-by-clause, problem-by-problem approach. We had run out of clauses, and the problems were too numerous to discuss without allowing recognition of the fundamental framework that perpetuated those problems.

Six weeks after the final hearing, a policy statement was tabled in the House of Commons. When it was seen that in six weeks the government had managed to write the report, translate it into French, print, proofread, and bind it, the rumours began to circulate that it had been written by departmental staff or outside consultants, depending on which version of the story you encountered, while the hearings were still in progress.

When the Indian Policy statement was tabled in June 1969, it set off such deep anger throughout the Indian community that by the fall the government was saying that it was not official policy. It had been put out only to test the response of public sentiment, the Indian community, Parliament, or whoever else might be made to

take the blame for a report that completely misrepresented everything that had been said for ten years.

"Aboriginal rights" was too vague a term to be used as a basis for
discussion. "Treaties" should be respected but were also regarded
as an anomaly. Equality of opportunity was defined so that it was
indistinguishable from assimilation. Multiculturalism for European immigrants. Bilingualism for French-English relations. And
assimilation for Indian peoples. If the government would not
adapt a policy for the needs of every people in this vast and diverse
land, it would at least find a people on which every conceivable
policy could be tried.

Indian lands, the statement said, should be given over to the
individual person who now occupied them. Termination. The
overwhelming experience of the seven American tribes who had
been terminated was as strictly ignored as our own words had
been. Or was it? The suspicion that the forced sale of Indian lands
that would surely follow was exactly what the government desired
had found sure and certain roots in their statement. The cry of
"cultural genocide" went out. The record offered no evidence to
the contrary.

Through a rare show of good taste, the government had avoided
using the term "White Paper." Indian people referred to the
policy statement as the White Paper because, like some over-
advertised brand of soap flakes, it proposed to make us whiter than
white. The government said that it was not a white paper because
it was not official policy. But *Indian Policy* was the title spread
diagonally across the green cover in orange letters. Mr. Chrétien
explained that if the Indians were not ready for his policy, he
would wait until we were.

My own opinion is that the *Indian Policy* statement was written
by the ghost of Mackenzie King.

> The height of his ambition
> Was to pile a Parliamentary Committee on a Royal Commission.
> To have "Indians if necessary
> But not necessarily reserves,"
> To let Parliament decide–
> Later . . .
>
> Let us raise up a temple

> To the cult of mediocrity,
> Do nothing by halves
> Which can be done by quarters.[31]

Mackenzie King's Indian policy had always been firmly rooted in the belief that Indians could not be allowed to vote or carry the other responsibilities and rights of mature citizens unless we signed away our identity, our lands, and submitted to enfranchisement. This may not have been so much a belief in our racial incompetence—which even an order from his government could not have affected—as a nearly mystical belief that every factor and consideration can be bargained and negotiated. Lands could be surrendered for the privilege of appearing before a committee that heard you without listening. Life within a community that had taken a thousand years and more to build could be negotiated for a vote, a welfare cheque, and a pension. Indian rights could be set over against human rights.

> Truly he will be remembered
> Wherever men honour ingenuity,
> Ambiguity, inactivity, and political longevity.

John Diefenbaker arrived at the remarkably enlightened position that Indian-ness, humanity, and perhaps even Canadian-ness could all be experienced by the same person. An Indian might vote and still remain an Indian. Our citizenship did not depend on paying taxes to a local government set up by a province whose main historic purpose had been the exploitation of land for the colonial settlers. We had paid our dues when our sovereign rule of the land was taken and were entitled to admission into the Canadian mosaic without further strings attached.

During the Joint Committee hearings there had been considerable division within the Indian leadership across Canada on the question of the vote. There were those, largely from the West, who believed that the vote was one useful way of demonstrating the political concerns of Indian people as *Indian people*. There were others who believed that accepting the vote would cut the thread that held the sword over our heads for so long. Those who favoured the vote, like myself, were no less concerned about maintaining our position as Indian people. Nor were the others really less concerned about making an effective presence felt.

Those who were most aware of the Mackenzie King experience, which had been felt most strongly in the East, would not accept the vote. Even if the present government has some good will for us, they argued, what will they do for our children's children when they are as dead and buried as we will be? We did not really have an answer. Those who were willing to accept the vote simply hoped that Mr. Diefenbaker's policy would continue for the generations not yet born. The old approach had not worked all that well. It had kept us together but at a terrible price. The new approach was not a surrender but an alliance.

There was no need to wait for our grandchildren to come of age. The Trudeau-Chrétien Indian policy confirmed every suspicion and apprehension that had been our legacy from the years of Mackenzie King, Charles Stewart, and Duncan Scott.

> Only one thread was certain: . . .
> Always he led us back to where we were before.

What was so bad was not that we were being governed by a deceased ancestor, but that in twenty years of rest he had learned no more than in twenty-two years in office. And the decade of consultation had served the purpose of making sure that his political descendants learned nothing. Now we learned that true self-government must extend in all directions. A free people must freely choose the wisdom of its own ancestors.

The attitudes and beliefs of the bureaucracy which so largely shape the policies of this government, and the relationship of that bureaucracy with Indian people, is nowhere more clearly reflected than in the committee that should have been the least political in nature. The advisory committee for the Indian Pavilion at Expo '67 was selected by the government without consultation with any segment of the Indian community.

I was on the community development training course at Laval University when I received word that I had been appointed. I accepted on condition that if there were any objections from the British Columbia Indian organizations I should resign. I went back to British Columbia and put the question to a meeting of leaders from all British Columbia Indian organizations, who reaffirmed that I should represent them.

The chairman had been appointed before the committee ever

met. Dr. Gilbert Monture, an Iroquois from Oshweken and a professional engineer, was a fine and able man. But if we could not be trusted to choose our own chairman there was not much value in carrying the work of the committee past that point.

When we were told that we could not plan our own agenda, I asked that the Indian delegates adjourn to another room. This was refused, and a small group threatened to walk out. Only by threatening to hold a press conference if we left were we given a ten-minute adjournment. After half a day's separate meeting we agreed to confirm Dr. Monture's appointment if we could draw up an agenda of our own. Our first day's agenda would include all the items on the original slate, but future procedure would be entirely in the hands of the committee as a whole. We also chose our own vice-chairman, Wallace Lebilois from New Brunswick.

On the second day of our meeting Dr. Monture invited a few of us to his home in Ottawa for supper. When we had eaten well and were feeling comfortable with one another he said, "I admire you for challenging me. I was caught in the same bind that the bureaucracy always creates. I was put into a position where the only way I could do my job was to paternalize my colleagues. The reason I called you down here is to tell you that I'm resigning tomorrow. The only reason I gathered this group here instead of announcing it from the floor is that I know you would fight me as fiercely on the floor if I resigned as if I made any other move. I don't want that to happen."

Gilbert Monture resigned and Wallace Lebilois became chairman.

The time came for the committee to select a design and theme for the pavilion building. Indian artists had been invited from all across Canada to come and present their conception of the pavilion to us. Of course, each artist had no other tools with which to work than the canvas and oil or sketchbook and pastels with which he was accustomed to work. No specifications had been laid down. No funds had been provided to build models.

At the meeting at which the design was to be selected, the artists' pictures had been pinned to the walls around the room. Accompanying each painting was the artist's own statement of his story line in cold, formal typewriter face on plain white paper. Near the centre of the meeting room was a large table with a cloth covering some large and bulky sets of objects.

When the meeting started each artist was asked to present his painting and explain the ideas he had for the pavilion. When all the artists had finished telling their stories and were waiting to have the decision, you could feel the anticipation in the air.

But first the departmental officials wanted to show us something. For over an hour we were shown coloured slides of a model pavilion building that had been designed on commission from the Department of Indian Affairs. When the designers had finished they asked what we thought of it.

Well, those slides made the artists' paintings look like pretty amateur stuff. I don't know how the artists felt at seeing us all being manipulated, but as one member of the committee I felt cheated and used. There was really nothing to say. In the deathly silence that pervaded the room the designers felt compelled to do something. They pulled the wraps off a scale model on the table—a completely finished and landscaped model of the building that had been in the slides we had been watching. Just the building of the model to that point had cost something in the order of a quarter of a million dollars.

Nobody could say that it did not look pretty. It looked like every cent of the quarter of a million it had taken to put it together. The building may have been built to scale, but the dollars had not been miniaturized.

Again we were asked what we thought of it. One Indian artist finally said what they all probably felt: "Well, since you have already spent a quarter of a million dollars to get this far you may as well go ahead. None of our works are worth a fraction of that."

It was the only way the artists could retain their dignity in dealing with people who engineered lives on that level. I was not an artist and could afford to speak more strongly.

"I should really blow this whole piece of conniving skyhigh. There is only one reason why I am not going to. All my colleagues who are more closely involved with this particular question than I am have given their approval. Because I have no claims to being an artist I would have gone along with whatever opinion the Indian artists here agreed on among themselves.

"But I want to go on record as objecting to your project. I object to it because you framed us and manoeuvred us into agreeing with you. You have already spent money that was credited to us for our development, our presentation. You have deceived the Indian people. When you put up this building you will deceive the Canadian people.

"You led us to believe we were going to plan our own pavilion when all we were doing was going through an exercise. I could never support this project fully. For instance, if this painting here had been used," pointing to a work by Gerald Tailfeathers, "I would have known that an Indian had designed the Expo pavilion. For the first time we would have had participation in a project that was genuinely Indian involvement. I would have gone across the country telling Indian people what we had done as a people. I would have been proud to tell my people that this building was designed by a fellow Indian.

"Now I will have to walk away from this meeting with a heavy heart. When people ask me I will not be able to lie to them. I will not like having to tell them."

Nobody else spoke out against the project during the meeting. But many people came up to see me later and expressed their support for my words.

When it came to a matter that touched on my own province, I ended up going a good deal farther. Before I was ever made a member of the committee, a non-Indian member of the committee had gone to Vancouver and had visited some of the better known totem-pole carvers of the west coast. The civil servant group had decided to commission a man called Bill Reid, who had already been commissioned by the University of British Columbia to do his work on the university campus—giving university students the opportunity to study his techniques as it closed the opportunity to Indian young people who wouldn't make it to university. The man who had made this recommendation was a federal government organizer who had never been exposed to Indian people and had never had the opportunity to become knowledgeable about totem poles.

By the time the decision was being made, I had completed the course in Quebec and had been posted to the Cowichan. The regional superintendent called me on the phone and suggested that I attend the meeting that was coming up in Montreal. He wanted me to come down to the regional office to receive instructions on what to do to support the man who had already been selected.

174

No carver had been asked to make suggestions about the kind of pole, the design, or any aspect of the work. My own people are not totem-pole carvers. I probably do not know much more about that art than the man who made the choice. I probably do know as much as he does about organizing, at least as it applies to Indian people and democratic decision-making. That was what was at issue.

The regional director instructed me to go to the meeting and support the nomination that was to be made. He also made an appointment for me to visit Bill Reid that afternoon. Reid was to give me the final briefing. I sat there like a real good wooden Indian and said nothing.

On the way over to Reid's, I went over to skid row and began to visit with that community of human rejects of all colours, races, and nations that had been destined to live together in Canada's most successful cultural mosaic. I became so caught up in their lives that I stayed there until the wee hours of the morning, and barely got out of bed in time to catch my plane for the East.

The totem pole was nowhere on the agenda. We went through all the items that required discussion. When there seemed to be no other business, the man who had selected the totem-pole carver told us, "You're probably wondering why the totem pole is not on the agenda. The reason is that all you Indians from Alberta or the East don't know what the totem pole is all about. George is the expert so we will just consult with him."

"Does Indians have feelings?"

The meeting adjourned. We went into another room. They put a paper in front of me saying Bill Reid should be given the commission. I refused to sign:

"Bill Reid is not the only good carver in B.C. There are many good carvers all over B.C. These people have a right to know what we are doing. They should be given an opportunity to bid for it."

There was no time to wait for bids to come in and make a selection. The pole was to be unveiled in a matter of months. This was how they justified railroading a decision that had been made years ahead. I thought of all those carvers who had never seen the sum of money being offered, $12,000, in their lives. I sat still.

"Your fare was paid here on the understanding that you told the regional director you would give your endorsement. We're going to do it with you or without you. So you may as well sign."

Diplomacy. Democratic decision-making. Consultation. Industrial training.

"You go ahead and do it as long as you do it without me."

The only way I was going to beat him was to get some allies within the organization. They had hired an English couple to design the interior of the pavilion. They were not very knowledgeable about the inside of Indian life, but they were capable of listening and did not expect to live off Indian Affairs the rest of their lives. They had professional careers and personal integrity.

When I went to see them, they told me that they had suspected that the involvement of Indian people had been pretty limited but they had not been able to find firm proof. They felt that involvement was essential to their own work and had come to put their skills at our disposal. They would go to bat for us. I found out later that when they did try to talk to the people making the decisions, they were told to mind their own business or they would be fired.

When I got back to Vancouver Island the next day, I dropped over to see an old carving friend of mine, Simon Charlie.

"Simon, you're a real good carver. Do you know about the totem pole they're going to commission for Expo?"

"Yes," he told me, and added some news I had not heard, "and the Indian agent said I would have a pretty good chance of getting the job."

"You'll never get it unless you write to the minister and tell him you would like to have a chance to carve that one. There are so many being considered, you'll never have a chance unless you write the minister."

"Maybe you could write that letter for me," he asked. "I don't write such good letters."

"Sure."

We sent copies of that letter to John Diefenbaker and Tommy Douglas. Meanwhile, the English couple had gone directly to Arthur Laing, who was then the minister.

When Mr. Laing began to get enquiries from all directions, he sent someone to see me. I walked into the Vancouver regional office. The staff there looked at me like I was a skunk at the Governor-General's tea party.

"What right do you have to make unilateral decisions? When

did you become an expert on who can and who cannot carve totem poles?" the regional superintendent wanted to know. Two weeks before, I had been introduced as the national authority.

Finally, the minister's man emptied a private office of everyone but himself, me, and a secretary to take minutes. Then he asked what I was after.

"Simple. All I want is for every totem-pole carver in British Columbia to be told about the pole and allowed to bid on it. And the best bid to get the job."

"We don't know all the names."

"The provincial government has had competition upon competition. They have all the names of at least the better ones. No problem to send a letter today. We can get the addresses this afternoon."

The letter went out that afternoon. Henry Hunts won the bid, with Simon Charlie as his assistant. They had put in a bid for $5,500.

Parallel with the formal consultation procedures that took place during that decade, there have been innumerable consultations on local matters. Whether the question is a small extension of a road right-of-way or a multi-million dollar building, the process is pretty well the same. When we make the decisions the Department desires, they approve the decision and commend us for our progressive thinking. When we object to the decision, they look for another representative, or set up a process of manipulation that demands far more energy than would ever be required to effect the initial decision.

The Expo decisions stand out as especially useful, because relatively small sums of money were involved and very few political ambitions needed to be put on trial. Expo was intended to be a grand spiritual statement of all participants. Each pavilion was to be a testimony to the world about the people who had built it. Touring Expo was meant to be like a miniature tour around the world. The Department saw to it that Indian people had the same voice in our pavilion that we had in our own lives. Scaled down to size.

During the Alberta School Boycott Jean Chrétien was questioned in the House of Commons about the Department's contracts with the local school boards for seats in the local high schools. He assured the House that the Indian people had participated in the decision.

The Department's definition of participation, which spokesmen gave to *Maclean's* magazine, is that a band council resolution had been passed confirming the decision.

According to Chief Blackman of the Cold Lake Reserve, the council had passed the resolution ten years before when more of their children were starting to go to high school. It was an experiment. After ten years of effort to make the arrangement workable, and after two years of telling the Department the experiment had failed, they had begun the boycott. The minister still had the ten-year-old resolution, authorizing his Department to make the contract. Not only had they not been a party to the negotiations at any time, but they were now being told that a decision once taken could never be changed. Not on a land sale, or the erection of a building, but on the selection of a school and the curriculum it offered to their children. Has any other legislative body in Canada ever found that it could not repeal a decision that the majority of people said had outlived its usefulness?

The belief that Indians do not really exist except as an appendage to the Department of Indian Affairs carries over from government circles into all aspects of non-Indian life in Canada. Most non-Indians rarely have the occasion to give the matter much thought. The lack of thought helps to perpetuate the stereotype the government communicates.

The press also helps to perpetuate the stereotype. About the time I began to do this book, I agreed to do an article for *Maclean's* magazine about the goals and aspirations of the Indian people. The editors asked the Department to verify the facts as I had tried to describe them.

The 1969 White Paper did help to quicken the growth of unity among the Indian people across Canada. It led the provincial and territorial organizations to come together and form the National Indian Brotherhood. Opposition to the White Paper led to a series of small grants that allowed the provincial organizations to begin a more systematic research into treaty and aboriginal rights than had been done before.

Many Indian leaders who had been as quick to criticize their colleagues as the government, and who had been tempted to spend too much time fighting organizations that competed with their own, began to put their organizations on a war footing. Small differences were overcome in the face of a threatened major aggression from outside. In the long run this will serve a useful purpose. The differences that are too small to be remembered will slip away in the mists of time. Many of the legitimate differences will be resolved as we work together. Those which cannot be resolved will be the valid distinctions between one Indian nation and another.

Still, the claim that the Trudeau-Chrétien administration has made that it is they who created Indian unity can be compared to Dwight Eisenhower and John Foster Dulles claiming credit for the success of the People's Republic of China. Shall we credit Mackenzie King with the purity of the Indian people because he would not let us dirty our hands with politics or money?

Indian people have come together in common cause wherever the need and the opportunity have coincided. There was sufficient cause for us to come together, pool our resources, and develop a more systematic research through our own organizational efforts without being threatened. Without needless aggression and verbal violence. We do not need an Indian policy that flies in the face of all the evidence. We do need a relationship with government based on a recognition and understanding of the past and present history of our people, and based on the belief that our people are living.

One of the early times when Indian people came together in common cause was a gathering of fifty-seven leaders from nineteen nations at an international council called to oppose the General Allotment Act of 1887 in the United States. The purpose of that act, coincidentally, was very similar to the Indian Policy of 1969. It proposed to break up reserves into individual holdings subject to the laws of the local states. The Indian nations at that conference were well enough organized that it took four congressional sessions for the government supporters to outvote those congressmen who understood what this law would do. The conference issued a statement that included the following paragraph:

> Like other people the Indians need at least a germ of political identity, some governmental organization of his own; however

crude, to which his pride in manhood may cling and claim allegiance, in order to make progress in the affairs of life. This peculiarity in the Indian is elsewhere called "patriotism", the wise and patient fashioning and guidance of which alone will successfully solve the question of civilization. Exclude him from this and he has little else to live for. The law to which objection is urged does this by enabling any member of a tribe to become a member of some other body politic by electing and taking to himself the land which at the present time is the common property of all.

How little has changed in the two European empires of North America since that day! Are we not entitled, those of us who have held on since that time, to claim some sort of victory? Is it not time to dance with the joy of life and recall the faces and wisdom of our ancestors?

Can Canada not develop any finer relations than those based on policies long ago discarded by the United States because they had failed so miserably? Is there nothing more to Canada than its pale imitation of one imperial power after another.

The poet says of Mackenzie King,

> He seemed to be in the centre
> Because we had no centre,
> No vision
> To pierce the smoke-screen of his politics.

Is that why Canadians have never learned to create their own ceremony to dance with the joy of life? Have they no joy? Have they no life? Are the fantasies that come from this uncentred life always to be projected onto us, as Indian people, because we are so few in number?

8

~~~~~~

The Daily
Struggle Now

WHEN THE ANTHROPOLOGISTS have tired of telling Indian people the proper way to smoke our salmon, dry our meat, or prepare our corn soup, the largest number of our Indian children will still go to bed hungry. When the civil servants have told the politicians for the last time that 90 per cent of our Indian people are below the poverty line drawn across the whole of Canadian society by Senator Croll's Committee on Poverty, we will still be the losing side in the bureaucrat's war on poverty; and the missionaries will still be trying to save our burning souls to the neglect of our frozen bodies.

This is the nightmare from which I have awakened countless times in the still darkness of strange hotel rooms as I have travelled across Canada, visiting Indian people in their own communities. When the sun is shining, the salmon are running upstream, and the buds of a new lease on life are everywhere to be seen, there are also innumerable signs of the ways my people are building a new life as we find ways to harness the technology that belongs to all men to the values and beliefs that have made our nations strong on this soil for so many centuries. But when I witness the suffering and degradation that still continues, I know that all these little signs of rebirth will not raise the future generations much beyond the daily struggle and passive resistance on which we have survived the colonialism of the past four centuries.

Unless there is some framework to lend support to all the little saplings of the rebirth, they are likely to be bulldozed and crushed in successive waves of expansionism. I am too young and too filled with hope to speak of dark prophecies. It is no less evil to cry, "Peace, peace," when there is no peace. I do not prophesy at all. I am only describing what I see wherever I travel.

The average age of death for Indian men in 1963 was 33.31 years, for women 34.71 years. When deaths occurring in the first year are left out, our men die at 46 and our women at 48. Canada's national average that year was 60.5 for men and 64.1 for women. The gap has not closed much in the ten years since then.

The average Canadian that year could obtain credit of $255. The average Indian had credit of one dollar. The causes of that disparity have remained almost unchanged.

The average Canadian was able to spend $90 on creating new housing or renovation for himself and another $90 for each of his dependents, while $21 was available to each Indian person for home improvements.

When the average Canadian earned $9,500, the average Indian worker earned $1,600. Inflation has changed these figures. The gap has widened.

It is no wonder that there is such a widespread temptation to describe the present state of the Indian world as a poverty problem. If the "Indian problem" is a poverty problem, the whole question of Indian identity can be treated as a disease curable by the rapid injection of large amounts of capital controlled by outside experts, financiers, and businessmen without reference to the reality of our world.

These statistics are all from government sources. You can find the same information on the faces of Indian children. Sometimes you see it on the faces of our homes when you drive through our reserves. Not always, because we have also learned to become part of the invisible poor. Our poverty breaks through the veil with occasional news reports of children who have died of

182

pneumonia aggravated by malnutrition. Or the man who has supported his family on the wealth of their river who suddenly drops dead of a heart attack with twenty times the safe level of mercury in his body.

The veil that makes our poverty less visible makes it easier for outsiders to ignore. This is a mixed blessing. People may choose to deceive themselves that our condition has changed. But the same veil has drawn an element of doubt, so that it is just that much more difficult to perpetuate the myth that it is the poverty that is at the heart of the present state of the Indian world.

In a world that believes in miracle-cures, instant coffee, instant dinner, and instant housing, the symptoms remaining from one social disruption become an excuse for another social disruption. If the patient can be called delirious, we do not need to listen to what he says to understand the source of his pain.

Yet there are other experts, few though they may be, who have taken the time to listen. Their studies have shown that the worst symptoms of the culture of poverty are in those Indian communities that are in the midst of having our own culture undermined. It is the Indian societies that have been forced into a transition through token consultation that have the highest rates of alcoholism, prostitution, welfarism, and suicide.

Indian people who continue to lead a traditional life in a community that clearly defines itself in traditional terms are not caught up in the culture of poverty. The cash they see in a year may be so small that they are poor in the most narrow and meaningless sense—like the trapper from Fort George whose trap lines are to be flooded by the James Bay Project, who said he sees $600 a year from the sale of his furs. He went on to estimate that the value of the two homes, the clothes, and food he provides for his family would cost him $10,000 a year in the city.[32] His figures are not far off an estimate by the Social Planning Council of Metropolitan Toronto.

Indian people who for all intents and purposes have assimilated into the mainstream of urban European North American society also do not reflect the conflict of loyalties and values and the resulting crisis of identity that produce the symptoms of poverty. They have made their choice. They know who they are. They set about fulfilling that identity in their daily lives.

Some of these have remained Indian in many of their inner and household values, while accepting another standard in their public and working lives. Others have simply adopted another culture. If the choice has been freely made, and if it can be a source of prosperity and happiness for their children, no one should begrudge these people their choice.

The urban ghettoes of North America are not filled with people whose choice was freely made. Many of our people have tried to become white Christian ladies and gentlemen. A few have made it, and though I would give my blessing, they do not need it. The thousands who have returned home or remained in the city slums are the ones for whom it just has not worked.

It has not worked because few people of any race or nation can long endure to stand with one foot in one boat, and the other in a different boat. When there is a parting of the ways, it is the person who has one foot in either boat who suffers. The helmsman, in either boat, is the one who is safe and can endure.

It has not worked because urban North America has not yet decided that it desires to build a bridge of lasting strength between communities of different cultural perspectives. Racism persists and flourishes throughout Canada wherever there is enough racial contact for people with the upper hand to decide how they want to respond in situations between man and man. The presence of human rights legislation has sometimes made the forms of discrimination in urban settings more subtle. In rural areas such legislation has gone largely unnoticed and unenforced. Nowhere has it changed the climate of public opinion. Neither has it touched those government agencies that are too often the worst offenders.

Twice, in my terms as president of the National Indian Brotherhood, I have seen well-dressed, sober, and polite delegates to Indian conferences turned away from hotels with empty rooms. On one occasion it was a CN Hotel owned by a federal Crown corporation. When a complaint was made to the Nova Scotia Human Rights Commission, the hotel issued a denial in a long press release. The local paper printed the release with no attempt to get the other side of the story. Neither the rules of *sub judice* nor those of fair play extend to Indians.

When a judge in Sudbury, Ontario, stated from the bench that "we have enough stupid Indians," Indian organizations across the country demanded his resignation. We would have taken it as a sign of sufficient good will if he simply disqualified himself from hearing further charges against Indian people. When similar remarks were made by another Ontario judge about Pakistani people, he was forced to step down.

All these matters arose in Ontario and Nova Scotia, the provinces with the most advanced legislation and the most dynamic Human Rights Commissions. Neither Commissioner will entertain a formal complaint against a judge or an officer of the crown.

When the remarks of the Sudbury judge were being debated at the convention of the British Columbia Association of Non-Status Indians, which was in progress when his statement was made, the mayor of Victoria, an invited guest at the convention, stood up to plead for cool restraint in our attitude, and told us not to be too harsh in what we might say about Canadian justice. He did not want to defend the judge; he only felt there was a need for patience. Is it so hard to understand those who, having gone home to wait patiently, tell those who ask, "This is how we were received in Victoria, Sudbury, Cornwall, and Halifax."?

This is only a short list from matters publicly debated at official conferences. The unspoken reality is the daily experience of any number of children bused from reserves to schools in towns where they are not welcome, while the $2700 of federal money that buys their seat is gladly accepted. Petitions in Winnipeg to limit the renting of houses to Indian families. Jailing and beating of Indian students in Wallaceburg, Ontario.

The height of Canadian racism is achieved in Canadian prisons, which even without the racial factor should be an everlasting source of shame to Canada. We have the highest rate of imprisonment, and the highest rate of repeaters, in the world. India and Sweden, which stand at the opposite extremes of the standard of living scale, have comparable rates of imprisonment at one-quarter of the Canadian average.[33]

Indian people, status and non-status, constitute a full one-third of the inmates of Canadian prisons, although we are only 4 per cent of the population. Ninety per cent of the inmates in the women's jail in Prince Albert, Saskatchewan, are Indian. More than 65 per cent in Prince Albert and Regina jails are Indians and Métis. Full

185

statistics on Indians in prison are not available except where there are native court workers. We do know that between 33 and 40 per cent of the deaths in federal penitentiaries are by suicide.[34] We can only speculate on the overlap between the third of the prison population who are native and the third of the death-rate that involves suicide.

Native people are not greater criminals than whites. Most of the offences for which Indians are jailed are either petty offences or crimes of passion; it is rare for an Indian to be charged with armed robbery, kidnapping, or any offence that is a serious threat to the larger society. We are jailed for minor offences that stem from the frustrations of living in a racist and colonial society. Sometimes these frustrations boil over and we take them out on the people who are closest to us.

The process does not begin in the prison. Ex-Corporal Jack Ramsay of the R.C.M.P. says that racism is built into the police system. It is more than the viewpoint of individual Mounties. "If ever senior officers want to use an example of an unsavory character, it's an Indian."

Where native organizations have succeeded in establishing court worker programs with translators and skilled but untrained social workers to work within a proper legal aid system, the conviction rate for Indian people has fallen close to the average for that court. Because of the easier access to resources, these programs have started first in urban areas. The farther north you go, the more common is "Mississippi justice." In one far northern community, the judge sentenced so many natives in one day that it took three days to transport them all to jail.

On another court circuit, the judge and Mounties were accustomed to sentencing one hundred native people each month. In September 1972, a lawyer unexpectedly showed up to defend the Indians and Métis. Almost all the cases were dropped. The judge resigned within the month. The Mounties remained. The jail remained. The absence of good and useful work from which a man and woman could raise a family in pride and dignity remained. *Industrial training!*

Just as it is the court worker programs that are stemming the tide sweeping our people into the claws of Canadian justice, within the prison system itself it is the Native Brotherhood Societies that are doing the greatest work toward long-term rehabilitation. With the help of a few friends on the outside, Native Brotherhoods, clubs formed by the inmates themselves, have been able to set up within the prisons educational programs and group activities that bring their members into social contact with both peers and community leaders when they get day passes. They are struggling to create halfway houses that will provide a real transition and not just carry the regimentation of the prison into the streets. There is the odd warden, like Pierre Jutras at Drumheller, who extends his office to help the Native Brotherhood programs succeed. Too many officials are prisoners themselves, caught between the bars of the local townspeople with whom they must live, and their superiors, who judge their performances by the extent of public complaint and their ability to achieve economy. Like Mounties and government-appointed community workers, the prison officials are restrained by a system designed by a vengeful society.[35]

When Dr. Howard Adams visited the Saskatchewan jails, he found that the average prisoner was a native person under twenty-five years of age. He stated his findings in an article for the Toronto *Star* on the unspoken issues behind the Canadian elections of October 1972. But how many Saskatchewan citizens have access to the Toronto *Star*? How many local papers attempt to report on the whole of their local communities?

The Senate Committee on Legal Affairs is studying the parole system. I hope they have started at the tail in the belief that that is what wags the dog. How can you study a parole system without looking at the police, the courts, and the prisons that go before them? At least the senators are sniffing in the right direction.

Racism pervades more subtle aspects of Canadian society. During the British Columbia provincial election of 1972, the Liberal candidate in one riding, himself an Indian, found that the people on one reserve had not been enumerated. Of the 450 eligible voters on that reserve, only those who had gone down to the post office and registered themselves were on the list. This, in an electoral system that pays enumerators so much per person enumerated. The candidate, Lawrence Gladue, says that when he brought the matter up with the enumerator he was told, "Why should we enumerate Indians? They don't know what this is all about anyways."[36]

Irene Peters, an Indian woman, did the enumeration on the other two reserves in the same riding. There were no complaints.

This is the same province in which the Evidence Act, in the last version of the revised statutes, provides that an Indian is a person of aboriginal descent, "ignorant of the knowledge of God."[37] A person's identity for purposes of the court rests equally on his proven spiritual knowledge and on his unproven ancestry. The pre-1951 Indian Act had been content merely to allow judges to caution Indians to tell the truth. Every witness had to make an oath. Indians were to be given instructions in honesty. The British Columbia Act raises doubts about whether we are capable of understanding those instructions.

The Canadian Armed Forces have been trying to recruit more Indian and Inuit people to serve in the north. Colonel Pierre Chasse, director of recruiting and selection told the *Globe and Mail*, "We feel . . . that perhaps we didn't offer them in the past the opportunities."

He went on to explain why the Forces were seeking more native recruits. "For rather primitive people, if you want, they're mechanically inclined. They're highly intelligent. . . . He has his own culture but he's the sort of man who could become Western very easily, become one of us."[38]

Perhaps his own words will explain to Col. Chasse why there has not been a longer line-up at his door.

The need for an armed presence in the North is itself somewhat hard to understand. Who is it we are to defend ourselves against? Foreign investors? Oil exploration? Northerners feel there is a very strong threat of external aggression. So far it has not come from the Soviet Union or the People's Republic of China. Nor are they yet convinced that armed force is the best way to resist it. If the present level of consultation continues they may well become open to that possibility.

It is not necessary to travel all the way to the Arctic to see the traditional colonial system operating with the full assistance of modern technology. Big Trout Lake is a major Hudson's Bay post for the most northerly and remote area of Ontario south of James

Bay. It serves the immediate Indian community and also a variety of outlying island settlements such as Kasabonika. The home of the Hudson's Bay staff is surrounded by a stockade. There are two separate churches—one for white government and Bay personnel, one for Indians. Will Anik open up more lines to the Creator? Or does He operate on a party-line system?

The local airline charges fifteen cents per pound to take goods from one island to another. The Queen and the beggar have the same right to ship their goods.

The old way of sharing still continues. A hunter divides the moose he catches among many different tables. But wildlife is getting scarce and children fill themselves with oatmeal twice a day. It is still preferable to the diet of Coke and chips that will come in when the airline rates go down.

When the mercury content of fish in the English and Wabigoon Rivers went up too high, southern tourists were told to "Fish for Fun." Native people who depend on the fish as their principal food were told nothing. Governments that were prepared to give grants to industry to locate on clean waters had no answer when native people asked, "What are we to eat?"

These are people who have become impoverished since the War on Poverty was begun. These are some of the people to whom Senator Guy Williams was referring when he told the Senate that poverty is worse today than when he testified before the Joint Committee that sat in 1947.

How do the outbreaks of typhoid fever[39] at Sachs Harbour and Tuktoyaktuk on Banks' Island differ from the smallpox that raged through the prairies and into the Kootenays in my grandfather's youth? It's true that the death rate is lower because of vaccination; I do not mean to gloss over such a difference. But northern people disposed of their sewerage efficiently for a thousand years. Europeans discovered the importance of public sanitation a hundred years ago. The failure to provide a system that would meet the needs of a growing and more stationary population must lie largely with those who have the resources and who have been encouraging northern natives to become less nomadic.

Schools, because they are the most widely shared and commonly experienced institution in North America, are where racism and discrimination are most commonly experienced. The

Indian child faces a cruel dilemma every day he goes to school. Failure to continue in school may mean that he continues the poverty and deprivation that have been forced on his parents no matter how hard-working and diligent they are. Continuing in school means creating a barrier between himself and his people. The barrier is often built of isolation for much or all of the academic year while he travels to a larger centre. Educators have pointed out for years that there is no economy in building larger schools; governments continue to build them. Even if the child stays at home, too much of the curriculum is unrelated to any rural life; the social studies and literature he must learn are degrading and dishonest. Most important of all, the entire structure and routine of the school represent a foreign way of life that acknowledges neither his culture nor the land from which it sprang.

The Hawthorne-Tremblay Survey found that 94 per cent of native children fail to continue school past the compulsory minimum age. The Commons Committee on Indian Affairs found in its report of June 30, 1971, that the transfer of 65 per cent of Indian school enrolment to the provinces from church-run schools had not provided a significant improvement in the amount of education received. The Department of Indian Affairs tells the taxpayers it spent $300 million in the same year on Indian education. The other taxpayers are cheated almost as thoroughly as the Indian child and his parents. We have seen already how much Indian involvement there is in the use of those funds.

It is not the teachers who have daily contact with the children who maintain the racial attitudes that characterize Canadian education. Perhaps some do, but many of them have joined hands with local Indian groups, to fight the worst aspects of the system.

Studies of textbooks in Manitoba and Ontario have shown that none of those approved for current use in either province gave a fair or accurate picture of Indian life. It is true that the ministers are refusing to approve new books that are not somewhat improved. How much money is being spent on developing new and more useful learning aids while the ones in use wear out?

Should an Indian child be learning Indian history and culture from a book written by a European, in a provincial school, under a good-hearted but non-Indian teacher?

Many children learn the *Volga Boat Song*, sung by the boatmen of ancient Russia as they pulled the boats along the Volga River. It is good to know the songs of many people. Now, suppose that you were going to school a mile from that river, and the school in which you were learning that song prevented you from going to the river from which the song was born. Then you would be an Indian child going to an integrated school in Canada.

If a white teacher in a white school with Indian children in attendance agrees to teach the corn dance, that may be a very kindly gesture on her part. But the corn dance is, for certain eastern Indians, one of the highest forms of thanksgiving to the Creator, because it is the corn He has given them that will keep them alive in the winter. It is a song that needs to be sung in or near the fields where the corn has been growing. It is not a song to be sung by children seated behind desks placed row on row so that they look like the poppies growing in Flanders' Field.

It is true that the Mass has been put to rock music. But that was done by Catholics who believe they are renewing and strengthening their own tradition.

A song can symbolize two different approaches to learning, but the matter goes deeper. Hostile educators have told us that culture should be taught in the homes or in Indian equivalents to Sunday schools. Such a misunderstanding of culture explains the system it maintains.

The culture of Indian people is every inch of our land and every event of our history. European culture is not restricted to the teaching of history classes and the memorizing of poems. It is taught in everything for which the school stands, everything it does. For example, much of mathematics was discovered by non-Europeans. It is not the content of the course but the manner in which it is taught that makes it distinctly European today.

The Canadian school systems serve the urban middle-class community extremely well. They should. It is the urban middle class who have designed them for the use and benefit of their children. The experience of the school is continuous with the experience of the home for many of those children. It is true that more and more children from the middle class are expressing dissatisfaction at the failure of the school to meet their needs. The danger, from our point of view, is that the schools will change in a direction that meets their needs without diversifying to give equal consideration to the needs that we have. So long as the schools are run by boards on which we have only token representation, if any, that is not so much a danger as an inevitability.

When Canadian statistics are lined up with ones from UNESCO, Canada ranks with Bulgaria, Czechoslovakia, Iran, Portugal, Romania, Thailand, and Turkey in the numbers of students graduating from secondary schools. Indians in Canada compare to Botswana and Guatemala, below the averages for Africa and Latin America in general. The only possible explanations for this that do not point to the need for a school system under the direction of the Indian community are too racist to be worthy of discussion.

It is not only politicians and bureaucrats who perpetuate a colonial education system. One reason for the lack of new materials—in addition to the lack of funds, and the refusal to allow knowledgeable Indian people who lack a degree to play a significant role—is the thinking of those whose training should prepare them to provide those materials.

Anthropologists have often been the tools of colonialism in North America, as in the Third World, but some members of that profession have claimed that there is no longer any danger because "colonialism has largely ended." Tom Gladwin, at the University of Hawaii, wrote an article replying to his colleagues who think in these terms that gives eloquent voice to what many Indian leaders have been saying:

> ... the new colonialism of economic penetration is if anything, more pervasive, probably more destructive, and is unwittingly served by far more anthropologists than the old. The moral issues of anthropology have not really changed ... ; they have just become more subtle.
>
> I see a significant parallel between the way [modernization] is being used, and the way in which a few years ago [the] concept of "the culture of poverty" distorted the lives ... of people less powerful than we.... By focussing on the lives of poor people, [it] legitimized an assumption that poverty was somehow caused by the poor people themselves, and therefore could be corrected without changing the larger, more powerful sectors of the society. This assumption unquestionably contributed to the failure of the "war on poverty."

To be modern comes out as somehow better than being traditional, and in any event, is inevitable. It is not inevitable.... As long as we who have the goodies pose our modern way as the only alternative to traditional backwardness, it is inevitable that modernization will have great positive appeal. The goodies include not only the consumer goods which soon make people the vassals of the industrial nations, but also better health, communications and other things no responsible leader would reject. Anthropological [scholars] seem often to say that these benefits can only be obtained at the price of accepting the rest of the modernizing package, that is, the dominant Western culture.

Yet there are other ways to achieve valued social goals.... Franz Fanon has written eloquently on the process whereby native elites perpetuate the colonial relationship in new ways and while paying lip service to tradition, ridicule manifestations of any new uniquely national culture.[40]

There is so much evidence in North American Indian relations both of "the new colonialism of economic penetration" and the racial bias that sees modern as better than traditional (and also as inevitable) and of the harm it does that those scholars who perpetuate the myths can hardly be called scientists. Yet it is they who lay the foundation for what is taught to our children—Indian and non-Indian children alike. Equality.

There are presently several economic penetrations into Indian land which have been initiated within the last four years and will, according to all the best information available, have as disastrous effects upon the people in the lands immediately affected as any Indian war of the nineteenth century. The James Bay Development Project, the Mackenzie Valley highway and pipeline, the strip mining of Black Mesa, the damming of South Indian Lake in Manitoba, all involve the seizure of lands from which Indian societies presently make a living for the purpose of satisfying the insatiable demand for power in the United States. All of these projects not only destroy a native economy in the name of somebody else's progress, they threaten to upset and distort entire ecological systems about which so little is known that the outcome cannot be reasonably predicted.

No major project, in even the most under-developed country, has ever been undertaken with so little study into the likely consequences as has been given to the James Bay Project. The first ecological study of that region was commissioned by the Indians of Quebec Association in the summer of 1972, a year after the National Assembly of Quebec passed Bill 50 authorizing the project. The information that should have been gathered through a public enquiry and through regular government channels is now being gathered through the cumbersome and awkward process of calling witnesses before a court on a motion for a temporary injunction to halt the construction now in progress.

When the single study that has been done on the economic effects of oil exploration on the people of Banks' Island was published, the Minister of Indian Affairs and Northern Development denounced the author as stupid, but was unwilling to have the report, a departmental publication, sent to a Parliamentary Committee for public discussion.

When the minister announced that work was beginning on the Mackenzie Valley highway, even the oil companies made public replies that their research was less than half completed. Knowledge of the area was so incomplete that uncertainty was expressed about whether there was an adequate supply of gravel to pour a roadbed, without ripping up every river bed near the route of the highway.

On Black Mesa the only pretence at a concern for either the Hopi and Navajo Peoples, to whom the land rightfully belongs, or for the environment are royalties at rates far below what any American state or private business concern would accept and a meaningless promise to restore the land to its original condition. Meaningless, because Black Mesa is sacred, the way Rome and Jerusalem are sacred to other people who would perhaps have strong feelings about strip mining under a Basilica, or an oil rig in St. Peter's Square.

Meaningless, because the demand for the Black Mesa coal and the Four Corners' power stations has been created as a direct result of the environment in California on the other side of the mountains, and an unwillingness on the part of the people in Los Angeles to consider why their air is unbreathable. State and local governments in California have prohibited such polluting forms of power production in their own territory but are quite willing to visit the same destruction on other people's heads—people who feel the natural beauty of their desert air, and who have fought

194

successfully for the past century to maintain the land in the state that they have always known it. If theirs is the only air in that corner of the continent that is far below a dangerous pollution level, it is because they have worked hard to keep it that way.

The James Bay Project bears the same relationship to southern Quebec and New York State. Although Premier Bourassa has denied that there are any firm contracts to sell northern power to New York State, he has also said that there are guaranteed markets for doubling the power production in a province where there is little reason to anticipate a similar increase in industrial production or population. New Yorkers mindful of their own ecological crisis have taken to the air waves proclaiming that James Bay will be their salvation.

Are we to die that they may be saved? Even if New Yorkers were as concerned for our environment as for their own immediate backyard it would be impossible for them to have any honest response to the situation with the information they are being given.

On March 12, 1972, Premier Robert Bourassa was heard to say to a CBC radio audience, "the corporation itself is presently making studies in conjunction with the Indians of the region as to their future and the way in which they could profit the most *from the project*."[41]

Whether the project was the way in which they could profit the most from the land was not something the government was prepared to negotiate. Further, Quebec in 1972, like the federal government in the 1920's, was setting some strict limits about the framework in which the negotiations would take place. On the same radio program Pierre Nadeau, then president of the James Bay Development Corporation, expressed strong resentment that the Indian people wanted to work through the duly elected representatives and the political structure we had worked so hard to create.

"We've tried to gather the chiefs of the different bands, as they call them up there," he said, without comprehending that "bands" are legally constituted bodies under federal law, ". . . and unfortunately the Association des Indiens du Quebec created some difficulties for us. They seem to oppose the fact that we want to inform the Indians directly without going through them."

When the representatives of the James Bay Development Cor-

Are we to die that they may be saved?

poration did try to meet with Indian people directly and distribute a pamphlet on the project, the people burned the pamphlet saying that if it was in Cree it was a dialect that was foreign to them.

Having refused to work through the lawful representatives of the people, Nadeau complained in the same statement, "You've got to establish some sort of a dialogue which has been impossible so far."

The chiefs of the area were already declaring that efforts at negotiation had broken down and were preparing for a court action declaring the work of the company unconstitutional, while Premier Bourassa was telling southern audiences he was still hopeful there would not be any major problems.

Respect for legal processes on the part of government officials in Canada still remains a one-way street.

These are not a series of scattered local events in which the federal governments of Canada and the United States have no particular interest, and can excuse themselves out of respect for local autonomy.

In the Northwest Territories where the Mackenzie complex will be built, the federal government is the local authority. It is also the major shareholder in Panarctic Oil, the company carrying on the exploration. The Minister of Indian Affairs promises that the entire project will be carried out in a way that will maximize the benefits for the Indian and Inuit peoples. The Minister of Northern Development sees that the vested interests of the oil companies and related industries are satisfied to concentrate their capital on a dubious project. The minister is one man with two bodies.

In the United States there is a similar arrangement without the formal partnership between private enterprise and government. The Bureau of Mines is the sales branch of the Interior Department; the Bureau of Indian Affairs is seen as the liability.

The role of the federal government has largely been played down in the James Bay Project as public attention has been focused on the provincial government, its development corporation, and the amounts of money that might be lent, spent, made, and lost. Yet the whole project would be impossible without the blessing of the federal cabinet.

The federal government has a constitutional responsibility for

"Indians and lands reserved for Indians," for navigable waterways, for migratory birds, and for airports. Any one of these interests would justify an active role, at least at the level of granting or withholding licence on different aspects of the project.

According to records that the government was not anxious to release, its own legal advisors had indicated that there was a clear responsibility on the federal Crown to protect the interests of the Indian people, and of the environment. This responsibility derives not only from the fundamental powers of the federal government, but from the whole manner in which the lands of northern Quebec were acquired.

When the Hudson's Bay Company sold these lands to Canada in 1871 for 300,000 pounds the order-in-council completing the transfer specified that Canada would assume the obligation to extinguish all aboriginal claims. When the lands were granted by Canada to Quebec, part in 1871 and the rest in 1912, at the same time that the other half of James Bay was given to Ontario, it was clearly set out that Quebec would make no use of the land until it had negotiated a treaty with the Indian peoples of the area. No province has ever been allowed to enter into a treaty of its own accord, and in international affairs Canada has intervened to prevent Quebec from attempting to exercise too strong a position on her own. The province could only negotiate a treaty as an agent of the federal government. The unlawful use of the land without a treaty being made is an offence by Canada no less than by Quebec, if one were to judge governments by a desire for law and order.

The federal cabinet, at one point, took the position that Quebec must respect the rights of the Indian people and be bound by her own agreements of 1912. Quebec refused. Canada compromised. The federal government demanded that Quebec seek licensing approval from the appropriate federal agencies. Quebec refused. Canada capitulated.

When the Indians of Quebec Association and the Inuit Association of northern Quebec decided to go to court to seek a temporary injunction, the federal government was repeatedly asked to intervene. Mr. Chrétien first tried to minimize the seriousness of the situation and to suggest that everything could be worked out through a cordial and happy three-way dialogue.

When Quebec found that the capital financing available was not unlimited, and decided to proceed immediately with only one phase of the project, Mr. Chrétien told the House of Commons, "I am happy to see now that because the Quebec government has decided to start working projects solely on the Grand-Rivière region only one third of the Indians involved will be affected." His commitment was not to help the Indian people determine their own destiny but to "help them benefit to the maximum from the development of the James Bay area."[42]

He refused to have the federal government represented at the court hearings for a temporary injunction to halt the project. The injunction was sought to allow time for a trial to determine whether the province of Quebec has the power to act independently to create such a project. Whatever powers do not lie with the province must be federal powers. That is the way the game works in Canada.

An intervention on behalf of the federal government's own interests would be "paternalistic" according to the Chrétien doctrine of equality. Did Duncan Scott and Mackenzie King in all their days ever find such a thin pretext for doing nothing? There is no doubt that the native people who brought the petition would want to be represented independently by their own legal counsel whether or not there was a federal presence. But how would it detract from our right to be independently represented at the court if the federal government undertook to fulfil its constitutional obligations.

There is a growing suspicion that the Nadeau philosophy—"5,000 of them and 5,000,000 of us"—has become the foundation of the new federalism. A few Cree and Inuit people can easily, if not happily, be sacrificed for the sake of peace between the "two founding races" of this great empire.

Mr. Trudeau has long publicly abhorred any recognition of special status either for Quebec or for Indian people. Caught in the squeeze between the weak and the mighty, he moves to the centre of power, yielding to every demand that Quebec might make while continuing to tell the people of Canada that his position has not changed.

When Quebec lets out the word that the northern rivers can be harnessed for two billion dollars, have they included the cost of welfare for the people whose livelihood will be lost, of medical care for the disease that will be spread, of law enforcement and prisons as the crime rate soars among people who have never before needed police power to help them keep the peace? When all these costs are included is this really the least expensive way to produce power?

Serious doubts have also been raised as to whether this is a very good way to produce electricity even if there were a clear title to the land and construction would not wreak havoc on the environment. Questions have been raised about the capacity of these rivers to produce consistently a fraction of the power that has been estimated. I leave such questions to those who make a business of measuring such matters.

It is clear that while this project may save the political careers of both Mr. Bourassa and Mr. Trudeau, it will not provide the 100,000 jobs that have been promised, and the last people who will get the jobs that are produced will be Indian and Inuit people.

There have been no training programs that will give native people the skills necessary to do any but the most menial jobs. Not that we are anxious to participate in our own destruction, but the number of jobs would be some indication about the seriousness of the promise that we are to share in the new wealth. Construction jobs will only last so long as the project is being built. How many carpenters, plumbers, graders, electricians, foremen, and managers will be needed to control a fully completed hydro-electric dam and generator?

The most accurate estimate available for the Mackenzie Valley pipeline is that on completion it will employ one hundred and fifty people in operation and maintenance. If all those jobs went to native people from the Northwest Territories it would not seriously affect the total employment picture in that territory.

Quebec has not even made an undertaking that either jobs or training will be given to northern people rather than importing people from the south who will expect "hardship" money for living in luxury houses that will be built on our land. And if the main aim of the project is to help Mr. Bourassa to fulfil his promise of 100,000 jobs for the unemployed in Quebec's own territory, he will not be able to make such an undertaking to the northern natives.

Perhaps it was mere coincidence that after the federal government had declared that the *Indian Policy* of June 1969 would not be official policy for the present, it proceeded to implement something indistinguishable from that statement in both the Northwest Territories and northern Quebec.

Within the last two years the government of the Northwest Territories has assumed virtually all the responsibilities for Indian people that elsewhere come under the Department of Indian Affairs. Settlement councils have been created to serve local needs and compete for the authority that properly belongs with the band councils. When the commissioner came to Ottawa to receive a decoration from the Governor-General, he stopped by the Canadian Club in Toronto to describe our culture to his fellow citizens. In his address to the club, he stated:

> But really, when you talk about retaining culture, what do you mean? Do you mean running behind a smelly old dog team, or do you mean living in an igloo, or paddling around in a kayak? Those are really only for amenities and I assure you that the people in the Canadian Arctic have the same ambitions as their fellow Canadians in the South. But what we are attempting to do in the way of culture is to let them decide how much of their culture they wish to retain, not us impose it from outside.[43]

Quebec has been attempting to set up an administration parallel to the federal government's in northern Quebec for all aspects of Indian life. In some areas the two governments have set up joint liaison officers to facilitate the transfer of responsibility. Quebec has been trying to train French-speaking teachers to become fluent in the Inuit and Cree languages before exposing them to the people. With no one to talk to, none of them has mastered the language well enough to carry on a conversation. The second language of the northern peoples has been English since they first had contact with Europeans. Now Quebec wants them to assimilate into a culture that refused to feed them in the famine years of the thirties and went to the Supreme Court to prove they were not a provincial responsibility, and that today still refers to us as "sauvages."

The first indication that the government seriously intended to shelve the White Paper Policy came in a leak of cabinet documents in the summer of 1972. One of the leaked documents was a memorandum to cabinet from the Minister of Indian Affairs and Northern Development.

> If the Government had shown willingness to entertain Indian concepts of aboriginal rights and had in place a cultural program to strengthen and reinforce Indian pride in self their attitude to the proposals might have been different and probably much more favourable. [44]

Translated from federalese that sentence should probably read that if the policy had been different we would probably have had a different response to the different policy than we had to the one that was, in fact, brought down.

Elsewhere in the same memorandum, the hope is expressed that the demand for special status will wither away with improved living conditions. If we all get a sufficient taste of the "good life" we will unanimously decide to stop being Indians. I predict that just the opposite will happen. Every improvement in our living conditions will free our people from physical bonds and allow them to demonstrate more confidently the strength of our culture. There is nothing incompatible between "the good life" fairly distributed among all our people, and an increasing sense of Indian identity. If the government believes they can threaten our culture by allowing us access to the basic physical necessities, I challenge them to try it.

Although the minister himself concedes that none of his programs has been more than mildly successful, he rationalizes the planning process by talking about the rising expectations. He absolves his office of any need to reconsider its position and is, inevitably, led to opt for reassurances to all concerned with a promise of a further review in a few years. In the meantime he suggests two small changes. First, that all programs relating to Indians from other federal departments and agencies come under his supervision, thus changing the pattern in which Indian organizations and band councils were learning to negotiate with the departments normally responsible for each service. Rather than going to Central Mortgage and Housing Corporation for housing programs, National Health and Welfare for medical programs, and so forth, we will now revert to the policy prevailing from 1880 to

202

1969. Second, it suggests that nothing be done, in a time which coincidentally was an election year, that could give rise to criticisms that could not be brushed off as a re-hash of old grievances.

The distinction between old grievances and new can only arise when attention is focused on each individual Indian situation, and each proposal, project, scheme, or contract for its solution as though they were isolated happenings and not part of some larger and longer-term pattern of events. It is not necessary that the authorities who continue to undermine our tomorrows deliberately plan the long-term pattern. They have only to refuse to listen to those who witness it every day of their lives. Although the form, detail, and personalities have changed over the years, the goal of the Indian peoples of Canada has remained constant throughout my lifetime and, I believe, throughout the longer years since colonization first touched us.

Our goal has never been any different from the goal of the English-speaking people of Upper Canada and the French-speaking people of Lower Canada in the early part of the last century: responsible government for the purpose of Home Rule within the framework of a partnership with our neighbours that encourages cooperation but does not foster the domination of the weak over the strong, and that allows each people to control its own resources within that partnership.

We have not made a national pastime of grieving or complaining. We have not made a national sport of stating problems that have no solutions. We have acted in the firm belief of our own humanity that our needs are as incapable of solution by external magic or outside domination as any other people's; and yet as capable of solution by our own efforts, given the proper resources, as the needs of any other segment of humanity. If we have spoken harshly it has not been to avoid the necessity of a realistic assessment of our goals, needs, and wants. We have made that assessment with care and diligence. It has given us strength which has helped us to endure. We have accepted with gratitude whatever has seemed likely to move us any little distance toward those goals, and have publicly declared our gratitude both to our Creator and to our fellow men.

Those goals have strong roots in both our own past and in some of our earliest contacts with Europeans. So many projects and proposals of Canadian governments have proven to be hollow shams, not because they were wrong in their diagnosis of isolated ills. Very often those diagnoses have been entirely correct. There has been and continues to be a need for education, for self-government, for community development. If each of these programs had been fully implemented and each had proven not to be the "ultimate solution," we could still point to a continuous line of progress through the past century. The tragedy has been that each program has been a bridge in the desert with no thought given to the construction of approaches, and no consideration of the path that the travellers choose to follow. The desire for uniformity, paper economy, and political convenience has meant that, even when the choice of medicine has been correct, we have been both under-prescribed and over-prescribed.

The Economic Development Loan Fund, which was introduced following the White Paper Policy, gave a reassuring answer to any bureaucratic fears that the traditions of Indian Affairs might seriously be altered.[45]

Real economic development is undoubtedly the most widely shared need of the Indian community. Poverty has been a common bond for us. Many of the programs that have been offered in the past become meaningful only when they have a material base. Education at any level is only possible when the economic potential of the community is being developed. Otherwise, the learning of the individual is either wasted or drives him away from the community to which he should be contributing. Self-government, even on its grandest level, without an economic base simply creates the economic colonialism we are witnessing throughout much of Asia and Africa today. We have already seen the hollowness of community development when it is not in partnership with economic development.

There are as many different kinds of economic development as there are different kinds of education. Once again, the question arose, "Is this economic development to solve our problems as Indian people? Or is it economic development to solve Ottawa's Indian Problem?" There was no doubt that economic development was an essential part of any prescription. The question was how great a financial commitment would be made to support our labour, and under what terms the funds would be prescribed.

The impact of the Economic Development Fund, or any other proposal for the economic development of Indian communities, must be measured primarily by the jobs they create. The average level of unemployment for Indian people across Canada on a year-round basis is 56 per cent. When the Canadian national average rose to 7.1 per cent it became a major issue in a federal election. Many commentators saw the level of unemployment and related issues, such as the uses of the unemployment insurance fund, as responsible for the loss of the clear majority the Liberal government enjoyed in the previous Parliament.

The 56 per cent of Indian people who are unemployed are not included within the statistics for Canada as a whole. (At least the Department of Labour recognizes our unique status.) And I do not know of one candidate—unless it was Wally Firth, the non-status Indian who was elected from the Northwest Territories—who made that fact a major part of his campaign oratory.

The government's own studies—the Hawthorne-Tremblay Survey—had shown that it would be necessary to put one and a half billion dollars into the economic development of Indian communities across Canada to create the industries that could provide employment and end the poverty that prevented the realization of many other goals. So we were told we would get fifty million dollars, a thirtieth part of the most realistic assessment that had been made. Still, with a thirtieth we might make a start. Whatever faults they may have, dollars, unlike principles, are at least negotiable.

When fifty million dollars turned out to mean ten million a year for five years, a thirtieth part became 1/150 part. Well, we've been down so long that even that looks pretty good.

Until you see that in the first year of operation, 1970-71, eight of the ten million went for civil servants' salaries, desks, stationary, and travel expenses. What was really made available to Indian people was $2.2 million. In the second year $10 million went to the civil servants and $3.9 million to the Indian communities across Canada. This economic development program promised a full reproduction of all the benefits that land surrenders had brought us in the last century. Northern Indian and Inuit peoples have an opportunity to enjoy both programs at the same time.

If even these funds had been given to us under terms that are generally considered workable when non-Indian people seek development aid, they might have brought some benefit to our people. The Canadian International Development Agency (CIDA), the economic development fund of Canada's External Affairs Department, gives fifty-year loans, free of interest, with an additional ten years to repay if needed. Its commercial loans are for thirty years at 3 per cent interest. Indian Affairs' Economic Development Fund offers us loans at 8.5 per cent for fifteen years.

The Department of Regional Economic Expansion (DREE) is supposed to do for the less-developed regions of Canada what the Economic Development Fund (EDF) does for Indian reserves. Prince Edward Island, with a population less than half the size of the Indian population of Canada (110,000 compared to 250,000) receives $725 million, which works out to $6,500 per Islander. I have seen P.E.I. There is no doubt they need that much to get off the ground. A smaller figure would leave them as immobile as an airplane whose maker could not afford wings.

Where does that leave us with a loan fund offering an average of $200 per person?

We are expected to create economic development without any of the things that CIDA, DREE, or the United Nations consider essential to real economic change: human resource development; a program to train and upgrade our manpower potential; proper educational facilities fashioned to meet local needs; improved community services such as water, roads, sewerage, hydro; total economic and social planning at the local level that will encourage people to stay in the area so that their technical and leadership skills will be there to be used.

These are the ingredients that are left out to arrive at the difference between $6,500 and $200. If some of these programs exist they are in a corner of the Department's programming far removed from the Economic Development Fund. The left hand has never come in contact with the right hand.

This program does not put money into the hands of any Indian who could not more easily obtain credit from a private lending institution—a bank. In fact, Indians who have created businesses, on or off the reserve, more often than not have obtained their funding from private sources. The fund is geared more to the exploitation of our natural resources by outside interests than to the development of our human resources under local management. It imposes an unnecessary dilemma between maintaining the security of our reserved lands or earning a few dollars.

After the 1972 election Mr. Chrétien declared that his government's "policies would not change; only our methods." The Economic Development Fund proclaims that its objective is "to facilitate full responsibility by Indian people for control of their economic destiny." That is a dream we all share. Like other policies, it is experienced only through the method in which it is offered and administered. It is another program that, on examination, proves only to have the ingredients for a nightmare, when it was promised to be the fulfilment of our dream. A change of method is a change of policy.

The unwillingness of the federal government seriously to reconsider the fundamental philosophy of the 1969 White Paper is nowhere better demonstrated than in the "Report on the Indian Loan Fund and Indian Economic Emancipation" which they commissioned from a private consultant, P.C. Laroque, and which he delivered to the Department in 1972.

Rather than developing an enlightened vehicle for social and economic development of the Indian people in tune with the Indian Act and with aboriginal and treaty rights, which could have gained the support and advocacy of Indian organizations all across the country, the terms of reference required Mr. Laroque "to provide . . . a proposal for an Indian controlled Loan Corporation, bearing in mind that this proposal must be within the guidelines established by Cabinet for the Indian Economic Development Fund." We have already seen how that fund fails to provide a financial service to Indian reserve communities that in any way resembles the conditions available to other peoples under comparable programs.

The authors use their status as government consultants to absolve themselves of moral responsibility to the Indian community, and our expressed goals and aspirations. The Laroque Report states that:

It is of course not our responsibility to negotiate the price which must be paid in enabling a permanent emancipation to take place but, to state [it] in another way, it is our mandate to try to suggest the kind of instrument that could best assist in sustaining this trust.

Nobody in the position of buying a service could be very responsible if he failed to consider the price he would have to pay. That is precisely the dilemma that Indian leaders have been trying to articulate for the last three generations.

A document such as the Laroque Report could have been useful and, prepared within a proper frame of reference, could be what the Indian community desperately needs if it is to develop a nationwide economic perspective on itself. Such a frame of reference is not hard to arrive at: it must assume the negotiation and settlement of all aboriginal and treaty rights; it must take its primary mandate from the Indian Act and use the full powers of that Act to resolve the contemporary concerns and apparent cultural-economic conflicts of the Indian community in Canada; the type and magnitude of the socio-economic needs must be considered before any program can be developed to make more effective use of the existing Economic Development Fund.

The keystone of the Report is the creation of a trust company with capital from the EDF and a board of directors composed of Indian people, and civil servants to represent the interest of EDF and the Crown. It would be hard to deny that there are advantages in channelling Indian savings through our own financial institutions, thus "assuring the Indian communities of the maximum use of their own funds by recirculation of the deposits" if there were a significant amount of money now in the hands of Indian people that they could transfer from present savings accounts to accounts in our own trust company.

Mr. Laroque admits that loans from trust companies are "usually restricted to those borrowers who are in a position to provide a high degree of security." Industrial, commercial, and residential loans, in their program, would only be obtained through first mortgages.

Indian people do not hold the legal title to their land, which would allow mortgaging or other demonstrations of security. The Indian Act states that the lands that are now reserved for us are held in trust by the Minister, "for the use and benefit of the Indian people." The White Paper proposal to create individual allot-

208

ments held in "fee simple"—the way in which land is held by non-Indian owners of land in Canada—provoked probably more opposition than any other specific proposal in that statement. Some Indian spokesmen have argued for a transfer of collective title from the Crown to some collective Indian body, most often the band. Nobody within the Indian community has sanctioned the idea that an individual Indian should be able to sell his allotment within an Indian reserve to a non-Indian. It is the very thing we have been trying to avoid. Mortgaging of the kind proposed by Mr. Laroque could only be done by repealing the very sections of the Indian Act we have most consistently sought to strengthen.

According to the Laroque Report, the trust company is to be used as a vehicle to "assist in the winding-up in the economic area of the Department of Indian Affairs." The argument for giving first priority to economic development has always been that people cannot become self-sufficient in any other respect until effective economic development has taken root.

Mr. Laroque believes, "it naturally follows that Indians should also constitute a majority of the Company's staff. . . . However this will generally not be immediately possible, at least at the management level." It is too easy to imagine the task force that will be set up thirty years from now to determine if the shareholders of the Indian Trust Company are yet ready to staff their own company from among their own members "at least at the management level."

Laroque and friends propose to provide for the emancipation of the Indian people with a loan from the government of $5.6 million for a period of thirty years, with five years additional grace, and a grant of no more than a million dollars. Its subsidiary loan corporation for Manitoba will "require no more than $175,000 of the $1 million proposed grant allocation." While the trust company is to be owned by the Indian people, all of whom would automatically be shareholders, the by-laws, lifted almost directly and with only minor amendments from the Canada Trust Company Act, would levy the standard rates for the management of band funds, the administration of estates, and real estate commissions. The government, in turn, will charge 50 per cent on the profits of the trust company. This is a plan to provide for "permanent and unalterable" Indian ownership and management.

Emancipation? Industrial training!

It is hardly surprising that the government has failed to excite the imagination of any spokesman elected to a position of responsibility within the Indian community by the release of the Laroque Report. So Indian Affairs has followed its own traditional, ingrown approach to democratic decision-making. When elected Indian leaders do not respond to government programs, the Department sets out to find or, if necessary, to create new leaders.

The Department has set up a task force that is presently going across Canada seeking out those few Indian people who have achieved some measure of economic success, and who are not involved in the structure of Indian political organizations, to attempt to sell them on a program in which they can play an active leadership role and which may also help their business concerns to find new capital.

The possibility that the framework given to Laroque, the same framework that dictated the terms of the 1969 White Paper, may be in error when judged by our reality is still not seriously entertained by any senior member of the Department. The possibility that democratic decision-making begins with a respect for the spokesmen elected by the people has not yet been applied by the government of Canada in their dealing with us.

One other major development since the White Paper Policy has been the birth of the National Indian Brotherhood as a federation of the provincial and territorial Indian organizations and the rapid growth of many of our member organizations. It would be unfair as well as pretentious, and perhaps premature, for me, having presided over the Brotherhood for more than half its short life, to assess the effectiveness with which we have worked. If discussion does not deserve another writer, it would at least require another volume.

For many of us, the founding and survival of the National Brotherhood was itself the fulfilment of a lifelong dream. The National Brotherhood has been the chief result of the growing trust and friendship, knowledge and understanding of local leaders from every corner of Canada. Whatever success it has had has been the result of a growing consciousness of our common bonds, which transcend both tribal and provincial boundaries while lending strength to the real and valid concerns of each region and tradition. We have by no means achieved the perfect model of cooperative federalism. Yet we share that dream with non-Indian North Americans as the one way in which such vast territories can fairly serve their collective and common needs.

It befits our own tradition of giving and sharing to develop that model. It has taken the Indian nations several centuries to decline to the low point of our spiritual and economic histories. If, in the five years of its existence, the National Brotherhood has moved only a few steps in an upward direction, we have at least laid the foundation, and perhaps helped to change the course of history for our people.

Yet there is a very real danger that our national and provincial organizations will become caught up in the same kind of dilemma that faces each reserve when it tries to develop an economic development program. Will we achieve a substantial control of our destiny for future generations? Or will we allow the funding that has made possible some of the real growth of Indian organizations to become a program of pacification for the younger generations of leaders?

Government spokesmen have expressed a strong desire to take credit for the success of Indian organizations because they have made possible the largest part of our funding. It would be easier to extend thanks if the demand for gratitude did not also obscure the fact that Indian organizations without funding did succeed in functioning for many lifetimes, at least to the extent of helping our people to survive. The value of the dollars we are receiving now should be measured by how much we raise our people above a standard of mere survival.

Three million dollars, for instance, can seem like a fairly impressive sum to a trapper, craftsman, or labourer whose family income is less than three thousand dollars. When the three million dollars is divided among ten provincial bodies, two territorial groups, and a national federation, we begin to find that it has provided for the cost of offices, and staff who might begin to develop programs and policies, but it has not really begun to cover the cost of a communications network that would make those staff workers readily accessible to every local Indian community. A field or communications worker program was designed that allowed one worker for every six thousand Indian people in Canada. These communications workers are supposed to help local communities to become aware of the services available to them from provincial organizations, government departments, and private agencies. Ideally, they could become the successors to the community development concept. No consideration was given to the different needs of small reserves with heavy concentrations of population. The figure of one to six thousand was arrived at without consultation with either the National Brotherhood or any provincial body. It is difficult to know what figures for the general population would bear a fair comparison. Urban people have such ready access to the centres of authority and to the media that no single figure would bear direct translation. We do know that the Canadian Bankers' Association proudly announced that there is one bank manager for every three thousand Canadians.

We also know that the total budget for Indian organizations represents a little less than three-quarters of one per cent of the money voted by Parliament for programs specifically for Indian people. And in the $300 million education budget alone there is a one per cent participation by the education committees of the communities in which that money is supposedly being spent.

We know that Indian organizations at every level have a lot to learn about making efficient use of scarce resources. We do not think those lessons are best learnt at the knee of the Canadian civil service. When the total staff employed by 2,300 band councils, twelve provincial and territorial associations, and a national brotherhood are stacked together, it can sound impressive. It is clearly not a number that has in any way improved the employment picture of the Indian community in Canada: 80 per cent unemployed in the winter, 56 per cent in the summer. I suspect that if none of the organizations had ever been formed, almost every person who is now on staff would have gotten a job some other place.

When a figure like three million dollars is stacked up against the figures of federal and provincial budgets, it can begin to seem pretty small. Three million dollars is one-half the cost estimated for the operation of the Senate of Canada in 1972-73, and one-ninth the cost of the House of Commons, in addition to the Divine Guidance for which they ask at the beginning of each session, when the Governor-General tells them they will be asked "to appropriate funds required to carry out the services and payments authorized by Parliament" for the rest of the country. It seems that we are still playing the game of the tortoise and the hare.

The danger that we face is that these funds will be enough to satisfy the appetites of those who benefit from the employment they provide, without being enough to build a foundation on which our people can realize our own potential for self-sufficiency. There is also the very real danger, which has already been experienced, that the government will reserve the right to decide which Indian organization represents the true sentiments of the Indian people. Economy-minded governments have found it convenient to fund competing organizations rather than have the local communities decide who is to represent them. Can you imagine both Quebec and Newfoundland receiving federal grants for the people of Labrador because both claim the territory?

There is also the danger of success, expressed in Mr. Chrétien's leaked memorandum as a hope, that our belief in a status that reflects our identity will wither away as our living conditions improve. We accept that challenge and offer his government another.

Mr. Trudeau has invited us to forget the past. We invite him to do the same and to allow us to develop our own rightful share in our land in the same way that his government has allowed the "two founding races" to enjoy their shares.

The Fourth World gives no more special status to the Indian peoples of Canada than is enjoyed by those who are already masters in their own house.

9

The Fourth World

THE FOURTH WORLD has always been here in North America. Since the beginning of European domination its branches, one by one, have been denied the light of day. Its fruit has been withered and stunted. Yet the tree did not die. Our victory begins with the knowledge that we have survived.

The celebration of the Fourth World, its real test of strength, and its capacity to endure, lies more with our grandchildren than with our ancestors. It is they who must cultivate the tree as a whole and honour the unique qualities of each root and branch.

Our grandfathers faced and endured the physical violence of wars, famine, and disease. They survived. We endured the social violence of legal disabilities and administrative oppression. We survived. Now there is the possibility that our grandchildren may yet face the danger of material success. They shall survive. Our past history and our faith in the future are united. We are neither the beginning nor the end.

The hope that we who could not be starved into submission may yet be assimilated by drowning in a sea of plenty ignores not only our own history but the present condition of the very peoples whose leaders harbour such hopes. Today in North America so many young people, whose own ancestors fled the plagues, famines, and wars of other continents, are trying to forsake the world they are in and find a world that will fulfil the promise of peace that they inherited from their grandfathers. Those who believe our values and culture have been preserved only through their own oppression should stop and reconsider. Do they think that if they stop the oppression we will stop being our parents' children?

Every Englishman knowledgeable of his own history knows that his countrymen have made their constitution grow and adapt to changing needs while the institutions that were the parts of their body politic, and the values that were their lifeblood and common bonds, endured. Such ancient institutions as the monarchy and Parliament were given major surgery rather than be allowed to die as happened elsewhere. Every schoolboy in the English-speaking world is taught not only to observe this pattern of growth and change but to take such pride in it that if he is not an Englishman by birth he becomes one by adoption.

At first the schoolboy may be disturbed to learn that neither the constitution of Great Britain nor of Canada has ever been codified, written down in a single document, from which all the majestic powers of his nation flow. He finds, for instance, that there is nothing in the British North America Act to describe, or even require that there be, an office of the prime minister. He finds that the provisions describing the Canadian Parliament begin by saying, "Canada shall have a Parliament similar in form to that of Great Britain." Yet there is no single British charter to say just what that will be.

If he continues his studies, he finds that independence has brought some important differences in form. "Similar in form" is only a point of departure from which the new generation could grow and take its strength in new soil, a different climate, and a new population. If the schoolboy were asked to describe his country's manner of government to someone who had never heard of Canada before meeting him, "similar in form to that of Great Britain" would not be a very helpful way to begin. He knows that without being told.

If he has had a good teacher he has been helped to discover that the peculiar strength of his country's constitution is that it has not been frozen onto a single handy paper to which he might point and say, "This is us." He comes to believe that if it were set down so easily and simply it would no longer be capable of that growth and change that has kept it strong and allowed it to endure nine hundred years and more. Constitutions that are alive and well are a collection of customs and practices that are recorded in whatever way seems suitable at the time that the practice was found good to the people who lived under it. Yet however loosely recorded, however many sources must be consulted to put together all the pieces, that constitution does stand as a valid symbol of the hopes and aspirations, customs and beliefs, traditions and taboos of the people who live under it at the present moment. It is more than a symbol; it is the very substance of the nation and its culture.

Why then should it be so hard to understand the root and branch of the Indian nations? Our claim to a special place in the past and future history of North America? Our belief that if the Canadian mosaic arises sensibly out of the history and culture of Canada, the case for Indian nationhood arises at least as clearly out of the history and culture that the Indian nations of North America have shared?

Our hopes for the Fourth World are at least as credible as the belief in a Canadian nation with nearly autonomous provinces, a diversity of languages and cultures, and a mutual respect for one another's view of the world. Indian institutions are as capable of growth and adaptation as any others. When anthropologists, government officials, and churchmen have argued that our ways have been lost to us, they are fulfiling one of their own tribal rituals—wish fulfilment. More often, bureaucrats have argued that it is simply impractical to work within an Indian tradition in a modern technological society.

It is also impractical for civil servants to work within a framework of parliamentary government with a House of Commons, a Senate, their time-consuming and tiring questions and committees, a cabinet who might object to the most minor administrative decision, a Treasury Board that watches every penny while developing only an intuitive view of where the dollars have gone. Those institutions have endured because they have been found to be useful tools with which to bend and shape and mould the technological and administrative machinery to serve the values and meet the needs of Canadian society. After all, the most common public criticism of Parliament outside of Ottawa, is not that it is impractical but that it fails to be an effective voice of the people.

The criticism that Indian people make is that even if the federal and provincial parliaments do serve the wishes of the great majority of Canadian people they can never fully serve the needs of our people. We do not doubt that these institutions might serve the purposes for which they were intended. We are saying that our own needs can be fully served only through the development of our own institutions.

There will be no significant change in the condition of unilateral dependence that has characterized our history through the past century and more until Indian peoples are allowed to develop our own forms of responsible government. The route to be followed to the Fourth World will be as diverse and varied as are the Indian tribes.

The Fourth World is not, after all, a Final Solution. It is not even a destination. It is the right to travel freely, not only on our road but in our own vehicles. Unilateral dependence can never be ended by a forced integration. Real integration can only be achieved through a voluntary partnership, and a partnership cannot be based on a tenant-landlord relationship. The way to end the condition of unilateral dependence and begin the long march to the Fourth World is through home rule.

It was the demand for home rule and responsible government in Upper and Lower Canada that gave rise to an enduring partnership among the provinces of Canada and between the dominion and her mother country. When Quebec and Canada were united as one province for twenty-five years they discovered that responsible government without home rule is meaningless. Confederation guaranteed local autonomy, at least for the two major powers participating. The smaller and poorer Maritime provinces demanded grants that would provide them with the economic power to participate in Confederation and allow a financial base on which to enjoy their local autonomy. Prince Edward Island and Newfoundland stayed out of Confederation until they achieved terms they considered favourable. The New Brunswick government, which agreed to terms its people found unfavourable, was defeated and a more responsible and representative government took its place. If the western provinces and British Columbia appear to have accepted whatever they could get at the different times they entered Confederation, they have never stopped pressing their demands since they have been allowed to sit at the negotiating table.

The demand of Indian people that we be allowed to sit at the table where our lives are being negotiated, where our resources are being carved up like a pie, is not really very different from the demand made by every non-Indian group in Canada who share both a common history and a common territory. The whole history of Canada has largely been one long negotiation about the distribution of economic and political power.

The Trust Company Task Force of which I spoke in the previous chapter is only one of perhaps twenty task forces that the Department is funding at the present time. Whenever a proposal is put forward by an Indian organization, or one is criticized that has been suggested by the Department, a task force is set up to travel across the country to study the people's response. Its purpose is to determine if the Department should claim the proposal as its own or disown it. Whatever material is gained by the task force surveyors is then interpreted by departmental staff within the terms of reference and political commitments laid down by the government.

When I testified before the Commons Committee on Indian Affairs in February of 1973, I suggested that it was essential to the proper growth of the political processes within the Indian community that we conduct our own consultations and develop machinery that will maintain that kind of effective liaison. The task force system of the Department is in direct competition with the legitimate function and role of the National Indian Brotherhood and its member organizations.

We must debate our own future in our own forums, and we must be enabled to live with the decisions that are taken in those forums.

"You imposed a system," I told the committee, "based on a simple majority instead of a consensus. Now when we take a decision you tell us we are not representative."

It is only with the guarantees of our rights and of the powers to make the decisions affecting our own communities that we can end the political manipulations which the trust company proposal has typified from beginning to end.

The way to end the custodian-child relationship for Indian people is not to abolish our status as Indians, but to allow us to take our place at the table with all the rest of the adults. Indian status has too often been described as a special status by those who wanted to create an argument to get rid of it. Indian status is neither more nor less *special* than those special provisions that have been made for different provinces, at Confederation and since, in order to make it possible for them to work within the partnership of Canada. These provisions were also the recognition of the unique needs of different peoples and groups. The provisions have been preserved because the differences have been found real. Yet everyone insists that they do not confer *special status* because they only *create conditions for the different groups to become equal partners*.

Why should there be a different kind of equality for us as Indian people than for the other groups of Canadians who share both a common history and a common territory that distinguish them from other Canadians? Of course, it is true that not all Indian people share a common territory in the way that a province occupies a single territory. Yet I can only imagine that our relationship with this land and with one another is far deeper and more complex than the relationship between the people of any province and their land, their institutions, or one another.

Nor can the Indian peoples be brushed off with the multicultural broom to join the diverse ethnic groups that compose the Third Element of Canada, that is, those who are neither French nor English. When the Englishman speaks of "the Mother Country," the French-Canadian can still reply "Maître Chez Nous," the Jew can build his freedom in North America with the faith that if it fails there is yet another Promised Land, and the Eastern European who becomes an ardent Canadian nationalist still believes himself to be in exile from his native land. It seems as if every element in the Canadian mosaic is carved from a split personality. This itself is enough to distinguish the Indian peoples from the multicultural society.

When we say, "The Earth is Our Mother," we are saying that Canada is our Promised Land. Where other people look "homeward" for the medicines to heal themselves, this is our home. If the exiled condition in which Eastern Europeans believe themselves can only be ended with a change in the relationship between their Mother Country and the neighbouring Great Powers, our exile can be ended only with a change in our relationship with Canada. We know that many of those people who have come to our shores to find freedom will not go home when their country is liberated. On that day their freedom will be the freedom to choose. This is the freedom of the Fourth World. We ask no more for ourselves than the many immigrant groups ask for themselves. We do expect the same freedom and autonomy in our Mother Country as they demand in theirs, and ours. This is equality.

Clearly, we are neither an ethnic group nor a province of Canada. Although there are elements in both models that are useful, neither one will really work very well. The imposition of models on those who did not have a hand in the design has been the problem throughout our history. Clearly, the right to design our own model is the first step toward the Fourth World. Home rule begins with the opportunity to build that model with all the ingredients that the tides of history have washed up on our shores.

What is useful in the provincial model is that it teaches us that constitutional provisions and agreements have commonly been used to guarantee local autonomy, the customs, traditions, and values of those people who have been able to make their political presence felt. The basic concept of making special provisions for special needs, far from being a strange anomaly as some contemporary political leaders have led us to believe, has been an accepted way of making room at the table for those whom the present partners were prepared to welcome.

The "ethnic model" teaches us that a Confederation founded on the belief in "two founding races" can broaden its perspective when it appears to be politically expedient to do so. That is a source of enormous hope and confidence. If Confederation can endure past the racial myths that were the midwives at its birth, there can be no finer proof that institutions survive through the will of men as much as through their purely economic virtues.

If there is no single model on which to build either a route or a vehicle into the Fourth World there is both a common philosophy and a common fuel.

The philosophy has been born from the desire to resolve two

dilemmas that have been imposed through the condition of unilateral dependence. We know that no Canadian government will ever deal fairly with the Indian peoples until we can negotiate from a position of strength. We also know that the kind of integration based on mutual respect, and acceptance of each other's values *as valid for the other*, will never happen until Indian people achieve the same standard of living as that enjoyed by city-dwelling, middle-class, white Canadians. The political and social dilemmas meet every time the Canadian taxpayers are told of the vast sums spent by their Department of Indian Affairs. Led to believe that the spending of this money is somehow directed for our benefit, the taxpayer resents the expenditure and wonders how people can be so foolish that they fail to benefit when so many hundreds of millions of dollars are spent on their behalf.

The energy to move away from this situation comes from the realization that the way to remain Indian is to dispel the myths that have given rise to these false dilemmas in the first place. Most Indian people not only want to remain Indian but do not believe that there is any conflict between wanting to live decently, and even comfortably, and wanting to maintain and develop our own way of life as Indian people. Remaining Indian does not mean wearing a breech-cloth or a buckskin jacket, any more than remaining English means wearing pantaloons, a sword, and a funny hat. Yet on ceremonial occasions all people dress in the manner of their forefathers to remind themselves where they came from and who they are.

"I don't need to wear an Indian costume. I am an Indian," was Buffy Ste. Marie's reply when someone at a concert asked her why she did not wear traditional clothing.

Remaining Indian means that Indian people gain control of the economic and social development of our own communities, within a framework of legal and constitutional guarantees for our land and our institutions. Without those guarantees, our people and our institutions remain in a defensive position, and our only weapon is passive resistance. With the constitutional and material support to carry on that development, there would be no dilemma. The racial myths that were created to justify the seizure of our land base will only be fully dispelled when we have received the legal recognition of our effective title to the lands that remain to us, and sufficient grants to compensate for what is lost that we can afford to develop what does remain. Only then will we be able to demonstrate that there is no conflict between wanting to live comfortably and wanting to develop within our own traditional framework.

The desire for legal recognition of our aboriginal and treaty rights has taken on a religious perspective. But, as in most natural or traditional religions, the spiritual has not been separated from the material world.

Recognition of our aboriginal rights can and must be the mainspring of our future economic and social independence. It is as much in the long-term interest of the non-Indian peoples of North America as in our own interest that we be allowed our birthright, rather than that governments and churches perpetuate the Christian conspiracy that renders us the objects of charity while others enjoy the wealth of our land.

Immigrants to North America have long been considered on the basis of their skills and their usefulness to the economic development of the country. Unfortunately for the Gross National Product, we did not apply at the Immigration Office. The skills that those immigrants brought with them were at least the portable portion of their birthright. We, the first people of the land, must recover our birthright so that we can choose whether to become a part of the North American economy or to develop within our own value system.

Since I started to write this book a number of events have occurred that have moved Canada close enough to a recognition of our aboriginal rights that we can look at some of the likely implications. The recent events also reflect the confusion and misunderstanding that still prevail among much of the otherwise well-informed Canadian public.

On February 1, 1973, the Supreme Court brought down a split decision in the Appeal of the Nishga Tribal Council for recognition of their aboriginal rights and native title to the Nass River Valley in British Columbia.

The first reports in the media said that the claim to aboriginal rights had been lost. Dozens of reporters phoned the National Indian Brotherhood asking the same question: "What will you do now that you have lost?" Finally, I decided to go over to the Press Gallery at the House of Commons and give a press conference. The decision to go through the courts had been the major long-standing difference between the Nishga Tribal Council and the Union of B.C. Indian Chiefs, who preferred political negotiation. But there was no denying that the court's decision would influence any political negotiations that might occur. The Union had submitted its position on native title to the Prime Minister in a brief shortly after the Nishga case had been argued in the Supreme Court in November 1971. The Prime Minister had deferred comment until the court made its finding.[46]

It was only after spending most of the afternoon meeting with our own lawyers, who had spent the morning studying the judgement, that I was prepared to tell the press we had not lost. It was a split decision. Enough had been said in our favour to leave the door open to further actions on both the legal and political levels.

What had actually happened was that three of the seven judges sitting found there were no aboriginal rights in law for the Nishga people. Mr. Justice Hall wrote a judgement, in which two of his colleagues joined, which reviewed much of the political history of British Columbia as it affected the west coast Indian nations and much of the legal history in which the courts of Canada and the United States have attempted to give definition to native rights. He concluded that the Nishga were entitled to the declaration for which they had asked the court, recognizing their rights. Mr. Justice Pigeon made a ruling, supported by the three judges who were rejecting the Nishga claim, which said simply that the Nishga had no right to sue the Crown of British Columbia without the consent of the government. British Columbia and Prince Edward Island seem to be the only provinces that have kept an old English rule that the Crown cannot be sued without its consent. (It was announced in the news the following week that P.E.I. intended to introduce legislation to abolish this rule.) Although a majority had agreed to reject the appeal that was before them at the time, exactly half the judges who said anything about the question of aboriginal rights or native title favoured recognition and found that there was a sound basis in the law of Canada and Britain for recognition.

When we declared that we had not lost, the extent of disbelief at the press conference was so great that neither national network referred to what was clearly the most important part of our remarks. They were kind to us. I was quoted as saying that the government must recognize our rights if the Indian people are ever to become part of the Just Society. There was no attempt to set our remarks off against someone who might have disagreed. Neither would they reconsider their own earlier reports declaring that we had lost, merely because there was sound legal opinion to that effect. Since I came to Ottawa, I have very often seen the press back off from a situation in which they were not hostile or unsympathetic, but simply found the story confusing because it was a departure from the standard formula with which they were familiar.

When the news is selected because it conforms to certain accepted conventions, and variations are rejected because they are too new, we cannot look to the press, as Senator Davey's Report on the Mass Media recommends, to prepare us for social change. The problem the media people face is a human dilemma, which may be magnified for them because they encounter it frequently and under great pressures. Even if they have some special opportunities to resolve the dilemma, the problem they face is the same one faced by every person who is somehow concerned with human relations or community development. Every Indian leader encounters it almost daily, and I can only assume it is no different for non-Indian leaders.

When we come to a new fork in an old road we continue to follow the route with which we are familiar, even though wholly different, even better avenues might open up before us. The failure to heed Lord Elgin's plea for a new approach to Indian-European relations is a failure of imagination. The greatest barrier to recognition of aboriginal rights does not lie with the courts, the law, or even the present administration. Such recognition necessitates the re-evaluation of assumptions, both about Canada and its history and about Indian people and our culture—assumptions with which people have lived for centuries. Real recognition of our presence and humanity would require a genuine reconsideration of so many people's role in North American society that it would amount to a genuine leap of imagination. The greatest preservative for racial myths is the difficulty of developing a new language in which the truth can be spoken easily, quietly, and comfortably.

Much of the distance we must travel to the Fourth World must be spent developing such a language, or all the talk of developing a meaningful multicultural/ecumenical dialogue will remain at the present level.

The week following the Nishga judgement in the court, when I accompanied the delegation from the Union of British Columbia Chiefs, I was reminded again of how we build barriers with words. Mr. Trudeau greeted us with the words, "You have more legal rights than I thought you had."

"Legal rights to what?" we tried to find out.

He had not changed his mind on the position he had taken on aboriginal rights in the White Paper Policy of 1969, but he was willing to recognize "legal rights to native title."

Mr. Justice Hall, in his judgement, speaks of "aboriginal right or title" as though the terms were interchangeable. In the Union's own brief it had spoken of "native title." Earlier papers, as well as a statement adopted by the National Indian Brotherhood in August 1972, had spoken of aboriginal rights. The use of one term over another had so far been largely a matter of convenience. As far as we were concerned, it was a distinction without much of a difference.

The Nishga Tribal Council and the Union of British Columbia Chiefs met with the Prime Minister on the same day. Within the week the Yukon Native Brotherhood presented its position in a meeting with Mr. Trudeau on which I accompanied them. By this time the implications of the Supreme Court judgement were becoming somewhat better understood. The result was that public reaction in Ottawa swung around to the other extreme and stayed equally clear of the mark. So strong was the temptation to believe that these events added up to a demonstration that the government had achieved new levels of agreement and understanding of our position, that it could be felt in corners of our own organizations as well as in the House of Commons.

In all the meetings at which I had been present, I had heard nothing that demonstrated a willingness on the part of the government to consider an approach that was significantly new and different from what we had seen so far. This feeling was confirmed when we appeared before the Standing Committee of the House of Commons on Indian Affairs on March 9, 1973. The Committee was using its study of the current estimates for the Department to receive representations on aboriginal rights. The purpose of my testimony before the committee was to present to Parliament the position paper adopted by the General Assembly of the National Indian Brotherhood on Aboriginal Rights in August of 1972.

We had already submitted this position to the government and only took advantage of the opportunity to go before the Parliamentary Committee in open session when we learned that the government was preparing a policy on aboriginal rights that senior officials of the Department assured us would be framed in the narrowest possible terms. Up to that point I had not believed there was that much value in bringing the matter before the Parliamentary Committee. The Executive Council and General Assembly had accepted my thinking on this matter.

The paper we presented simply reviewed the history of the aboriginal rights claim and proposed a definition and description of those rights based on that history. We did not attempt to go into the details of each dispute. Nor did we try to estimate the specific value, either in land or in dollars, of the claim. Where every previous government of Canada had accepted the basic concept of aboriginal rights, the aim had been to reach a point where detailed negotiations could begin. Faced with a government that had so long denied the concept, we felt it was necessary to establish the basic principle before any detailed negotiations could begin.

We told the committee that we would not be prepared for detailed negotiations—even when the principle had been accepted—until the detailed studies being carried on by each provincial and territorial organization were nearing completion. These studies are assembling the specifics of the time and circumstances under which each loss took place. We know, for instance, that in the province of British Columbia the McKenna-McBride Commission cut large amounts of land off many different reserves. Other areas covered by treaty suffered similar losses. Some treaty promises for land have not been fulfiled. These are the details that require documentation before negotiation is possible. But if the fundamental principle of aboriginal rights is not acknowledged, there is no point in discussing the detailed history of each band and each piece of land.

Joe Clark, a Conservative MP from Rocky Mountain, Alberta, moved that the committee recommend to the House of Commons that our paper be adopted as a description of aboriginal rights. The

New Democratic Party members of the committee, Tom Barnett, Frank Howard, and Mark Rose, indicated they were prepared to support the Conservative motion endorsing our position.

Ian Watson, the leading Liberal member of the Committee, and the author of the committee's report on Indian education which we had endorsed, asked us what it was we really wanted. I held up my copy of the brief and said that we wanted recognition of aboriginal rights based on the description offered in our paper. Although Mr. Watson himself said he could go along with that definition and had no quarrel with it, all the Liberals on the committee abstained from voting.

When the committee's report came before the House of Commons on a motion for adoption, both the Minister, Jean Chrétien, and his parliamentary secretary, Len Marchand, opposed the motion because, they said, it left open a great many questions of detail. Mr. Chrétien argued that he could not accept an over-all policy statement such as this because it would have different implications in different parts of the country. Yet the whole history of Canadian-Indian relations has been that the specifics of each tribe and each territory have differed. Could it have been otherwise?

His most spurious argument—a pure attempt to play with people's minds and words—was that whole cities in British Columbia might be found to be on land that was not Canadian. There was nothing in the paper that challenged the underlying title or fundamental authority of the Crown. The Opposition critics were entirely correct when they replied that this kind of statement could bring out a white backlash by posing a false threat to other people's security.

Len Marchand had opposed the motion in committee on the ground that it was necessary to hear from other Indian groups. The vote on the motion was postponed until that evening so that the Native Council of Canada, representing the Métis and non-status Indians, could be heard. They accepted the basic concept as we had outlined it—probably because their representatives had sat in on some of the drafting sessions. Every provincial and territorial organization representing status Indians had been represented at all the drafting sessions. They, in turn, had consulted with all the bands in their territory. This was the only way we could ever have

227

reached the level of agreement necessary to gain the approval of the Brotherhood's General Assembly. Mr. Marchand never specified just which other Indian groups he desired to consult.

In the House he abandoned this argument and simply expanded on the minister's desire for the additional detail that could only come forward when we reach the negotiating table.

The Liberal party made sure they never voted directly against the motion in the House by seeing that it was talked out. Conservative and New Democratic members offered to reduce the time allotted to each speaker, and even to give up their right to speak to allow time for the motion to come to a vote. The Social Credit members offered their support for the motion. The Liberals simply found more and more members to repeat their initial reservations. They looked the issue squarely in the eye and stepped aside, voting neither for nor against, saying they agreed with the concept of "aboriginal rights," but preferring the name "native title," and questioning whether either term implied a real obligation on their part. The present government's position is, "Native title if necessary, but not necessarily aboriginal rights."

It is no coincidence that the Liberal government moved from a complete unwillingness to discuss the matter to this position during the occupation of Wounded Knee by members of the Oglala Sioux Nation, who were demanding nothing more than a fulfilment of their treaty rights and a congressional investigation into the corruption of the U.S. Bureau of Indian Affairs. Although they said they had dropped their White Paper Policy a year and a half earlier, the Liberal government had avoided telling Parliament what their present policy was until pressure from the majority in Parliament and the decision taken by half of the judges on the matter in the Supreme Court, at the time of the Oglala occupation, moved them to this present position.

I do not believe the thinking, "What will it cost and we'll see if we want to pay it," represents the thinking of the people of Canada. The White Paper had wide popular appeal among the non-Indian population mainly because it promised equality. The majority in Parliament, in supporting the Brotherhood's position, is simply recognizing that the White Paper cannot deliver on that promise without recognizing native title. Better welfare schemes are not preferable to recognizing native title to resources than can

228

really provide equal opportunity. An opinion poll taken across the United States found that 54 per cent of the American people supported the demands of the Oglala Nation at Wounded Knee and only 18 per cent were opposed. I cannot believe that Canadians have a sense of justice inferior to that.

The primary objection of Indian people to the White Paper was its desire to see the constitutional responsibilities that result in a unique status for Indian people and our land terminated. The willingness of the Parliamentary Committee to recognize native title could open up the possibility of negotiations. The negotiations for which we have been waiting since the hearings of 1968-69 were concluded, and for which British Columbia Indians have been petitioning since British Columbia joined Canada, and which non-status Indians have been seeking since Louis Riel was refused his right to sit in the House of Commons. The negotiations can be all these things if recognition of native title is to be the mainspring and material base of responsible government for the Indian peoples of Canada.

No negotiation is possible that does not begin with an exercise of imagination that permits a good deal of give and take to reshape the present framework into something mutually acceptable. The first exercise of imagination — even if the spirit of good will now present in Parliament is transmitted to the government — will be to realize that any settlement must necessarily be a long-range process, and allow the retention of a strong land base on which we can develop a viable economy for Indian people. The Indian and Inuit peoples have learned from the Alaska settlement the dangers of entering into an agreement before there has been a sufficient involvement of the local communities directly affected, with research into both the historical background and current needs of the people, and the potential of their natural resources for their own economic development.

Following the round of meetings with the Prime Minister, I talked, on a phone-in radio show with a nation-wide hook-up, with the mayor of the North Slope Borough that had been created in the Alaska settlement. The mayor is an Inuit and has been involved in a good deal of their negotiating. He was firmly convinced that the details of their settlement resulted not so much from the considered needs of the people but from a consideration of what would be acceptable to a majority of U.S. Congressmen.

Just what the mayor meant can be seen by contrasting the Nixon administration's bill to settle the Alaska Native Lands issue with the natives' own bill and amendments to the Administration Bill that supporters in Congress proposed. The Administration Bill would "turn over," according to one wire service report, forty million acres to the native peoples. It also proposes to pay $925 million over an eleven-year period. The total can be described as $17,000 plus 750 acres per capita. If the normal objectivity of wire services is presumed, it turns out that the native people are *turning over* 525,000 square miles for $925 million, or $1600 per square mile, or three dollars an acre. When you look at the prices for which lands were surrendered in the last century, taking inflation into account, there is a real opportunity here to calculate in precise dollar-and-cent terms just how much social change has transpired in Indian/non-Indian relations in the past hundred years.

The most important element in the natives' own bill, besides more cash and greater land reserves, is a provision for "2% royalties on federal and state income from minerals and surface resources *in perpetuity*." I am told that in many states people whose land title includes mineral rights receive 10-per-cent royalties. Many Third World states now receive 35-per-cent royalties on mining rights of foreign companies. Two per cent seems like a modest proposal.

Part of the lands that will be surrendered under the Administration Bill will be retained in public ownership. New reserves will be created and existing parks and game preserves will be enlarged. The Udall-Saylor amendment would have created a joint state-federal planning commission with representatives from all sectors of private and public life, including the Alaskan native peoples. Here was a chance for a partnership in the sharing of common lands.[47]

Congress defeated this amendment and in its place put a weak state-federal land planning commission with only an advisory authority, and for which the Alaska legislature failed to vote any funds.

The referendum that created the Alaska North Slope Borough as the world's largest local government was passed 595-33. The response of the oil companies, who may find themselves paying property taxes on $320 million worth of property within the borough, was to ask the State Supreme Court to declare against the borough's legal authority. Seven oil companies, some of them among the largest and most powerful in the world, called it an illegal grab. Their brief gives many reasons why the oil companies are afraid of the new borough, but they all seem to boil down to one: "Despite the unquestioned sincerity of its proponents the implications of the proposal [for responsible government and home rule] are so far reaching that the full account must be taken of the enormous opportunities and temptation to misuse and abuse power to overstep the restraints of responsibility."

It seems as if the oil companies feel about us much the same as we feel about them. Whether a native/non-native partnership makes sense depends very much on whether federal, state, and provincial governments are more dedicated to serving industry or people.

The Inuit people of the North Slope Borough, for instance, want to collect taxes from local industry mainly to support a local school system. At present, their children must attend classes hundreds of miles away at the south end of Alaska or enroll in the BIA institution thousands of miles away. This is a problem with which Indian and Inuit people all across Canada are familiar. The solution that was proposed was consistent with the way schools have traditionally been supported throughout European communities in the United States and Canada. It was a solution designed well within the overlap of native and European traditions, values, and goals. Friends of the oil companies charged that the borough would be a "racial enclave" because it would be predominantly Inuit. The executive-director of the Arctic Slope Native Association replied that "the existing borough-governments in Alaska are white, racially-defined enclaves . . . reservations for white folks. . . . If borough government is good for white racist entrepreneurs why is it bad medicine for poor Eskimos?"

The dislike for law-and-order that does not work to their advantage and the presence of state and federal governments who have an air of studied neutrality, or what Richard Nixon elsewhere described as "benign neglect," has raised racial tension—in a territory where there are so few Europeans that such tensions could easily have been avoided altogether—to the point where the Eskimos responded to the oil companies' court action by asking their southern brothers to boycott Mobil, Amerada-Hess, Amoco, BP, Humble of California, Phillips Petroleum, and Union Oil of California.

There was nothing either impossible or utopian about an Alaskan settlement. The Indian peoples of Canada have been ready to negotiate such a settlement for a long time. While it is true that we cannot make a precise statement of either needs or rights for a particular community until there has been enough research and communication, there is still a basic framework on which almost all native peoples agree and which will be present in every negotiation.

Our identity as Indian peoples must be enshrined in the fundamental law of Canada. We do not need either the British North America Act or the Indian Act to give us our identity. We need them to tell us what Canada's attitude to us is likely to be. We cannot talk about a partnership that is not written down on a paper that all parties understand and that is put beyond the easy grasp of governments that change from day to day.

The reserved status of our lands must be reconfirmed in a way that will assure us that it will no longer be played with by every prospector, highway builder, and politician. If the legal rights in the Nishga case appear unclear, there is no doubt that legislation and agreements binding the federal and Quebec governments in regard to James Bay lands were clearly set down. The question is whether the rights of Indian communities will be as well respected in the courts of Canada as the rights of power producers.

Canada's willingness to honour the spirit in which the treaties were made and to take account of changing knowledge and technology will be a measure of our welcome into Canadian society. In public discussions on the Mackenzie Valley complex, government has repeatedly said that it will respect the rights guaranteed under Treaties No. 8 and 11 as they apply in the Northwest Territories. But continuing research by the N.W.T. Indian Brotherhood has indicated that the Indian people who were present at the signing did not understand—were not told—that it was more than a treaty of peace and friendship. The Indian parties to the treaties do not agree that they surrendered their land. The research is not yet

232

complete, but it does raise the question of the willingness of Canadians and their elected representatives to be influenced by the evidence. It is a question that has just as profound implications for Indians in southern Canada as it does for those in the "remote north."[48]

Our rights to hunt and fish are logically a part of our right to the land, no different from mineral rights, timber rights, or other rights to use land in a particular way that might sometimes be usefully separated from the main title. But the legal protection of these rights has been inconsistent and far from uniform. In the prairie provinces, where natural resources were kept in federal hands for some time after the different Acts of Union were passed, these rights were reconfirmed in the various natural resources agreements that stand as amendments to the BNA Act. The courts have found that the treaties on Vancouver Island preserved hunting rights. But even these guarantees have been watered down by the Migratory Birds Convention Act without consideration either of our needs or of a fair and public hearing to determine whether any particular species might, at different times, be endangered. Yet the model for guaranteeing our rights through a constitutional agreement has laid down. Let it be fully developed and respected.

The Indian peoples who are dependent on hunting and fishing for their livelihood are as concerned as any urban conservationist or any public servant for the preservation of endangered species. We are also concerned with the forms of pollution that make fish and game inedible while continuing to allow them to live. An urban man who is deprived of his livelihood is entitled to fair notice. Under certain circumstances, such as expropriation, he can demand that the proper authorities demonstrate to the satisfaction of a court of law that their decision is in the public interest. Both in expropriation matters and in negligence cases he is entitled to just compensation to allow him to live as comfortably after the loss as he did before. Many provinces have now adopted "the house-for-a-house" rule in expropriation. One benefit of this rule is that local authorities will give very serious consideration before depriving a man of either his home or his livelihood if a realistic estimate of the cost is made. A similar respect for our hunting and fishing rights would be a form of equality in which all parties could

233

believe. It would be less expensive—both in terms of dollars and the value of lives and human dignity—than the present policy which provides welfare and medical costs for mercury poisoning.

Nor are hunting and fishing rights likely to lose their importance in the future if the animals are treated with the respect they deserve. Cooperative experiments have been conducted with a fair degree of initial success for the first years of operation in the development of industries directly related to these rights. The largest number of such experiments have been cooperative fishing experiments from Eskasoni, Nova Scotia, through northwestern Ontario to British Columbia. Secondary industries, such as packing plants and small wood mills for producing crates and other specialized products, have developed alongside and sometimes as part of these cooperative enterprises.

These are not miracles. They are carefully planned programs that require the same careful cultivation as any sophisticated farm. Nor is their success to be judged entirely by the first year's profit sheet. But they are a demonstration that the way to bring about equality is not to abolish these rights but to enhance them. The greatest single drawback to these experiments so far has been neither a lack of labour nor a lack of good planning. It has been a lack of capital. If trapping, fishing, and related industries were as well subsidized as mining, the low income of our people would be described as a bookkeeping problem rather than one of endurance. If there were as much support for cooperative enterprises as for oil exploration, the reduced need for welfare, unemployment insurance, and prisons might more than offset the cost of subsidies if the scale of measurement encompassed the normal life-span of a man.

The number of examples available in which the technology of the global village has been harnessed to traditional Indian values and culture are necessarily limited by the lack of opportunity that has been available so far. The way to test our belief in the Fourth World is not to argue with a theoretical model but to help us to develop the material resources we will need to make it succeed. When an outsider walks in and proclaims to our people, "Your land is not really suited for economic development," we know that there is something lacking in his development program. Perhaps there is something lacking in his whole concept of economics.

234

One great Indian leader of the last century gave a fair and loving reply to the then unborn generations of economic development officers when he said, "The Earth and myself are of one mind." When you understand that the Earth is his Mother and mine you will not begin your discussions of our welfare with us by saying that she cannot bear fruit because she rejects your seed.

The strength of all Indian cultures in the past has been achieved through working on a communal or cooperative basis. I think it is no coincidence that a hundred and more years of church and government officials, with all their preaching of possessive individualism, have failed to cultivate an entrepreneurial class of Indian people. Those few Indian people who bought that idea moved to the cities, where wealth could be had in that framework. Yet even many of them have returned to work with their people. It is just not the all-embracing model that white administrators from John A. Macdonald to Arthur Laing have tried to make us believe.

There is no better demonstration of the willingness to use modern technology to serve our own needs and wants than to count the number of portable tape recorders at any Indian meeting, whether it is a local pow-wow, a traditional unity caravan wending its way across the continent for several months, a general assembly of the National Brotherhood, or a meeting with an agricultural representative. If there are things being said that are good and useful, most of our leaders want to share those words with their people. And most of those people want to learn whatever will help them to live their own lives in a happier, more comfortable, more secure condition. So long as they are our lives to live, we will celebrate our customs, dance to our beat, and be best served through the development of our own institutions.

When Sitting Bull was travelling with Buffalo Bill's Wild West show, after he had been defeated and there was no more respectable way off the reservation, he had a chance to observe the number of white children who were begging for pennies in Chicago and other big European cities of this continent. He observed that a people who allow their own poor to suffer so much can hardly be expected to take much interest in the Indians. He also observed that white people had learned to produce goods in vaster quantities than anyone else, but they had not learned very much about distributing them.[49]

Although his appreciation for the relationship between production and distribution may have been as keen as his contemporary, Karl Marx, it would be unfair and misleading to call Sitting Bull a socialist. A big, central government with unlimited authority to intervene in local affairs would have horrified him as much as it would the staunchest conservative. Nor could it be said that the Sioux leader came from a culture where individualism was less highly prized than collective action. No people were more radically individual than his.

The difference is that the structure of organization and the style of leadership with which Sitting Bull, or my own grandfather, was familiar did not set up a conflict between the individual's unique personality and the community's need for cooperation. So long as that conflict continues within European society, people will earnestly debate the merits of one form of action over another without pursuing either one very vigorously. That is a problem European societies in North America will have to work out for themselves. We will all be interested in hearing of the outcome. Meantime, if we do not all rush to sign up when the military, the police, or industry advertise "Become one of us," we are only waiting while a clearer definition of what that means is worked out.

The increasing contact of Indian youth with the young people of other disenfranchised groups may, on the other hand, point to a whole new set of examples from which we can learn and benefit. An unwritten alliance is already emerging between the Indian, black, and Chicano youth across North America. White youth who are recognizing Sitting Bull's truth are also reconsidering their role in building the future. The alliance has already crossed the oceans and gone beyond the bounds of our own continent.

It was an African diplomat who pointed out to me that political independence for colonized peoples was only the Third World. "When native peoples come into their own, on the basis of their own cultures and traditions that will be the Fourth World," he told me.

My own first trip outside of North America was to meet with the Maori people of New Zealand and the Aborigines of Australia. I felt so much at home with the Maori people that I kept referring to them as Indians, and they kept referring to me as a Maori from North America. In Australia it was so difficult to meet with the aboriginal people without some official being present that I knew how a reporter on an official government tour of Indian reserves eighty years ago must have felt.

The Maori in New Zealand and the Aborigines in Australia are at almost opposite poles in their relations with the governments of their countries. With the possible exception of the Lapps in Sweden, the Maoris have achieved a better material standard of living, by their country's standard, and a better relationship with their European neighbours than any other aboriginal people. The reason for the relative success of the Maori seems largely to be the willingness to make these rights into something of the kind of mainspring to which I am pointing. Like any other model, its usefulness lies in the general concepts that have proven successful, not in a formula that can be transplanted and imposed, nor in the particular details.

Maori lands, for instance, have been secured through trust boards that are elected directly by the Maori people who live in or come from the region. The need for a trust board arises because there is nothing that corresponds exactly to our reserves as a political unit. What is important is that lands have been reserved for native people, with the title placed directly in their own hands rather than in the name of the Crown, as has been the case in North America, and without breaking the land up into individual lots on an English model.

Perhaps the main reason why the Maori people have maintained a reasonable relationship with the New Zealand government is that for over one hundred years they have elected four Maori members of Parliament. The country is divided into eighty-two ridings for European voters. The same country is divided into four ridings for Maori voters.

I had several opportunities to discuss the use of this political power both with Maori leaders and with a political scientist who has made several extensive studies of the impact of these seats. Maori members of Parliament have served as acting prime minister on four occasions. The Maori MPs have held the balance of power on at least four other occasions. More important than these dramatic moments in the parliamentary life of the country is the simple knowledge that every Maori person has a representative in Parliament to speak for him—a representative who has been sent

237

to Parliament to represent the interests of the Maori people. That is altogether different from a member of Parliament who is concerned and interested in our problems but who must look elsewhere for his votes.

Indian people have often had friends in Parliament. I have quoted two governors-general who spoke out on our behalf. Sir Wilfrid Laurier was not the last prime minister to say that we should have a fair and judicial hearing on our rights. John Diefenbaker introduced two bills to establish land claims commissions. Lester Pearson promised legislation that would go even further in recognizing aboriginal rights. If there is an anomalous position it is the one taken by the Trudeau government.

Nothing came of any of those promises, not so much because these men were insincere, but because Indian people have never had the political power to establish our claims as a priority that demands attention and consideration. I do not think it depreciates the kind support we have received from a very small handful of MPs to say that their voice on our behalf has been a spare-time activity. The demands of their own constituency had to have a higher priority. Their debt to the party that funded their election also had to have a higher priority.

In the Parliament elected in 1968 we had one Indian MP. In the Parliament elected in 1972 we have two Indian MPs. Their situation is not really any different from the position of the non-Indian MPs who have supported our cause throughout the years. They cannot extend their commitment to the Indian people to the point where there might be a conflict with the wishes of either their constituents or their party. If Wally Firth finds less of a conflict representing the native cause in the Northwest Territories than Len Marchand has as the MP for Kamloops, it is because the greatest number of people in the N.W.T. are native people. The conflict of interest has been lessened.

Real legislative change that reflects the presence of the native people as part of the partnership of Confederation is far more likely to come about when the conflict of interest is resolved for the rest of us. Northern Indians are not more numerous than those in the South. They simply represent a higher percentage of the total population in their territory.

The bureaucracy in New Zealand is not naturally superior to

that in the rest of the world; nor is ours naturally worse than theirs. I am not even sure that Indian Affairs' structure is impossibly worse than the rest of the government's. The most important role that a Maori MP fulfils is the ombudsman role that any MP serves for his constituents. The knowledge that he is there to act on their behalf is shared not only by the Maori people, but also by the civil servants. Indian Affairs staff have operated for a very long time with the knowledge that nobody will seriously question their conduct unless they have been playing a role so sympathetic to the Indian people that it offends someone else. The presence of Indian MPs who are sent to Ottawa to pursue our interests would do no more than introduce the same element of responsible government into Indian Affairs as has shaped the course of decision-making in every other department of government.

Far from being a departure from the whole idea of giving the vote to Indian people, it would be the next logical step. Nor is the idea without precedent in other fields. Until 1941, Quebec was guaranteed that it would not receive fewer seats in any future redistribution than the number with which they began. The smaller provinces have had much the same guarantee by the provision that they will never have fewer seats in the House of Commons than they have in the Senate. Many provincial legislatures make special provision to assure that the rising urban population will not swamp the rural representation. Federal redistribution generally tries to separate rural and urban areas so as to minimize conflicting demands on the same member of Parliament. Where Indian people are in the most remote areas, the distinction between rural and remote would be only a further step along the line drawn between rural and urban.

If the government cannot see that these Canadian examples add up to a clear precedent, perhaps that explains why we have not been better served in the past. A real partnership requires that we open our minds to wider possibilities than can be derived from one partner's past.

I doubt that there has ever been a time when there have been more than half a dozen MPs who were seriously knowledgeable about Indian Affairs. Four would be a more common figure until the last Parliament. When I see Prince Edward Island represented by four MPs and four Senators, Newfoundland by six and six, I think it is not unreasonable for us to believe that we need somewhat more representation than that to serve the needs of an equal number of people spread across the whole map of Canada.

Even before he gave Indian people the vote, Mr. Diefenbaker appointed James Gladstone as the first Indian Senator. Shortly after Senator Gladstone's death, Mr. Trudeau appointed Guy Williams. So far as this gave us a foot in the door of Parliament, it was a good and useful start. Senators, like MPs, have one pass a week to travel by plane or train to their own home town and back to Ottawa. Even the youngest, most energetic man, completely free of party ties, would be somewhat limited in his ability to cover a constituency as wide as Canada singlehandedly with such limited financial resources.

Even in the valuable committee work that seems to be the most time-consuming part of the Senate's business, a single man cannot be in all places at once. There is as much need for an Indian voice in the shaping of science policy as in the Report on Poverty. The Joint Committee on the Constitution must become as important to us as the current study of the parole system.

The fate of the many Senate committee reports rests not with the Senate but with the government of the day. It is not enough to be represented next door to the centre of power. Governments are made and broken in the House of Commons. Although we may all wonder who has control of the purse strings, there is no doubt that power nominally lies with the elected House. Ministers respond to the questions MPs ask about their departments' operations because the money to run those departments must eventually be voted by those MPs.

The whole system of responsible government is founded on a series of exercises in collective self-interest. Its critics say it does not work very well. Its defenders say it works better than anything else they have found. They are both right. If the interests of the Indian people are to be served within the framework of a Canadian Confederation, we must be allowed to join in the same exercise of collective self-interest.

The laws governing the Maori electoral districts say that a Maori is any person with a Maori ancestor. Even more all-encompassing is Sweden's definition of its native peoples; a Same (sometimes called a Lapp in English) is defined as anybody who says he is a

240

Same. The definition of an Indian under Canada's Indian Act is the strictest and narrowest definition of a native person in any country in the world. It is a definition that has been made narrower and stricter with the passage of time.

The earliest legislation governing Indian people in Canada included a provision for recognizing as an Indian a person "reputed to be an Indian." Today we are faced with a situation where half the Indian people of Canada lack a legal status recognizing their rights as Indian people. As I write this, lawyers for eighteen different parties are arguing in the Supreme Court of Canada whether certain provisions of the Indian Act violate the Canadian Bill of Rights, namely the provision that an Indian woman who marries a non-Indian loses her status as an Indian under the Indian Act. There is no doubt that the provision is unjust in many ways. Yet we cannot accept a position where the only safeguards we have had can be struck down by a court that has no authority to put something better in its place.

The tragedy of this situation, like so many others, is that it never needed to arise. For all the lack of uniformity with which our hunting and fishing rights have been preserved, and all the inconsistency of recognizing aboriginal rights in places where it seemed expedient, and ignoring them when that was more convenient, both Parliament and the civil service have had tremendous zeal for uniformity where it least applies. Indian customs of inheritance and for defining identity have varied from nation to nation according to political and economic structure and religious beliefs. Many trace through the mother's line, some through the father's. My own people work through a mixture of both, as do many of our neighbours.

Strict patrilineal descent seems to have crept into Canadian law from the customs of the church. The Indian Act took the general measure of Canadian law and applied it to us—but only when it was found to be convenient to narrow the group to whom services would be provided under the Act. The same act that recognized persons reputed to be Indians made a distinction between Indian half-breeds and non-Indian half-breeds.

One was to receive scrip with which to procure land. The other was to receive membership in the band to which he already belonged. The promises made to one group were no better kept than those made to the other. The point is that the early legislators in Canada had no grave difficulty in distinguishing between the two.

Even today, there are still two definitions of "Indian" in Canadian law. The definition that is generally known is the one in the Indian Act. But the federal government's authority to pass an Indian Act comes from its powers under the BNA Act, which provides exclusive federal jurisdiction for "Indians and lands reserved for the Indians." The courts have said that Inuit people and non-status Indians are nonetheless Indians within the meaning of that section of the BNA Act. The Indian Act definition simply says that while Parliament has the power to legislate for all Indians, it chooses to make laws only for some. This rule gets somewhat bent in the Northwest Territories and Yukon, where territorial ordinances, which are a form of federal law, do make special provisions for "Eskimo" people.

The BNA Act definition of "Indian" could be as wide as the New Zealand definition of "Maori" or the Swedish definition of "Same." When the National Indian Brotherhood adopted a statement on aboriginal rights, we said that these rights apply to every person who is an Indian within the meaning of section 91(24) of the British North America Act. Parliament cannot dispose of our rights simply by saying that we are no longer Indians. Neither can it fulfil its constitutional responsibilities by repealing the portions of the constitution it does not like.

The way to resolve the difficulty is not to introduce a court action into an already over-complicated situation. If Parliament fulfiled its responsibilities, there would be no need to go to court to return status to some small portion of those from whom it was taken away. Indian tribes in the United States have long been allowed to draw up their own constitutions. This is true for some who have never stopped living under their own constitution, and under the Indian Reorganization Act; it applies to those who adopt a new constitution by referendum. A part of writing your own constitution is a right to say who will be included within your tribal roll or band list or whatever form of register you choose to keep. Indian peoples who have this freedom do not seem to be either better or worse off in any other way. They do have the knowledge that the membership of their particular group is neither broader nor narrower than the children of their ancestors choose to make it. It is up to them to develop a sound "immigration" policy.

Canada already has a general list for Indians who are not on the list of any band. The rights that Indian people have that do not relate to membership in any band are enjoyed equally by those on the general list. Many non-status Indians live in Métis colonies on land to which they have no title, and which is not reserved under the Indian Act. Alberta has moved to give some recognition to these colonies, but it is beyond the power of any province to give these people their just entitlement. Métis people have estimated that there are two million acres that were promised to them when the treaties were made, and they received land scrip for which they have never received title.

Whether the lands to which the non-status Indians are entitled should become reserves under the Indian Act is a decision the local Métis community must make. They have suffered as much from the policies shaped by the centralized cookie-cutter in Ottawa as we have.

The question of definition must be an important part of any over-all negotiation. But it is the whole relationship between Indian and non-Indian that must be redefined. The question of getting on either a band or a general list cannot be separated from the question of what it means to be included on that list. We cannot have our land base being eroded by governments at the same time that the courts extend the list of people who can occupy those lands. Only the federal constitution can secure our land base. Only the people can identify their brothers and sisters. It is no better to have both ends of the blanket pulled up from under you than to have only one end pulled up.

There are only three barriers to granting full Indian status to all those people who fall within the meaning of the word "Indian" in the BNA Act: (1) The good will of the government and the people whom they represent needed to increase the size of the reserved lands and the federal budget in proportion to the increase in numbers; (2) the creation of the administrative machinery that will allow the transition to be made as smoothly as the settlement of refugees has so often been done; (3) the individual and community decision as to which identity people wish to choose.

I did not really appreciate the identification between our situation and that of Third World Peoples—although my own children had tried to point it out to me often enough—until I went to Tanzania. Here was a nation where the subject peoples had outnumbered the Europeans but were nonetheless controlled by them. Here were a people who were fortunate enough in their leadership to realize that political independence was not the coming of the Messiah; it was only the beginning of the struggle for economic and social self-sufficiency. Political independence only gave them the tools of sovereignty with which to begin to build their nation. And Julius Nyerere finds a way of reminding his audience of this every time he speaks. Yet he does not speak in a way that perpetuates violence, incites hatred, or projects the temporary failings of a new and young nation on some minority group who can be made a convenient scapegoat.

He tells the students graduating from the university that their studies have been made possible through the labour of the common people in the village. Now that they have completed their studies, they have a debt to pay. They must return the knowledge to the people who sent them to find it. And he shows them what he means by going out in the field himself with a pick and shovel on a regular basis. If my grandfather had seen this man he would have pointed him out to me as an example to be copied at every turn.

At first, I found it strange to be in a world without television, and where the foods to which we have grown most accustomed are not the standard fare at the corner restaurant. But when I went into a grocery store I found that a can of salmon that might have been spawned in my own river in British Columbia was available for one-sixth the price my daughters must pay in Vancouver. Then I knew that there were ways modern technology can be adapted to traditional values. The state did not own the retail outlet, and certainly had no control over the British Columbia or Japanese canneries. They could and did control the middle man who establishes the distribution system and sets the final price. Luxury goods, such as after-shave lotion, were sold at inflated prices to cover the cost of providing a stable and nutritious diet to children. Somebody had made a judgement about national goals and community needs and found that feeding children, of all ages, was more important than pampering the faces of aging men.

The decision to postpone the development of a national televi-

244

sion network had been made in order to leave the limited funds available free to develop eight local radio networks that could accommodate all the local languages. That was multiculturalism.

A few months before I went to Tanzania, their High Commissioner to Canada came to the General Assembly of the National Indian Brotherhood. After lunch one day we persuaded him to speak to us. Until our executive-director, who had spent four years in east Africa, sought him out, he had never met any Indians in three years in Canada. He told us something of Tanzania's struggle for independence. It was a short speech that touched only on the highlights. He did not belabour the evils of colonialism or spend time in a polemic against foreign oppression. When the assembled delegates rose to a standing ovation his good judgement was proven. There was no need to tell fifty-six Indian leaders what was wrong with someone else running your life. It was good to hear how others had dealt with the same problems we have.

Tanzania is such a good example of the difference between the Third World and the Fourth World because neither the people nor their leaders have been content to produce a new society that is merely a darker imitation of the world of their colonial masters. Perhaps there are any number of other Third World countries that I have not visited where there is a similar struggle going on. There is a strong temptation, however, for a newly independent people to believe that their paper constitution is their proof of identity, their ticket on the train to the next world. Even within the past four years we have seen newly independent people colonize their smaller neighbours, or continue to keep them in subjection, because they are using the symbols of power left behind by the conquerors to establish their own status.

The hardest task in the struggle for the Fourth World is to learn to produce that new reality that reconstructs a tradition in which people can hold a common belief, and which uses all the benefits of a global technology. When the colonial powers set out to justify their Manifest Destiny, they created a myth that would give legitimacy to the new economic system. The myth was begun by creating a scarcity of goods far greater than any natural scarcity. Attached to the scarcity was a belief in racial supremacy. Some of the most racial aspects of the myth have now been dispelled. Today we know that the appearance of scarcity is created by the failure to harness technology for the effective distribution of plentiful goods. The way to destroy the myth that remains is to build an economy that bears a relationship to the Fourth World. Out of the act of building will come a myth that celebrates that healthy relationship.

Of all the models of economic and social development that I have seen, Tanzania is the closest example to my understanding of the way that Indian people want to develop. The material goals are not really any different from those of middle-class urban Canadians. It is a structure and style and economic organization that allows the whole community to share in those good things, and to decide which are the higher priorities in moving toward that ultimate goal, that distinguishes the Fourth World.

The present condition of the Indian peoples in Canada is without even a single defender. The Indian people have expressed dissatisfaction at every possible opportunity. If there is any merit in the government's *Indian Policy* it is in its determination to end the paternalistic nature of its relationship to us. There is neither scholar nor citizen in any corner of the country who finds it to his advantage. The debate is not about whether that condition would be changed. It is about who should do the changing; and in what direction we should move from here.

The fastest way to bring about change among an oppressed people is to put the decision-making authority, and the economic resources that go with it, into their own hands. Only then will there be a line clearly drawn between the evils of external control and our own normal human errors. So long as external control is the dominant fact of life, the line distinguishing the two faults does not really exist. After all, the line merely separates the human problems on which we can act from those on which we must act through less direct means.

Genuine integration will begin to take place when this line is apparent to everyone. Its visibility will be proof that we have control over our own destiny and are making good use of it. The respect for one another's personal and community identity will grow from there. As long as Indian people are materially disadvantaged and the decision-making over our lives lies in someone else's hands, there can be no integration. The human concept of acceptance has not yet developed to a level where people who live

246

comfortably accept those who live below their material standard, or hold a strongly different religious or political view.

Of course, there is the isolated individual whose unique life is the exception to prove the rule. Just as there were four white men who helped me in my early life from their own basic goodness, there is always the odd humane individual who can be cited for example. Any man who has made a success of his life has been helped along the way by at least one of these humane people.

It would be most foolish and unwise to place our hopes for the future on the off chance that such people will come more often. The way to find so many good people is to change the day-to-day experience of the common man.

We know who won the last war on poverty. The minute a budget is created by the rich to help the poor, or by people in power positions within the church or government or labour unions, they immediately set up an administration to look after those funds that saps away both the financial resources and the growth of any kind of leadership and initiative within the community that can speak for the people who need the help.

If the Indian peoples in Canada are to win the next war on poverty, we must define the philosophy, the objectives, and the broad terms of reference of a development program that is both social and economic, on a local and regional basis. We must determine the size of the total national program from a realistic assessment of local needs. Within the framework of a national program, we must put the initiative for planning and decision-making into the hands of local communities, who will make their decisions with the support of a technical staff employed to serve that community's interests and no other.

The present provincial organizations have already begun to fill the need for competent technical advisors to assist bands in preparing their own budgets. This is something that the Department has said it has been doing for several years. The problem with departmental advisors, as we have known them so far, is that they work according to a preconceived formula established in Ottawa without the involvement of the local Indian community. Most of what finally comes out of that budget-making process is really determined before the advisor ever arrives on the reserve. Apart from the band administrator, the chief, and a few councillors, the people never become involved because the process that had been set up had made no room for them.

Of course, a good deal of budget-making is a deadly dull question of detailed accounting. That is what creates the need for competent technical advisors. There is another part of the process that has so far been generally overlooked. Anyone who has looked even briefly at the course a budget follows through the House of Commons knows that a budget is really a statement of goals, priorities, and direction for the next year, two years, or five years. For a developing community a budget is the program for development on which the community has agreed.

Those provincial and territorial organizations that have made a start in providing technical assistance have taken the first step toward allowing the community control over its own resources. If we give advice without passing on the skills behind the advice, we perpetuate the colonial relationship by replacing one central bureaucracy with another. But we cannot devote the time and energy that each individual reserve requires so long as we have one communications worker per six thousand people.

The Department of Indian Affairs has a real role to play if it chooses to support the local initiatives developing on each reserve by finding the expertise and other resources to place at our disposal. There is no doubt that other government departments have worked with outstanding efficiency to bring together people and materials from the most diverse sources. Examples abound from the Wartime Prices and Trade Board to the recent airlift of Ugandan Asians, from the Veterans' Charter to DREE programs. If the resources the Department assembles, once delivered, were to be left in the hands of the local reserve, the Department would work itself out of a job far more realistically than by transferring ineffective and undeveloped services from one department to another, or from one level of government to another.

There is far more possibility of such a philosophy emerging in the field of education than through the discussions of aboriginal rights as the government's position has developed so far. In December 1972, the National Indian Brotherhood presented a brief outlining its position on education to the Minister of Indian Affairs. This brief was the result of resolutions adopted at our General Assembly in Edmonton in August of that year. It was the first time that the Indian people of Canada, through their own organization, had presented to the government a single document stating their position on a matter vital to our daily lives.

Our basic position is that any Indian community that wishes to do so should have the opportunity to control its own education. This position was also taken by the Commons' Committee on Indian Affairs in its Report on Education. We went further in describing the need for achieving a real and authentic involvement by the community. We also went further in describing the goals of education.

Our schools must provide what Julius Nyerere has called an "education for self-reliance" within the first seven years of study. The curriculum must be flexible enough to allow a person the choice of going on to higher education or of returning at the end of elementary school to his own community with skills that will permit him to begin making a real contribution. Regardless of what level of education a student has achieved by some abstract and universal standard, when he returns to his community the real measure of his learning will be his capacity to further the goals of the community through his unique contribution. That means that a valid curriculum can only be designed in harmony with the local economy and the goals and aspirations of the people. It also means that the school environment can only be as healthy as the general community atmosphere.

In some instances, this will mean establishing our own school authorities and administering our own schools. Elsewhere, it may simply mean that the Indian people become the first party to any federal-provincial negotiation for the purchase of services on our behalf. That depends largely on whether the services needed by a particular reserve community can be obtained through negotiation.

Some bands may not even want to exercise this option right away. Our aim is not to replace one imposed program with another. It is to allow our people the same voice in the education of their children that non-Indian North Americans have in the education of theirs. This is our understanding of equality.

In February 1973, after a series of meetings with the minister and his senior advisors, the National Indian Brotherhood received a letter from Mr. Chrétien accepting our position as the policy of his department. If the principles of our education brief are allowed to carry over into other aspects of Indian life, this can represent the beginning of a new relationship between the Indian peoples and the federal government.

This change in direction for Indian education does not have to involve an immediate major increase in spending, only a shift from giving grants to provincial school boards to giving them to Indian bands. One of the first experiments in building community-based secondary schools was started in the remote villages of the Philippines following World War II. Otherwise unemployed teachers were recruited by the government and trained to work with the local community. The community undertook to raise the necessary resources. Often this meant using an elementary school after hours, or improving the condition of a community hall to the point where it could double as a learning centre.

One of the earliest workers in this program, writing in UNESCO *Journal* in 1972 said,

> If we had waited until all was well provided—buildings, textbooks, science equipment, well qualified teachers—the 250,000 children and young people who are now enrolled in some 1500 barrio high schools, 45 community colleges, and 500 pre-schools would still be waiting.

Our children are still waiting for such an opportunity, when there need be no lack of resources. The $2,700 per seat that the federal Department now pays local school boards is surely enough money to secure a worthwhile education. What is needed is to make effective use of the resources now available.

Apart from an inflation factor, the total budget only needs to increase as our present drop-out rate of 94 per cent falls off to something resembling the national average. At that point we will be asking the government and Parliament as a whole to extend the same credit to Indian education authorities who want to control their own education, as they have in the past to provincial school boards that wanted to sell surplus seats to the Department of Indian Affairs. When the good will and cooperation that allowed an initial agreement to be made between the National Brotherhood and the federal Department is experienced in each reserve community, then the Indian peoples will believe that we have begun to participate in the Canadian mosaic.

Education is the first key to the Fourth World. Without the knowledge and understanding, skills and training, both traditional and modern, we will continue to find ourselves hobbled in any attempt to move forward. Still, education is only the first key. The school has always been a miniature of the society whose children were sent there to learn. We cannot move our school system very far in a new direction without acting on our understanding of who we are through our social, political, and economic institutions.

There is an abundance of studies to demonstrate that equalizing formal educational opportunities will not do very much to equalize results. Even if we were interested solely in equalizing opportunities for economic success, making our schools more nearly equal to the Canadian or North American average will not help very much all by itself. Creating our own education opportunities is important for the lives of our children. It may not contribute too much to their opportunities as adults; we will only begin to move toward economic equality when we change our economic institutions.

Many of the plans for the development of Indian communities related to the 1969 policy statement were based on the hope that Indian communities would begin to tax themselves. Certainly, as our standard of living begins to rise, we will need to support many of our own programs from our own income. In one sense, this is nothing new. Indian people have always supported our own institutions and organizations, long before we were made dependent. Throughout this past century of struggle, Indian people have raised vast sums of money to support their leaders. We would never have survived through this past century if we had been entirely dependent on government handouts and lacked our own tradition of giving and sharing.

The difference is that tradition took the particular forms that had been found good and useful by the people of each tribe and nation. Our different ways of sharing grew naturally out of the different forms of wealth that various nations enjoyed.

The decision of the California Supreme Court, in 1972, that the system of taxing property for the main support of local school systems is in violation of the equal protection clause of the Ameri-

251

can Bill of Rights is not likely to slow down those who feel that the way Indians must join into North American society is by learning to pay such taxes. In *Serrano* vs. *Priest* the court found that "this funding scheme invidiously discriminates against the poor because it makes the quality of a child's education a function of the wealth of his parents and neighbors."[50] Saying that, the court struck down in its own state a pillar that has supported the education systems in North America since the first public schools were created. Yet there was nothing new about the criticism it made of the system.

In his *Autobiography*, Thomas Jefferson regretted that the Virginia statute creating a system of public schools had left it to the county judges to implement the legislation. "One provision of the bill," he wrote, "was that the expenses of these schools should be borne by the inhabitants of the county, every one in proportion to his general tax rate. This would throw on wealth the education of the poor; and the justices, being generally of the more wealthy class, were unwilling to incur that burden, and I believe it was not suffered to commence in a single county."

Indian people are not anxious to adopt a system of sharing that was stillborn almost two centuries ago. We only have to look at the level of other public services in wealthier municipalities compared to poorer ones to realize that a tax system that has served the public schools so poorly has done no better for public health, fire and police protection, water and sanitation systems, or any other local concern. The whole of North America must develop new ways of sharing our surplus wealth if "equal opportunity" is to become something more than an empty political slogan. It is no conceit for Indian people to believe that this is one area in which our traditional techniques are at least as advanced as anything Europeans have developed in North America or brought with them.

The traditional argument for the assimilation of Indian peoples has always begun with the belief that the way of life that European man called "progress" was not only good but inevitable for all mankind. The changing attitude to the land on the part of many non-Indian North Americans in the past few years suggests that the trend in the future may be in exactly the opposite direction.

The recognition of the sacred value of the land, the air, and the water because they are the source of all life, and the suspicion that it is wrong for any small group of people to monopolize the primary sources of life for the whole community, is no longer restricted to Indian religious thinkers plus a few long-haired philosophical academics. The *Serrano* case in California and the land use and land ownership legislation introduced in several provinces across Canada during the past year suggest that such thinking has grown strong enough for governments sensitive to all the various forms of pressure and opinion to take at least some note of this thinking.

The idea that centralizing landholding in the hands of a few big agricultural industries will increase efficiency and thereby serve the common man is a myth. If it ever was believed, the myth has been thoroughly exploded in recent economic studies and in popular newspaper and magazine articles. A two-hundred-acre farm, properly equipped and financed, can produce as abundantly and as efficiently as a thousand- or five-thousand-acre farm.

Landholding, even outside urban areas, has gone almost full circle since the start of colonialism. Land that had been held in common by the Indian tribe who lived on it was at first broken up into small holdings held by each family. In this step there was at least some consistency, since the immediate family was the functional unit of people working the farm when European agriculture first took root here. As some people, following each major war, left for the city, or did not come back from the war, their lands were taken over by their neighbours. But within their neighbour's family the same relationship with the land continued.

Now the land is more and more being held by corporations that are often larger than the state or province—Imperial Oil, International Telephone and Telegraph. If a local family continues to work the land, they do so as employees of a massive bureaucracy that has no real relationship with either the land or the people. Landholding is moving under the control of multinational corporations, which have all the worst aspects of state control and none of the virtues. The next logical step is to complete the cycle and return the effective control of the land to the local community, with the legal title held either by that community or by some larger community such as the province—or for Indian lands the federal Crown.

The land use and land ownership legislation introduced in

several provinces across Canada during the past year is the most concrete and specific evidence of the growing awareness that landholding is not an abstract notion that can safely be left to lawyers and politicians to manipulate. The community's relationship to the land has an immediate and direct influence on the lives and work of farmers, labourers, and housewives.

The British Columbia legislation is, perhaps, the most far-reaching proposal so far. Where other provinces have focused their attention largely on restricting the right of non-residents to own land, the Barrett government is proposing to regulate land use within each region and district of the province so as to control urban sprawl and encourage the agricultural and forestry base of the economy of the province.

Explaining the purpose of his own legislation, Dave Barrett accurately described the situation when he asked, "Why tie up all the land [in river valleys, plateaus, and other flat lands], when there are all those hills to build on?"

There might be a greater initial expense to build on rock but it makes sense to preserve the land and to solve the problem of flooding by not building in flood plains in the first place.

In central Canada I have observed the same problem. The news reports state that the Great Lakes have reached their highest level in the past century. These reports were followed a few days later by statements by land resource experts within the Ontario government that people who build near waterfronts take this calculated risk.

When I first came to Ottawa the complaint about waterfront land was that cottagers buying up waterfront lots were depriving the general public access to the beaches and the water, which have traditionally been held in common. It is tempting to wonder if the floods have provided some kind of natural justice. But then, I wonder how much effort was made to inform and educate people about the dangers of what they were doing before they built? I also question whether people were offered alternative sources of water if they did not build beside a lake or river. Who was to account for the increased cost of roads to houses built on hillsides rather than on the flatlands? I'm not sure that Justice would point a finger at the individual small-holder.

Mr. Barrett's Bill 43 is the kind of measure that can open up these alternatives to individual families and local communities. On a broader scale it opens up the possibility of preserving the family farm as an important social and economic unit—as a way in which people can maintain an all-embracing relationship with the land while enjoying the fruit of modern technology.

Measures that do no more than restrict ownership to residents of the province will do very little beyond speaking to the growing sense of Canadian nationalism. By themselves, such measures cannot encourage the productive use of land and discourage speculation. Only measures that discourage speculation by making it unprofitable are likely to return the effective control of land to the people who live on it.

When you really think of it, the idea of land ownership does not make much sense. Anything else that a person might own is somehow or other the fruit of his labour. If the present owner did not make it himself, he exchanged what he did make for goods another person made. However sophisticated the system of exchange becomes, the basic principle continues. There may be any number of inequities and means of unfair exploitation in the system of exchange that cry for correction. And the more complicated and sophisticated the exchange system is—the more turns and twists in the road—the greater the opportunity for one person to exploit another. Still, ownership of most things can always be related to the fruit of human labour.

With land that is not so. Land and water are the sources of life. I might exchange my labour for land that another man holds. But neither he nor any of the previous owners had a hand in the creation of that land. For him or for me to claim more of a title to that land than the right to use it while we have need of it is a presumption and an affront to our Creator as well as to our community.

We are learning today that, even with all the benefits of modern technology, there are immediate and severe limits to the mineral and fuel wealth we can extract from the land. The timber industry in central Canada is dying because there is no longer the supply to justify replacing old-fashioned equipment. Pollution and over-harvesting have threatened our fish supply.

If land and water were like the goods man produces by his own labour, we could repair or replace what was exhausted and make more to meet our growing needs. We know that this is not so. We know it so well I wonder why I should have to go to such lengths to point out what everyone can see with their own eyes.

The traditional relationship of Indian people with the land, the water, the air, and the sun has often been praised because of its spiritual nature. People seeking their own roots have praised it because it is a tradition they can grasp. But its real strength historically for our people, and its growing appeal today both for our own young people and for non-Indian people concerned for the generations still coming toward us, is not a romantic notion. Its strength lies in the accuracy of the description it offers of the proper and natural relationship of people to their environment and to the larger universe. It offers a description of the spiritual world that is parallel to, and in fact a part of, the material universe that is the basis of all our experience.

The land, the water, the air, and the sun are sacred because they are the source of all life. They are the limbs of the Guardian Spirit. Their sanctity is recognized because of their importance to our survival.

Even the capitalist recognizes that the value of land comes from its limited supply. The difference is that he chooses to exploit this value for his own personal ends and finds himself in a society that encourages him to pursue this exploitation. Little people are beginning to realize what the capitalist and the spiritualist have always known.

The growing pressure on governments from environmental movements to preserve the land, to exploit it with wisdom, and to assure that its riches are open to the poor as well as the wealthy is a small move in the direction of the values of my grandfather. People are starting to realize the threat that is presented to their daily lives by the continuing abuse of their environment.

The Indian doctors and spiritual leaders used to say that if man abuses the medicines of nature for too long they will refuse to work for him. People in a more technically sophisticated and more spiritually primitive society might choose to express themselves differently. Whatever language people might use, there is no doubt that the wisdom of this thought is finally being understood and accepted.

More and more Christian religious thinkers, whose spiritual

256

ancestors were dedicated to calling down my grandfather's world, are now saying that non-Indians in North America must either learn to live like Indians or they will destroy themselves. The experience of salvation is becoming a social, collective, and earthly activity.

The ancient Indian prophecies are just as likely to be heard in study groups at colleges and community halls in the cities today as in the Big Houses. The speaker is as likely to be steeped in Asian or European traditions as in our own; perhaps he has just been listening to the still small voices in his own retreat.

Those who do his word proclaim our victory.

While it is heartening to go to a college campus and hear students express these concerns, it is in the *doing*, not in the talking, that the victory lies. And while those who have been handed down an understanding of nature by their families have a real advantage, the victory will lie with those who do the doing.

If the Indian people face the danger of success, the ecologists face the danger of teaching those who do not share their concerns how to put their garbage in somebody else's backyard. This is one lesson of the Four Corners Power Plants fed by the coal from Black Mesa to power the homes of people protected from the pollution by an entire mountain range. Similarly, people concerned with the environment of New York City have hailed the James Bay Hydro Project as their salvation without considering the price someone else is paying.

If only the environments of the middle-class people who are in a position to give initial leadership to a movement are saved, there will be no victory. The concern for a life related to the land, the water, and the air cannot be separated from a life related to the other human beings—the poor, the unfortunate, the disabled—with whom we are or should be in contact. A materially comfortable environmentalist cannot tell himself that he is recycling his possessions and avoiding waste, when he uses the poor as the recipients of his hand-me-downs without asking why they are poor.

The need to redefine our relationship with the land cannot be separated from our need to find more effective and far-reaching ways of redistributing wealth across regional and provincial boundaries as a matter of right and without preconditions. In return for limiting the percentage rate at which they taxed their own residents, the provinces, during World War II, were guaranteed they would receive the tax revenues equal either to their own provincial average or to the national average, whichever was the higher. No province, no matter how poor, would have revenues less than the average rate of income tax payment for the whole nation, in proportion to their own actual population. Although this formula for equalization payments created a new concept by raising every region to a national average, the basic idea had roots in provisions of the original British North America Act which allowed for certain guaranteed annual payments to the maritime provinces, as well as for the sharing of debts of all provinces through the federal treasury for areas of responsibility that would be federal concerns for the future.

For many years after the war ended there was a growing tendency for the federal government to offer grants-in-aid to the provinces for undertaking works which the federal government chose to encourage. A province could receive, for instance, 75 per cent of construction costs and 50 per cent of maintenance expenses for vocational schools built under the Vocational Training Act. ARDA, FRED, PFRA, and other programs all worked on a similar basis.

The Joint Committee of the Senate and House of Commons on the Constitution, in its First Report, recognized that the grant-in-aid approach had much the same fault in federal-provincial relations as property tax had on a local basis. The poorest provinces lacked even the 25 or 50 per cent they were expected to contribute. When the province had to raise the whole amount, with the federal subsidy arriving at the provincial treasury when all or part of a project was completed, the province was forced to borrow money it could not raise through taxes. When the subsidy did arrive the province was left with the interest still owing on the debt which the subsidy repaid, and no money in the treasury for future development. Grants-in-aid were another scheme in which the rich got richer.

The Joint Committee recommended that, at the discretion of each province, the option be created of allowing a larger part of the total tax bill to be shared on the basis of the equalization formula. Rather than having 30 per cent of the national tax dollar, for instance, distributed on the equalization formula, with the provinces coming hat-in-hand for another 20 per cent on the basis of grants-in-aid, if they could raise the initial capital, this committee of federal legislators saw the wisdom of giving 50 per cent of the national tax dollar to the local governments as a matter of right, thus ending the beggar status of the poor provinces.

Perhaps this program has its limits and drawbacks in how the income-tax dollar is calculated in the first place. How much do corporations contribute in contrast to the donations of the working poor? The strength of the program is that it recognizes the national average as the minimum standard below which no partner in Confederation can be expected to participate. There is also no guarantee that the larger provinces are willing to apply the same principle to the poorer regions within their own vast territories.

If the same program were applied to the total Indian community in Canada, based on our present population, we would be receiving no more than what is now paid as a matter of right to Prince Edward Island. But the sum would be several times what we now receive. The wisdom and discretion with which it would be spent would be our own. If leaders at any level spent funds in ways that their people found unwise, they would have to face their day of judgement at the end of their term of office in the same way that federal, provincial, and local governments must ultimately answer to their electors.

We can have neither home rule nor responsible government so long as Indian leaders are elected to band councils and provincial and national organizations by voters who do not have the same role in shaping the budget to the support of their organizations as Canadian people have in the financial support of their governments. But the form of support must be one that is consistent with our way of life and also with the general Canadian standard. If a resident of one province works in another, he pays taxes only in the province of his residence. An Albertan who works either in Saskatchewan or in British Columbia is in no different a position than his neighbour who works in his home town. An Indian who works on his reserve pays no taxes. His Indian neighbour who works in the neighbouring town pays both federal and provincial tax, although the province has no obligations for bringing services to his home. If Indian people were to share in the general re-

259

venues of Canada on the same basis as residents of Saskatchewan, Prince Edward Island, Quebec, or Newfoundland, we might then begin to develop the economic equality needed to make Indian communities in Canada strong.

At present a corporation that locates a plant on an Indian reserve in Canada would not have the problem the oil companies in the North Slope Borough of Alaska are facing. They would pay their taxes to the neighbouring, provincially constituted municipality. It is true that they may be paying a rent to the band council—at a fraction of the rate they are paying taxes to a municipality that has no particular concern for the development of our lands. Urban areas that have succeeded in providing public services on the strength of their property taxes have done so precisely by relying on the contribution of large industries.

I doubt that we want so many wealthy industries on our land that we can grow rich off their tax payments. Nor are there enough such industries to go around. But I would hazard a guess that the taxes paid to outside municipalities by industries located on reserves today more than offset any income tax not paid by Indian people whom they employ.

The lands that belong to us by native title, and the compensation for our aboriginal rights, are our birthright as the aboriginal peoples of North America. They are not about to be sold for a mess of pottage. The equalization payments, tax benefits, parliamentary representation, and local autonomy will become our entitlement when we are welcomed as equal partners in the Canadian Confederation.

To those who say we demand too much, we say, "Count up more carefully what you and your neighbours have received. We are asking neither more nor less than what is already received by the 'two founding races.'"

There are others who will say, "Your demands are just and reasonable. But be careful how you make them known. If you press your demands too strongly, however just and reasonable they may be by all the standards of natural justice, *you will create* a backlash."

We say to them that a government that tolerates 56 per cent unemployment for Indian people by leaving our communities out of the national figures already represents a backlash. The minute you allow one group of people to be so materially disadvantaged compared to the national standard you have created a backlash.

If what is meant is that we must speak with care and precision, giving fair and just replies, and not inciting against others the racial hatred they have brought against us, I agree. If the statement means what it says, I ask those who make it to reconsider. If our claims are true and our needs are real, are we not entitled to seek justice through all the means that have been open to men since the beginning of time? Do you think the new technology has created a new standard of truth. Consider, just once again what the truth might be.

My belief in the Fourth World is an act of faith. But it is no illusion. I have told you of the strength of my ancestors. My faith is simply that the strength of the present generation and those who are still coming toward us is no less than the strength of our forebears. The Fourth World is far more of a Long March than an Eternal Resting Place. My faith is that we, and our children's children, are willing and able to take up the burden of our history and set out on our journey. Were there no more to it than that I should ask no more of other men than to let us pass freely.

There is more to the Fourth World than that because it is a global village in which we live. If we cannot forget the history of past centuries, neither can we forget the events of recent decades. Our lives are too bound up with yours for either of us to go entirely our separate ways. We have heard your children crying in the night for peace and comfort as much as we have heard our own.

I have set down here our own needs as Indian peoples for the Fourth World. We know that we cannot move very far in that direction unless you also choose to move. Do you know how far you can move without us? The Fourth World is no less open to others than it is to us. We must each march to our own drum. We must each travel in our own way. I have spoken of our own needs because it is to my own grandchildren that I most want to speak my heart. I cannot speak of the needs of people I have hardly known. I can only believe that they are as real as our own.

We cannot become equal members in *your* society. We *can* become a member of a new society in which everyone chooses to share. But that cannot happen until you begin to reconsider and reformulate your understanding, and your view of the world, as we have begun to reformulate ours.

My friend and colleague, Vine Deloria, wrote "An Indian Plea to the Churches" which brings all his studies of law and theology to bear on what I am saying:

> It is not the documented and footnoted answers that you can use to justify your position that I seek to evoke, but the beginning of honest inquiry by yourselves into the nature of *your* situation. And that situation is that I believe that you have taught mankind to find its identity in a rewriting of history and not an affirmation of it.
>
> It is this tendency, more than any other, that now confronts [North] American Indian peoples in their relations with the United States [and Canadian] governments. We are content to live under the laws of this country. But the . . . government has learned to continually change those laws with respect to us by viewing its own history as it chooses and not as it was. And I would be so bold as to suggest that the government learned to do this by following the lead of its religious community.
>
> Early missionaries, for example, told us the story of Adam and Eve . . . regaled us with accounts of the Resurrection, the Exodus, and the Tower of Babel. . . . We recognized these stories as myths by which a people explain how they came to consciousness as a national community. When we tried to explain our myths the missionaries grew angry and accused us of believing superstition.
>
> At each point and in every respect you refused to confront our ideas, but chose instead to force your opinions, myths and superstitions on us. You have never chosen to know us . . . . It is this tendency to continually pervert the experiences of life that you have passed on to the federal government that has created our present difficulty . . . .
>
> Wishing that something happened long ago does not change what did happen at that time. Believing in myths does not give them historical reality. Indeed, it shields one from ever knowing that reality or from learning from it. So it is with government, so it is with religion.[51]

The way to change the historical reality is by acknowledging it as our common heritage. Let me give one example. When the prime minister of Japan stepped off the airplane in Peking in the spring of 1972, it was his first visit to China since he went there with the invading forces in the Second World War. His first words, when he greeted his Chinese counterpart, were, "We are sorry."

When he said that, the two men—the two nations—could truly embrace each other.

What makes that so much better than Pierre Trudeau's advice, in his Maniwaki speech, that Indian people should forget the past, is that he shows so little willingness to change the present reality and to make a new beginning. Pierre Trudeau has often been accused of arrogance. I do not consider that the Japanese prime minister, in saying those words, humiliated himself. He just spoke and acted with humility. That is the alternative to arrogance.

> A disclaimer of the traditional Christian understanding of history would carry with it the demand of the peoples of the West that all institutions honestly attempt to appraise the present situation in its true historical light. . . . We could all come to the necessity of facing ourselves for what we are. We would no longer have a God busily endorsing and applauding the things that we are doing. We would have to be on God's side in our dealings with other peoples instead of being so sure that God is automatically on our side.[52]

The church has so long been the treasure-house of values for western European people that it must have a role in the Fourth World. It is as difficult to live without the church as it has been to live with it. For all its faults, no other institution has a greater potential for building bridges between different societies and different nations. But I doubt that the church can do very much to address itself to our condition until it first solves the Christian Problem.

Perhaps we can help them to solve their problem by showing what it means "to counsel together until all are of one mind." Churchmen who want to play a part in the spiritual development of the people they pretend to serve could learn a great deal about living a spiritual life in the world of the here and now by examining the Indian religions they have worked so hard to destroy in the past.

It is not necessarily the details of ceremonies—they are only the technology of religion—that they should study; it is the values lived out in everyday human, social, and political relationships, and celebrated by those ceremonies, that must be understood and shared. Every Indian religious ceremony that I have seen, and I

263

should think the celebrations of most other natural peoples are not so different, is a way that people have of coming together to give thanks for the special gifts they have received, whether from the Creator, from nature, or from another person. To celebrate the joy of being able to give, which some would call creating, that is the basis of all human relationships. That is the joy of the elders who can teach the youth who carry our spirit on in this world. For though we may believe in another world, we prefer not to talk so much about what we cannot know. It is bad for our children to see elders insisting on what we cannot explain.

If the church wants to play a role in the spiritual development of our people, it must begin by learning and sharing our values. I am told that the church is presently engaged in a serious reappraisal of its own work. I do not mean to be unkind when I recall that the government has been engaged in a serious reappraisal of its role in relation to Indian people since long before Lord Elgin's speech against his own regime. We have learned to wait to see. It is difficult to respond to these rumours of reappraisal until we see the reality emerge in a new relationship between the church and the Indian people, in each local parish and as a nation.

How can we expect the people, or the governments that represent them, to believe that "a leader must stand no taller than the rest of his people" when their whole spiritual structure is a pyramid standing in the light of our sun.

A leader who stands no taller than the rest of his people stands in the centre of a circle and speaks the voice of the minds and souls he hears around him. The Christian view of the world, as we have received it, is a vertical triangle with each level of leadership being closer to God. The state, as we have seen it, is the perfect mirror image of this triangle. This is not the shape of our world. It leaves no room for the things we think are most important.

I do not believe that Christianity has to be seen this way, or I would not speak of its role in the Fourth World. It will be easier for us to believe that it can take on a shape that more closely resembles the world around us when we receive a sign that the leaders of the church have joined in the dance of life.

Perhaps when men no longer try to have "dominion over the fish of the sea, and over the fowl of the air, and over every living thing that liveth upon the earth," they will no longer try to have dominion over us. It will be much easier to be our brother's keeper then.

There is, I believe, a whole variety of kinds of giving. The kinds of giving are as many and as varied as the gifts and the givers. Most difficult to satisfy is the person who gives to you because the gift for which he hopes in return is his own identity. It is unlikely that you can give to him what he is seeking. And there is a great temptation to give him your own identity instead.

I was in that position myself when I first came to Ottawa. If cabinet ministers had been willing to meet with me then, I would have been ripe for being absorbed into their high-powered methods. It is so easy to allow a person whose status and power you admire to impose his style and values, whether or not that is his intention. Nobody has to organize the effort to buy you off when you are certain of your own direction.

I would like to think that, if they had been willing to receive me, I would not have been so easily absorbed. Still, I am human, and as capable of weakness as any other man. I count it a blessing in disguise that they ostracized me right from the beginning. Then I had no choice but to give whatever strength I had to my people. This was not a selfless act. There was no other way that I could increase my strength but to give it away to receive it back double.

The Indian peoples have a tradition and a culture to offer to the world. We have tried to take on other peoples' ways and found that they just did not work for us. Today, more and more European people in North America are finding that their own culture cannot meet all their own needs while they live on this land. It is not only young people who are trying to retribalize European society by building communes and developing other forms of extended family. They are trying to re-create a situation in which everyone is related to everyone else, a situation in which everyone says, for better or for worse, "These are my people."

I hope these people have the patience to work through the generations it must have taken our ancestors to reach the level of stability and cooperation for which they have been so much praised. It is a good model for the global village. It is not likely to be built by a community development worker who is only on a two-year tour of duty. Still, if he comes by, have him in for coffee. He may be helpful.

Indian people have never completely left our Old World, the Aboriginal World which I have tried to describe. European North Americans are already beginning to work their way out of a value system based on conquest and competition, and into a system that may be at least compatible with ours. If those values are really shared, technology can be harnessed to them to make the transition both easier and less painful. But I think technology will never be harnessed to our ways until we respect it as we have been taught to respect the animals, the water, the land, and the air. Not that it is exactly a living thing in itself. But it is an extension of the things that live.

Teilhard de Chardin, the French philosopher, I am told had only one sentence in all his books related to North America. "If the white man also stays in North America another 10,000 years, he too will become Indian. If you think I mean wearing buckskin and living in wigwams, you are mistaken. I mean in gaining a feeling for this land. It is your only survival." I hope he is wrong. We do not have anything resembling ten thousand years remaining to us to make that transition if we are to survive. Either you or I.

These are my words. Now, I must pick up my burden and go with my children and their children. I hope you join with us along the way. Please understand if we do not feel we can wait for you. These are my words.

Notes

~~~~~~

[1] Tape recorded interview with Dr. Marie-Francoise Guedon of the National Museum of Man of Canada.

[2] For a fuller discussion of the migration of horses and the development of their use as a means of travel see, Richard Erdoes, *The Sun Dance People*, Knopf, 1972. His account is consistent with my own understanding of the arrival of horses in the interior. I recall stories from my grandfather and others of his generation, tracing the arrival of horses to trade with the Kootenay people to the southeast of the Shuswap. My grandfather was already a mature man and had worked some years hauling supplies from the Hudson's Bay store at Kamloops before the first horses were available. He was born about 1830, and may have been over thirty by the time he first worked with horses.

[3] Quoted in Erdoes, and also in Dee Brown, *Bury My Heart at Wounded Knee*, Holt, Rinehart and Winston, 1970.

[4] For an excellent brief outline of British Columbia native history see, Wilson Duff, *A History of the Indians of British Columbia*, Volume I, Provincial Museum of British Columbia.

[5] Duff, *ibid*.

[6] Tape recorded interviews with Wilson Duff and Henry Castilliou, April 1972.

[7] Based on an interview with Henry Castilliou tape recorded by Posluns and available, as are all other sources listed here, from the National Indian Brotherhood. Henry Castilliou has practiced law and collected historical material on the Indian peoples of British Columbia for many years. He has travelled to almost every Indian community in B.C. and worked with a number of Indian organizations.

[8] The details of British Columbia history, which are explored in greater detail in a later chapter, are based on three principal sources: *Native Rights in Canada*, Douglas Sanders, editor, Indian Eskimo Association; F.E. Laviolette, *The Struggle for Survival*, University of Toronto Press, 1961; and *Proceedings* of the Special Committees of the Senate and House of Commons Joint Session to Inquire Into the Indians of British Columbia, 1926-27, Queen's Printer.

[9] Terms of Union, quoted in Laviolette from the Report of the Royal Commission on Indian Affairs for the Province of British Columbia and in *Native Rights in Canada*.

[10] For a detailed chronology of the activities of the U.S. Cavalry, see Dee Brown, *Bury My Heart at Wounded Knee*.

267

[11] The only written source in which we have seen the concept of mutual dependence at least partially developed is Wilson Duff's *History of the Indians of British Columbia*. Both Wilson Duff and Henry Castilliou expanded on the concept in recorded interviews. Ray Fadden's analysis of east coast Indian history in his recorded speech, "Three Messages," seemed so consistent with Duff as to suggest a similar pattern. "Three Messages," published on tape by Akwesasne Notes, Rooseveltown, N.Y., 1970.

[12] The terms "band," "tribe," and "nation" as they are used in discussions of Indian matters often appear confusing to those unfamiliar with this context. We have tried to use them in the way that Indian people most often use the terms among ourselves. "Nation" refers to any group who traditionally thought of themselves as one people and governed themselves accordingly with a common language, territory, and social structure, e.g., the Shuswap Nation. A "band" is a group who commonly lived and worked together as a unit, or who are presently constituted as a band under the Indian Act, e.g., the Neskonlith Band of the Shuswap Nation. Many Indian groups in the United States refer to themselves as a "tribe," and the term is often in the general sense interchangeable with "nation." The main value of the term as we have used it is to stress a "tribal" way of life.

[13] *Johnson v. McIntosh*, 1810, quoted at greater length in *Of Utmost Good Faith*, an anthology of legal documents edited by Vine Deloria Jr., Straight Arrow Books, San Francisco, 1971.

It was pleasing to find, shortly after we had written this chapter, that Mr. Justice Emmett Hall, in his 70-page judgement in *Nishga Tribal Council*, begins by quoting from Marshall in *Johnson v. McIntosh* and comments that a great deal has been learned since Marshall's time, so much that he would treat this classic statement as mistaken.

[14] Shortly after we wrote this chapter, the Supreme Court of Canada brought down its decision in *Calder et al*, often referred to as *Nishga*, which we discuss in more detail later. Almost at the outset of his seventy-page judgement, Mr. Justice Hall refers to *Johnson v. McIntosh*, and finds that Chief Justice Marshall's understanding of Indian life has been set aside by the greater knowledge of history that we possess today. We think that is a scholarly and judicial way of affirming the opinion we have offered here.

[15] Laviolette, page 70. Throughout this chapter we follow Laviolette's account of the Potlatch Law and its application. Many of the individual stories were already familiar to us, but his work pulls together the pattern of events as it unfolded across a vast territory, and relates it in depth to the events in Victoria and Ottawa.

The letter on page 75 is part of a letter from an Indian agent at Metlakatla, B.C., on January 22, 1889, as quoted in Laviolette, p. 58. The settler's complaint on page 79 is quoted in Laviolette, p. 107.

[16] For a full discussion of this case see Michael Posluns, "The Nations of the Iroquois," Akwesasne *Notes*, June 1971.

[17] From a letter by Chief Billy Assu, a Kwakiutl of Cape Mudge, to the editor of the *Fisherman*, reflecting on the loss of Indian health, fishing and hunting rights, land, and capacity to care for the sick and elderly which he had seen in his 75 years of life up to 1922.

[18] *Native Rights*, page 126.

[19] Much of the specific material on the B.C. Land Claim is drawn from Laviolette, although our interpretation differs and goes somewhat farther. Where we draw on other sources we will indicate.

268

[20] The conditions, as presented here, are our own condensation of correspondence appended to *Proceedings, Reports and Evidence of the Senate and House into the Indians of British Columbia*, Queen's Printer, 1927.

[21] *Proceedings*. Points one and two are our own condensation.

[22] The dialogue quoted here is taken in each case from *Proceedings*, the original source.

[23] *Statutes of Canada, 1927*, Queen's Printer.

[24] *Special Committee of the Senate and House of Commons, 1960, Proceedings*, Queen's Printer, Submission of the Aboriginal Native Rights Committee of the Interior Tribes of British Columbia.

[25] "Hawthorn Report" refers to *A Survey of the Contemporary Indians of Canada*, Part I, ed., H.B. Hawthorn, Indian Affairs Branch, Ottawa, October 1966, IAND Pub No. QS-0603-020-EE-A-18.

[26] Wes Modeste, from a tape-recorded interview.

[27] Quoted in Jerry Gambill, "Indians, White Men and I," *The Humanist*, reproduced in mimeograph by the Company of Young Canadians.

[28] Lord Elgin, quoted in Indian-Eskimo Association pamphlet, *Community Development Services for Canadian Indian & Métis Communities*, 1968.

[29] *Citizens Plus*, Indian Association of Alberta, Edmonton, 1970. *Citizens Plus*, more often referred to as *The Red Paper*, was the official reply of the All Chiefs Conference of Alberta to the government's *Indian Policy*, sometimes known as *The White Paper*.

[30] There is presently a bill pending before the United States Congress to reinstate the Menominee Nation as an Indian tribe under protection of federal laws.

[31] F.R. Scott, "W.L.M.K.," *The Blasted Pine*, An Anthology of Satire, Invective and Disrespectful Verse Chiefly by Canadian Writers, ed., F.R. Scott and A.J.M. Smith, Macmillan Co. of Canada Ltd., 1962. All poetry selections in this chapter are from this poem.

[32] From a CBC radio news special program available through Akwesasne *Notes*, *Concern of the James Bay Cree*.

[33] Jean Vanier, "On Violence in a Violent World," speech delivered at the First Unitarian Church of Ottawa, February 11, 1973.

[34] *Hansard*, Senate of Canada, February 8, 1973, appendix.

[35] Toronto *Star*, article by Dr. Howard Adams, October 21, 1972.

[36] *Indian Voice*, article, August 1972.

[37] B.C. *Evidence Act*, Revised Statutes of British Columbia, 1960, quoted in Hawthorn.

[38] "Armed forces recruiting Indians and Eskimos to help in Arctic," Toronto *Globe and Mail*, September 23, 1971. James Wah-Shee, president of the Northwest Territories Indian Brotherhood, in a reply appearing in Akwesasne *Notes*, Autumn 1971, said he agreed with Gen. Walsh on the need to assert sovereignty in the North but questioned whose sovereignty should be asserted.

[39] Steve Hume, "Two Arctic communities hit by typhoid fever, rabies," *Edmonton Journal*, November 3, 1972.

[40] Reproduced by permission of the American Anthropological Association from the Newsletter of the American Anthropological Association, Vol. 12, No. 8, October '71. Reprinted in Akwesasne *Notes*, Early Autumn, 1972.

[41]From a CBC radio news special program available through Akwesasne *Notes*, *Concern of the James Bay Cree.*

[42] Commons' *Hansard*, May 17, 1972.

[43] Speech at the Canadian Club, February 1973, heard on the "CBC World at Six" National News.

[44] "Development in Indian Affairs" Cabinet Document, 747/72, released to the press through unknown sources and reported by Stanley McDowell, Toronto *Globe and Mail*, August 11, 1972. Reprinted in Akwesasne *Notes* under title, "Canadian Government 'leaks' New Indian Policy: Plans to Start Being Nice," Early Autumn, 1972.

[45] This analysis of the Economic Development Fund is based on a research article prepared for the National Indian Brotherhood by Resources Management Consultants Ltd., "Indian Economic Development, A Whiteman's Whitewash," October 1972, and is developed at length in a speech given by George Manuel and reported in *Indian Voice*, November/December 1972, and two subsequent papers, one prepared by Resources Management Consultants Ltd., and a second prepared by Eugene Seymour.

[46]Mr. Justice Judson and Mr. Justice Hall wrote the two major opinions in the Nishga case. It should be stressed that Mr. Justice Judson did not disagree with Mr. Justice Hall on the basic concept that aboriginal rights or native title were firmly embedded in English and Canadian law. The question on which disagreement arose was whether that title continued to apply to the lands of the Nishga. Judson, and the two judges concurring with him said that it had been extinguished by a series of legislative enactments. Hall, and the two who concurred with him said that such an interpretation would allow the legislature to accomplish by an indirect and backdoor method what ought to be done by mutual agreement. Nonetheless, the meaning of native title as a concept of Canadian law was not a major difference separating the two major opinions handed down in the Nishga case, (*Calder et al*).

[47] This discussion of the Alaska settlement is based partly on two articles reprinted in Akwesasne *Notes*, Early Autumn, 1972. It has been pointed out to us that corporations such as the oil companies might very well have contested the validity of the legislation establishing the North Slope Borough no matter who the voters were. Perhaps. What is important is that according to the articles referred to, and a variety of other sources, the case was not treated as a simple tax appeal but became a racially charged political issue. The oil companies' brief itself questions the competence of the people who do live in the North Slope Borough to run their own local affairs while avoiding "any temptation to misuse and abuse power to overstep the restraints of responsibility." Let he who is without guilt drill the first well.

[48]After we had completed writing, Mr. Justice Morrow of the Supreme Court of the Northwest Territories found there was sufficient evidence based on the testimony of interpreters, witnesses and participants to the treaty negotiations—who all testified that there was no surrender of land—to uphold a caveat indicating the Indian interest in the land and effectively prohibiting development until the Indian claims are settled. The federal government at first challenged the authority of the Northwest Territories court to hear the case. When the court's authority to hear the case was upheld on an application to the Federal Court of Canada, the federal government refused to be represented at the hearings before Mr. Justice Morrow. The court then appointed a lawyer to represent the government. Mr. Justice Morrow granted the motion sought by the Northwest Territories Indian Brotherhood. He later ruled that the caveat not be filed until all appeals from his ruling

were exhausted. Since then the government of Canada and the Northwest Territories Indian Brotherhood have agreed to negotiate and have postponed further appeals.

[49] Dee Brown, *Bury My Heart at Wounded Knee*, page 427.

[50] Erwin Knoll, "Five Crises in Public Education," *The Progressive*, December 1972.

[51] Reproduced by permission of Vine Deloria, Jr., from his article "An Indian Plea to the Churches," as printed in the Los Angeles *Times*, February 6, 1973.

[52] *Ibid.*

Index